Class Matters

Class Matters

The Strange Career of an American Delusion

STEVE FRASER

Yale UNIVERSITY PRESS

New Haven and London

Published with assistance from the Louis Stern Memorial Fund.

Yale University Press books may be purchased in quantity for educational, business, or promotional use. For information, please e-mail sales.press@yale.edu (U.S. office) or sales@yaleup.co.uk (U.K. office).

Set in Minion type by IDS Infotech, Ltd.
Printed in the United States of America.

Library of Congress Control Number: 2017948003

ISBN 978-0-300-22150-3 (hardcover : alk. paper)

A catalogue record for this book is available from the British Library.

This paper meets the requirements of ANSI/NISO Z39.48–1992 (Permanence of Paper).

10 9 8 7 6 5 4 3 2 1

For Richard—Long may he ride through his heart's pastureland
For Sabina, someday
In memory of Vev

Contents

Acknowledgments

In one way or another much of what I've written about over the years has involved the role of class in American history. I might have come up with the idea of writing about why class matters on my own. But I didn't. Steve Wasserman, then an editor at Yale University Press, suggested I tackle this subject. I had known Steve through his various incarnations as a discerning editor and literary agent. When he broached this, I knew I wanted to give it a try. But I wasn't sure how to approach the project. I threw out a slew of ideas about how I might go about it and Steve was my first sounding board. So I am grateful to him both for the genesis of this book and for helping me through this period of what I hope turned out be productive confusion.

Others were equally helpful in listening, criticizing, and offering their own ideas about how to grapple with a topic that offered up almost too many tempting ways in. My long-time friends Josh Freeman and Paul Milkman were among those early listeners and commentators. I have relied on their judgment for every book I've written. That is true as well of my wife Jill. I also called on the three of them again to read and criticize initial fragments and whole drafts of some of the first chapters as well as for other advice and help once the book was complete. My good friend Rochelle Gurstein also read some early material and as always provided sharp, sympathetic criticism. When I had about half the book drafted I grew nervous about the approach I had adopted. I asked another friend Marshall Rafal, and two superb historians, Elaine May and Nelson Lichtenstein, to react to what I had done. They did so with alacrity, and combined critical commentary with encouragement that the approach I had chosen seemed to be working.

When I had a complete draft in hand, Yale University Press asked the distinguished historian Gary Gerstle to provide the Press with a critical reading. He produced a wonderfully inciteful and sympathetic critique and then subsequently shared with me the knowledge that he was its author. Gary is not only a talented writer and historian, but an editor as well; indeed, he and I have edited two books of essays together. *Class Matters* benefited immensely from all these readings, but especially from Gary's.

Many people I don't know or barely know–scholars and laymen alike—made indispensable contributions to this book. *Class Matters* covers six subjects about none of which can I pretend to have expert knowledge. Without the work of historians, social scientists, and journalists whose work is cited in the endnotes there is no way I could have written this book.

Other good friends helped along the way in discussing possible titles, jacket designs, and other matters dear to an author who is also a once, and now and then still an editor. Thanks to Robert Boyers, Tom Engelhardt, Corey Robin, and Geoff Shandler as well as a good number of the people I've already thanked above.

I am in debt of course to several people at Yale University Press. When Steve Wasserman left Yale for another publishing position, Yale's Editorial Director Seth Ditchik graciously took over the project. I have valued his advice and warm support for my orphaned book. His assistant Michael Deneen has been unfailingly responsive to every noodling question and anxiety that impatient and anxious authors often are apt to express. Robin DuBlanc is a superb copyeditor and also knows how to hold the hand of a self-doubting writer. Margaret Otzel epitomized professionalism in her work as the book's production editor and, like Robin, made that production process seem less impersonal than it sometimes can. I want to thank as well my publicist Brenda King. And finally at Yale I want to thank Mary Valencia for her perceptive visualization of the book's mood and purpose in her design of the book's dust jacket.

As always, my family has been my most precious asset. They helped in specific ways, but most of all by being there for me. Without Jill there would be no books nor much of what I value. My son Max and his wife Elena are dear to me, not least for bringing into the world my brand-new granddaughter Sabina who is hilarious and a thrill. I can't imagine my life without my daughter Emma. My brother Jon and his husband Marco have enriched my life and the family's in so many ways. And to that group I must add my last remaining uncle, Arthur Oluwek who shared with me information and memories of his father, my grandfather, that find their way into Chapter 3. To all of them thanks is scarcely enough.

Introduction
The Enigma of Class in America

I am sitting down to write this two days prior to the inauguration of Donald Trump as the forty-fifth president of the United States. So I am tempted to compose the shortest book on record: The answer to Why Class Matters is "Duh." And thank you for your time and you can thank me for mine.[1]

Debates over how the inconceivable happened will stay hot for years to come. But the triumph of "the Donald," everyone seems to agree, had something vital to do with the surfacing of a rebellious working class, in particular a "white working class." Suddenly class seemed to matter a great deal in a country long grown accustomed to relegating matters of class to some musty attic of national memory.

Trump doesn't deserve all the credit, however. In the run-up to his stupendously unanticipated victory, the notion of class had been worming its way to the surface of public life. Across the Western world, from London to Athens, the norms of public life were being shattered by right- and left-wing populisms fired by class animosities. Here at home, people had become acutely sensitive to the specter of the class divisions in our midst, faintly reminiscent of that specter Karl Marx invoked when he penned *The Communist Manifesto.* Worries about runaway inequality have commanded headlines, generated reams of government reports, and turned scholarly tomes into best sellers over the past decade. Some people occupied Wall Street. Cities and states rushed to pass minimum wage and living wage ordinances. The economy nearly fell apart at the seams, and all of a sudden capitalism itself stood before the bar of public judgment. Our vocabulary filled up with references to "the 1 percent and the 99 percent," and "financial vampires." We christened our era a second "Gilded Age," pockmarked by poverty and extravagant displays of wealth. Polls regularly recorded that a large majority of Americans believe government services the rich with little left over for working people. Everybody lamented the vanishing of the middle class, that special class that is no class, the victim of bipartisan abandonment.[2]

Everyday life in every way bears the stigmata of class. Who lives longest and who dies soonest, who goes to jail and who is free, who is healthy and who sickly, who learns and who lives in ignorance, who gets bailed out and who goes under, who pursues happiness and who goes off to fight and die, who lives with rooms to spare and who six to a room, who breathes clean air and drinks clean water and who is poisoned, whose children thrive and whose barely survive, who looks to the future and who lives moment to moment, who is secure and who in peril, who rules and who obeys? Answers to these and other life-and-death questions depend to a very considerable degree on just which niche in the class hierarchy you inhabit. Reports and research studies periodically remind us of these stark realities.[3]

Even without the help of investigative journalists and social scientists, however, we know. How could we not? Social life is mapped with this knowledge. A restaurant—fast food or gourmet—is wallpapered with the compulsory deference and suppressed resentment of its wait staff. Emblems on our cars tell us where we stand on the highway to preferment. Driving may entail passing through or avoiding the wrong neighborhoods. Logos on pants and T-shirts, handbags and footwear, are brands that brand us as belonging to some distinct inner or outer sphere of the social cosmos. Skin color darkens the closer we venture down to the bottom of the economic pecking order. Disembodied voices from the telecom recite sales messages to dial tones while in drear warehouses the messengers are surveilled, disciplined, and live in fear. Lush landscapes are tended by intimidated migrants who daily line up at Home Depot, eyes averted. Window shopping, on- and off-line, in magazines and TV dramas excites our admiration and secret envy of those who have reached the summit of wealth and power. The housoleums and helipads and private islands of the 1 percent are the insignia of both their superordination and our frustrated desires. Others get by in trailer parks, row houses, or in the back seat. Children "race to the top" or fall by the wayside. Passengers fly with ample leg room or are vacuum sealed. We live reminded over and over again at the sports arena or theater, in the "'hood," at the mall, on the links, or on the pockmarked asphalt of inner city parks that we are traveling through life either in business class or coach. Blue-collar workers fend off contempt. We genuflect before "winners" and show the back of our hand or a piteous sneer to these "losers." Workers don't produce, they serve. We are a servant society that demands. The demand is that we respond to every nuanced prompt that tells us America is after all intensely rooted in the deference, jealousies, resentments, and aspirations given life by the combustible energies of social class.

So of course class matters, at the very least in the public arena and, one suspects, at the subatomic level of private life as well. America, after all, began on the premise that social class counted a great deal. About this its earliest settlers, people like John Smith in colonial Virginia, had no doubt. The captain explored the Atlantic coast of the New World searching for an escape from the Old World's fixed hierarchies, a place where "every man may be master and owner of his owne labour and land." That dream would abide for generations, even though from the days of the earliest settlements class insinuated itself into the tissues of settler America.[4]

Still, even a decade or so ago, in the years before the global financial meltdown and "Great Recession," many would have denied those cleavages existed or were important or would last. We had lived for decades during a conservative ascendancy that treated even the traces of class animosity as a sacrilege. Metaphors of class did not compose the lingua franca of everyday life. Class differences were less abrasive, if they registered at all. As a category of social life class seemed a leftover from some bygone age—if people even remembered that far back. And this too is hardly surprising. America has spent most of its short life denying it was a society in which class mattered, or if it did that it was a strictly temporary condition. Living in denial has ever since required great political, intellectual, and imaginative resources to keep the lid on that incendiary paradox.

Class is the secret of the American experience, its past, present, and likely future. It is a secret known to all, but a source of public embarrassment to acknowledge. It lives on all the surfaces of daily life, yet is driven underground every time its naked self offends cherished illusions about how we deal with each other.

Our economy is and always has been a set of architectural variations on the hierarchy of class. But at the same time its avowed purpose has always been to abolish class. As a material matter that is what the American Dream promised, a country so richly endowed that no matter how low down you began the resources to rise and rise again were there in abundance. Here too, however, the paradox lived on underground. The hawking of goods and services, from the days of patent medicine ads in daily tabloids to today's agora in virtual reality, has mined the subtlest distinctions of social status. Yet this invidious pursuit of inequality happens under the smiley face of equality for all. Officially we all subscribe to the American Dream. But as we also all know, as George Carlin once bluntly put it, "They call it that because you have to be asleep to believe it."

More than in any other realm, in the United States the political system has worked overtime to expunge class from our public vocabulary, to keep it from shaping legislative proposals, to prevent its organization into independent parties, and to stigmatize any open ideological articulation of class interests. Largely successful in that effort, the two-party system, so celebrated for that accomplishment, has nonetheless been chronically troubled, sometimes nearly overwhelmed, by questions of class it veers away from answering.

Thinkers of every species and subspecies—historians, political scientists, sociologists, anthropologists, philosophers, scholars of the law, social critics, and theologians—have filled whole libraries with proofs that class in America doesn't exist, or is going out of existence, or is an intellectual dead-end. Still, that those libraries even exist, that over time they expand rather than shrink, confounds their premise that class is ephemeral, a hallucination, a categorical mistake, a profound misunderstanding. One might say they do protest too much.

From Bartleby to Gatsby to Willy Loman our literary imagination has been populated by characters caught up in the compulsive flight from the antinomies of class. The typical

American hero—in popular and "serious" fiction, in a thousand westerns and post-westerns, in the romances that pass for journalism, inlaid in the tissues of every organ of popular culture from sports to music—is a solitary, steely, emotionally truncated male at odds with the social order. Both his sense of freedom and his estrangement are rooted in an antipathy to the constraints, protocols, dependencies, and emasculations felt to be the psychic ransom of social stratification and the submissions it commands.

"Lighting out for the territories" has always been more than an economic escape mechanism, more than a second chance at democracy, more even than a cutting away of the spider webs of social entanglement that suffocate the free spirit. Out there is the ever-renewable promise of an Edenic rebirth, a paradise as classless as anything ever dreamed of by Marx. Here metaphysics meets sociology. Here utopian desires, which after all are always about transcending the social antagonisms forever plaguing humankind, can themselves live forever. Before Marx thought of it the New World had already set sail for a future without classes.

Some say Joseph Stalin invented the notion of American exceptionalism in one of those unkind moments of intellectual dictation he was so well known for. He was actually reprimanding an American Communist whom he accused of falling prey to that native delusion that the New World was exempt from the universal laws of class conflict. (If Stalin was indeed the godfather of "American exceptionalism," one can't help but relish the irony that it is nowadays the favorite catchphrase of conservative ideologues.)[5]

Others maintain the notion goes way back generations before the general secretary stalked the earth. Whether or not the phrase itself came over on the *Mayflower* or the *Arbella*, clearly the New World offered itself to its first European settlers as a way out. It was a passway with multiple exit ramps, some leading its voyagers closer to the divine, some to a virgin land immune to the social and moral pathologies afflicting the steeply hierarchical Old World. For some heaven and earth met here, heaven on earth would happen here. American exceptionalism is the nation's sanctification. It confronts the specter of class by stopping it at the water's edge. It is our native form of class consciousness, a consciousness that the curse of class may be exorcized but only at the price of eternal vigilance.[6]

American exceptionalism has also functioned as a kind of promissory note to the rest of the world. Our plenipotentiaries carry it in their diplomatic pouches. Its reach is global and meant to be exemplary. We can tutor the rest of the world on how to avoid the pain and suffering, the civil wars and international Armageddons that have bedeviled all ancient civilizations—from Europe to the Levant and on to the Far East—because we have discovered the secret of democracy and equality and abundance. Social jealousies, class resentments, all those cravings for pelf and power that make up the warp and woof of life outside our borders can be domesticated, even eradicated, if only nations would imitate what we are and do. But this is strikingly odd, of course, because the United States also stands before the world today and long before today as the globe's principal imperial power. Such a position presumes overlordship and subordination. Yet American imperialism, like our peekaboo relationship to class here at home, is a reality that dare not speak its name.

There was a time when this shyness was not so pronounced. During the first Gilded Age our nouveau riche were so exquisitely class conscious (precisely because they were so nouveau) that they concocted preposterous fantasy lineages and masqueraded as aristocrats to prove and justify their superordination. Across the great class divide where the "other half" struggled to survive, where the "dangerous classes" assembled as a reasonable facsimile of Marx's specter, where the nation seemed poised on the precipice of a second civil war, class consciousness was a familiar idiom within the American lexicon. Yet even then and there the "dream" lived on. The stigmata of class, however anxious they made people, could be treated not as indigenous to the New World but as viruses imported from the Old, temporarily toxic but soon enough rendered harmless by America the Abundant.

Nowadays, our nouveau don't act out a charade of class superiority. They do the opposite—dress in bib overalls, ride the range in Range Rovers, and suck on bacon rinds in order to efface from public view their power and privilege. Both getups—the costumed and bejeweled pretenders of the Gilded Age and the good ol' cowboy-hatted billionaires of today—are ways of being that express a chronic fixation on class. Indeed, class consciousness, either as an affirmation or as a strategic repudiation, has been a more conspicuous and continuous feature of daily life for our country's elites than has been the case for those further removed from the centers of wealth, social preferment, and political power. That's as it should be. Under normal circumstances, those empowered to deploy a society's resources, to steer its political institutions, to shape and guard its means of cultural reproduction also create, as a matter of course, justifications for their right to be doing these things, their right to rule, and do so with confidence. If they lose that confidence, if the justifications begin to ring hollow, the circumstance are no longer normal.

Are we edging closer to such an abnormality? Inequality is once again a political incendiary. Under more settled conditions, the chosen way to expunge class from our public life has been to invoke America as the land of the middle class. Now such references are at best aspirational. Instead most lament the vanishing of that class and the looming up of a social vacuum. A creeping premonition grows that a world of the downwardly mobile and dispossessed is gathering on one side of that vacuum, the overly propertied on the other. Is America headed back to the future, to a time long ago when social classes squared off against each other with such venom that, American exceptionalism notwithstanding, consciousness of class mattered so much it could not be anesthetized?

It's a Mad, Mad, Mad World

Class matters in America precisely because the country has labored so hard to pretend it doesn't. Has that imparted a distinctive dialectic to American society and if so, what have been the consequences? Living in denial is generally considered a danger to mental well-being. Psychoanalyzing an individual is a problematic enough undertaking. Trying to do that for a whole society would be a fool's errand. However, without supposing the existence of some collective mind, it may still be possible to take the measure of class and the erasure of class in American life, to sketch its social pathologies.

Hamlet-like, the upper classes can't decide whether to be or not to be. At one moment they parade their prerogatives like the feudal stanchions of some yesteryear. Wealthy and wise, they assert their fitness to rule. Then again, susceptible like everyone to the egalitarian mythos of the land of the free and worried they might be dangerously offending their less blessed compatriots, they flee grandiose pretension. Better to remember their parents and grandparents coming over in steerage, sweating in steel mills, cleaning up after the careless and idle rich. To and fro they go, trailing behind a perverse form of faux democracy, moneyed but anti-statist, populist yet engineered, credulous but cynical.

Those of wealth and power always have it and always will feel skittish about exercising their outsized wherewithal inside a democracy. Electoral and parliamentary protocols can't be ignored, and managing them is not simple. But matters must have moved to an advanced stage of deterioration and psychic disorientation when elites feel it necessary to stir up incendiary passions directed at themselves. Say what you will about ruling classes, they hold things together. When they are psychologically as well as politically unable to, the abyss looms. That might be welcome news or not. Trump's victory suggests a gloomy prospect.

Sisyphus would have sympathized with the infinite frustration of the American middling classes: always climbing, chronically afraid of falling, sentenced never to attain the summit. Such are the wages of a peculiarly American sin: the yearning to be not only equal but first among equals. If the Sisyphus complex doesn't show up in the DSM, it is nonetheless a social malady that's been a plague practically from the beginning. The race after invidious distinctions observed trenchantly by Tocqueville in the early nineteenth century has delineated the middle ranks of American life ever since. It is the dark matter lurking beneath the civic commitment to a classless equality—namely, the equal right to become unequal.

What might be called the Sisyphus complex, the peculiar pathology of this heterogeneous milieu, has left the middle class politically malleable and at a cultural in-between: a politics oscillating between *spread the wealth* and *keep what's mine*, a cultural persuasion part bourgeois self-advance, part bohemian off-road. "Personality disorders" lend piquancy to TV sitcoms and melodramas, to novels of familial dysfunction, to the ceaseless back-and-forth on Facebook and like social media, and to the self-regard and self-surveillance that suffuse the middle-class psyche. By definition, this preoccupation seems to originate and reside somewhere far away from the outside world. What's it got to do with that other realm of big bureaucracies, professional associations, corporatized universities, faceless insurance companies and banks, white-collar sweatshops, ateliers of digital innovation, a brazen plutocracy, or the invisibles of über-America who serve them? Where and when do these private and public spaces have intercourse? What offspring emerge?

Maladies of the interior life may be routinely diagnosed as arising from within the suffering individual and consequently are ministered to at that site. However, this is tenable only so long as the "individual" is accepted as the elementary particle of the social cosmos. What if instead the "individual" is a social fiction assembled out of an assortment of building blocks of which class is a cornerstone? Still, everything about middle-class life conspires to uphold the fiction of the autonomous individual; it's a primal unreality and a faith.

Bossed yet self-invented, children of choice but shaped from birth into bureaucratic and professional functionaries, meritocrats who network just in case, captains of consciousness in thrall to experts, creatives under surveillance, free agents yet under duress from an armada of institutions in which they are embedded; this is a class whose constitutive illusions leave it unmoored, at sea. Such is the psychic dispensation for those who work so hard to put in the shade all that might encumber their fragile selfhood.

A society riddled with social fissures but one that seeks to hide them from view makes casualties, economic but also psychological, of its subalterns. They in turn may act out or internalize the wounds. A blue collar has long been a stigma. Faux Bubbas from among the upper crust may sport one to effect a kinship with those down-home. But it's the quaintness of food, drink, and dress, the frozen-in-time picturesqueness, the masculine caricature of the backwoodsman that is being offered up as a spectacle and masquerade. The celebration is an insult.

The insulted may internalize the contempt. So "the hidden injuries of class" can fester into malignancies of shame. They are crippling, disempowering, ending in quiescence. Unschooled, living in dreary, passed-over districts, eating wrong, playing the numbers rather than the stock exchange, condescended to, superannuated, out of fashion in every way, the socially invisible tunnel down into zones of self-reproach.

Or they may not. Instead those wounds may flare up as an infectious resentment. The political psychology of resentment, anger aimed at circles of privilege and power, will often couple, as it does today and has at times in the past, with a fury deflected downward at the mudsills of American society. Nobody plays by the rules, neither the snobs nor the incorrigibles. Latte sippers and welfare queens, pinstriped bankers and the zebra-striped incarcerated defile the homeland, mock what is sacred, diss those who do still fuck, marry, reproduce, and work the way you're supposed to. This is a form of class consciousness, to be sure. And it has its points. But it is one terminally tainted with jealousy and envy, fear and loathing. It is an escape route that dead-ends, a movement that remains fixed in place.

What was once identified as "the blue-collar blues" may, however, assume yet another psychological profile. Rarer, it subsumes and can eventually extinguish resentment by a yearning for emancipation. The social psychology of emancipation—

something our ancestors of the late nineteenth and early twentieth centuries were familiar with, something many of us today can still remember from the era of black liberation—is a generous emotion. It embraces the whole social order. It is also a class consciousness but one trying to escape the pathology of class.

Nothing much like this exists today. Still, its embryonic presence may be observed. Invariably it surfaces where the politics of resentment also show up. Occupy Wall Street was ecumenical in its indictment of capitalism and the system's multiple indignities and servitudes. But it was also caught up in its own anarchical individualism and identity group resentments. Schoolteachers, relentlessly and maliciously made the scapegoats for the squalor and poverty of deindustrialized finance capitalism, find common cause with students and parents. This is social outreach into the unknown but also a tactical maneuver for securing a square deal in the here and now. The Sanders campaign elicited the once unspeakable—there may be life after capitalism in which the needs and desires of the commonwealth take precedence—yet its more quotidian programs and platform rhetoric enunciated a vision just left of the New Deal and its ex-communication of "economic royalists." Inside trade unions empathy and solidarity cohabit with I'm alright, Jack. Environmentalists may find capitalism and the health of the earth incompatible, or on the contrary lobby for a "green capitalism" as the best medicine.

Class consciousness is everywhere and at all times a form of social pathology trailing a variety of psychic ailments in its wake. This is true even when it inspires the sentiment of emancipation. Class has always mattered in America. That our society so often compulsively denies that is not only politically and economically problematical but also leaves it damaged in the

heart, afflicted in the brain. Only in the case of class consciousness as liberation might it function as the healing agent for the
wound it created.

Into the Heart of Darkness

There's an adage in Great Britain advising that if you're pondering a social dilemma, the first place to look for answers is that
country's exquisitely intricate class structure. In America that
would be the last place to look. One sociologist has called this
aversion "America's forbidden thought." Committed to the notion that class in America is everywhere and nowhere, I decided to take the measure of class where it is least likely to show
up, where the heart and soul of Americanism is thought to
reside, free of any tincture of class.[7]

Iconic events and documents and images in our national
history comprise the raw material of my version of why class
matters. I've selected six: the settlements at Plymouth and
Jamestown; the U.S. Constitution; the Statue of Liberty; the
cowboy; the "Kitchen Debate" between Richard Nixon and
Nikita Khrushchev; and the March on Washington and Martin
Luther King's "I Have a Dream" speech. Each in its own way
enjoys an exalted status. All are emblematic of the American
credo and deeply lodged in the national imagination. They
capture something essential about what many would agree is
at the heart of the national experience, summarizing its best
intentions or most fervent yearnings.

None of them appear to have anything much or essential
to do with class; class does not seem to matter. Scholars might
see them differently, aware that their histories are entangled
with the social division of labor or the unequal distribution of
power and wealth or the rise of capitalism. For most people,

however, they stand as monuments to individual freedom, self-reliance, tolerance, democracy, racial justice, and equality. And in some sense they do. By looking for telltale signs of class, I do not mean to argue that these are really camouflaged landmarks of the class struggle. What I do believe is that class mattered in their origins and evolution and the space they came to occupy in our national life. And if that is the case for what many consider instances of immaculate conception in our national narrative—defining moments when class didn't matter—then it might be that class runs in the American grain. However much the country has dedicated itself to effacing that blemish and however deeply embedded and hard to discern that grain might be, it's there like Henry James's "figure in the carpet."

My six semaphores are not the only ones signaling the country's exceptional immunity from the contagion of class conflict. I might have chosen "the New World" or manifest destiny or Horatio Alger or family values or the Declaration of Independence or the Empire State Building or "the Free World" to serve the same purpose. All are equally well known. Whatever else they might conjure up, they evoke a universe that operates free of the constraints and abrasions of class.

What I deliberately avoided selecting were memorable moments that recall times when the lineaments of class were clear for all to see: the Haymarket Massacre, or William Jennings Bryan's "Cross of Gold" speech or the Flint sit-down strike, or Shays' Rebellion, or the châteaux imported from their European homesites by Gilded Age "robber barons" to line Fifth Avenue and the seashore at Newport, Rhode Island, or the Bradley-Martin Ball where "the 400" masqueraded as European nobility while outside the barricaded Waldorf Hotel "huddled masses" floored by the depression of the 1890s scavenged to stay alive, or the uproarious denunciations of "economic royalists" during the New Deal, or Teddy Roosevelt's scorn for "malefactors of great wealth," or Jacob Riis's photographs of the urban misery in which "the other half" lived, or utopian and dystopian best sellers like *Looking Backward* or *Caesar's Column,* about a country ravaged by class antagonisms, or *The Grapes of Wrath,* or of course the battlefields where the fate of slave labor was decided, or the Emancipation Proclamation that made abolition official. However imperishable at least some of this inventory from the past might be, none of it registers as an all-American theme, if only implicitly, in the creation of an exceptional nation. On the contrary, they live on as aberrations, departures or interruptions that were gotten past, their lessons learned, the ruptures they caused in our public life transcended.

I picked my six icons in part because they first appeared during distinctive periods in the country's life. Those eras roughly coincide with phases in the economic evolution of the New World. Plymouth and Jamestown as well the Constitution are products of the seventeenth and eighteenth centuries when the future of the country as a capitalist society was not yet settled. Alternatives coexisted alongside the emergence of market-centered arrangements. The earliest colonial settlements as well as the document that definitively put an end to that era were marked by this pre-capitalist condition, which profoundly influenced just how class mattered and just what class signified.

The Statue of Liberty and the cowboy are figures of the nineteenth century. Then a way of life that might be characterized as family capitalism flourished. It nurtured romantic notions of unfettered individualism and sometimes Napoleonic delusions of grandeur. In this "new world" the hierarchies once assumed to organize social life before capitalism were now expected to get erased. Yet family capitalism brought with it the specter of proletarianization and unanticipated modes of subordination. Both the myth of the cowboy and the statue were initially molded by that encounter.

What some have called corporate capitalism or the corporate welfare state overshadowed (although without extinguishing) family capitalism in the twentieth century. Relations between classes were engineered out of existence, their incendiary potential defused, their boundaries crossed and eroded away by the flood tides of the "affluent society." Triumphant postwar America accomplished all this so effectively that the nation's founding utopia as a "city on a hill" seemed to have taken on the flesh-and-blood secular reality of a country without classes. Vice President Richard Nixon boasted as much in his celebrated encounter with Soviet premier Nikita Khrushchev in a model kitchen at a commercial exhibition in Moscow. Not long after that hundreds of thousands assembled in Washington to march for "Jobs and Freedom" and listened to the most honored speech of the twentieth century. Martin Luther King's "I Have a Dream" and the movement it spoke for seemed then and even more emphatically since then to mark a further historic step forward on the road to realizing the promissory note of equal rights for all originally issued with the Declaration of Independence. That road might run straight through the barriers of racial exclusion, but it bypassed the hidden fault lines of class. The political economy of midcentury America had less and less use for the stigmata of race so long as they might be erased without igniting the fires of class conflict.

Pre-capitalism, family capitalism, and corporate capitalism are rough categories I am imposing to counteract the tidal momentum of the more conventional staging of our national history. This nation—any nation, for that matter—inherently understands itself as rising above whatever internal fissures may lie beneath the surface of national unity. The tensile strength of that conceit is especially strong here in the New World; that's part of what made it new. But it is my claim that distinct political economies, full of flesh-and-blood social divisions, shaped the way the nation originated and evolved. Having said that, I do not pretend here to describe or analyze those political economies, but merely to use them as demarcation points.

Finally, my purpose is not to write histories of these six cardinal pieces of Americana, an absurdly ambitious undertaking even to contemplate in these short essays. Rather, they are focused strictly on how class mattered in their makeup and nothing more.

The Personal Is Political

Class has mattered to me as it has to all of us. When Yale University Press first asked me to undertake this book, it made what I considered an odd suggestion. Why not, the editors proposed, include or even organize the book around the experiences of your own life? The fame and commercial success accompanying Ta Nehisi Coates's letter to his son (which became a best-selling book under the title *Between the World and Me*) no doubt encouraged this thought. I rejected the idea out of hand and the press accepted my decision.

Then, as I began work, I rethought the proposal. My own life span, it occurred to me, might be conceived as running from one postwar moment, when class still occupied a prominent place on the surface of public life after World War II, to a second postwar moment after Vietnam, when class was already rapidly receding into the background, becoming a kind of dark matter. Perhaps introducing this vantage point into the treatments of my six iconic moments might enrich the larger story. It could offer a personal way of embodying Faulkner's much-quoted adage that the past is not only not dead, it's not even past.

Moreover, I've spent a good portion of my life engaged in political affairs. That naturally influences the way I look at events like the Kitchen Debate or the March on Washington, at which I was present. Unlike Zelig, I can't say the same about the foundation of the Jamestown colony or the arrival of Lady Liberty. Yet it would be naïve to think the opposite, that because I didn't come over on the *Mayflower* or ride the range with Buffalo Bill, my views of those times are unmarked by my own political and even personal experiences.

When I was first asked to tackle this project, I thought immediately of all the reams and reams of paper devoted to more analytical and theoretical as well as empirical accounts of class. Many are of immense value. I didn't want to replicate that approach, however. Going personal was therefore also a kind of end run.

Consequently, each chapter contains material from my own life. This shows up in no special sequence, sometimes at the opening, sometimes at the closing, sometimes here and there throughout any particular chapter. If a thread runs through it all, it might be called one man's encounter with the proletarian metaphysic.

The Elephant in the Room

I was born into a world where the notion of class enjoyed a relatively distinct meaning. To the degree it was an operational part of everyday language, it pinpointed where a social group stood in the system of production. There was a class of owners, a class of wage earners, and in between floated a broad middle strata of professionals, administrators, self-employed businesspeople, and farmers. The terrain was always more complicated than that, of course. Middle managers, clerical workers, the marginally employed, the idle rich, and the idle poor fitted into their own special places, situated in a hierarchy grounded in the way American society organized its capitalist economy. Even in America, especially in the one just emerging out of the Great Depression, it was common enough to contemplate the country's future by anticipating how the tension between workers and bosses would be resolved.

However, as even this simple schema suggests, there were then and before then and since then alternative ways of defining class. Already in the post–World War II world in which I came of age, class was being refigured in terms of income distribution, varying standards of living, and competing styles of consumption. Social scientists referred to social strata rather than classes. They noted the impermanence of what were once thought of as firmly rooted class divisions. These status distinctions were often seen as invidious ones, even if highly liquid. They might give rise to resentment, jealousy, imitation, snobbery, fawning, envy, emulation, or even renunciation. What they did not take into account openly (but nonetheless embedded) were relations of power and subordination.

Power and subordination are at the forefront of the way class is deployed in these six essays. Before it was reduced to an abstract economic category, capital first of all existed and continues to exist as a vessel of power, a political relationship between those who have it and those who, because they don't, must submit. In that sense, I remain a child of the proletarian metaphysic. That outlook for a long century, beginning with the advent of the industrial revolution, imagined the new class of propertyless wage workers brought into being by that revolution to comprise the generative social division of modern life. Moreover, that working class was perceived as the principal agent of historical transformation, the class that was nothing destined to become everything, to paraphrase a famous anthem.

Recent times belie that anticipation. The political alignments that were supposed likely to emerge from that class configuration have not formed, or where and when they did they soon dissolved. Other developments similarly undermined older expectations or forebodings. In an idea stretching as far back as midcentury and resurfacing today, social observers have spied in automation or cybernetics a logic that will do away with classes by making most human work superfluous. One theorist, André Gorz, put it so: "Work—the defining activity of capitalism—is losing its centrality both to exploitation and to resistance." Even stopping short of Tomorrowland, work (and its relationship to class in contemporary life) suffers an ambiguous status; glorified yet steeply stratified, inviting a badge of honor yet disguised so as not to appear like common labor, which is perceived as dependent, dumb, undignified.[8]

Classes conceived instead as congeries of consumer behaviors and aspirations is perhaps the most frequently used map of our social geography. This is true even in this new age of Trump, when most of the superheated populist rhetoric zeroes in on the cultural pretensions of elites. The "relations of production," to use the Marxist term of trade, have largely subsided beneath the surface of public life, no longer quite as visible to the naked eye. I am preoccupied with refocusing attention on power and subordination in these six explorations into why class matters. In that sense, the essays are about both the past and a return to the past. However, interrogating who runs things and who doesn't necessarily expands the boundaries of class well beyond the economic sphere. Dependency may originate or be nurtured there, but it naturally and inevitably spills into political and cultural life. That is where social classes make their presences known—and, more profoundly, is where they actually take shape. The chapters that follow thus pursue the hunt for class into these realms.

We live in an ostensibly democratic society whose political protocols, institutional mechanisms, and creedal beliefs reflect those democratic commitments, however often they are breached. But the forms of democratic life may work to obscure class boundaries. Is capitalism compatible with democracy always, at times, never? Are "the people" a class; are they the 99 percent? These are the formulations of a populism that may or may not converge on class divisions as they are molded through the "relations of production." The American political genius has at times overmastered those underlying "relations" and at other times laid them bare, as these six explorations may show.

Those "relations of production" may seem bloodless, arising out of the mathematics of the otherwise antiseptic intercourse of labor with capital. It has become a commonplace, however, to note that race and gender muddy those waters. That they do is self-evident. The subaltern status of African Americans, women, and others of the wrong color or nativity decidedly inflect the nature of class in America (and of course elsewhere as well) at work and away from work. This interlarding of racial and class subordination has never been clearer than it is now with the metastasis of the carceral state. As the economy has deindustrialized, it has produced a swelling surplus population largely, if not entirely, made up of people of color. Millions have ended up jailed. One social observer has noted, "From the point of view of Capital 'race' is renewed not only through persistent racialized wage differentials or . . . occupational segregation . . . but through the racialization of the unwaged surplus or superfluous populations."[9]

Less frequently noted, however, is that class itself tends to biological interpretation on the part of ruling classes. One of the great achievements of the American Revolution was to strike a blow at the stigma born by the mass of laboring humanity since Adam's fall. Yet Thomas Jefferson, that paladin of democracy, voiced a hoary commonplace when he wrote to his friend John Adams noting the existence of a "natural aristocracy among men" marked by "virtue and talents" who should run society. A subordinate status within the "relations of production" has again and again been associated with a basal inferiority, apart from any tie to a specific "race" or other organic identity. Such was the case within the fractious Jamestown community, among those hoping to save "Lady Liberty" from the "huddled masses," and with the upstanding farmers and ranchers who warned off proletarian cowboys, even those of pure Confederate stock, brash enough to want to marry their daughters. "White trash" then and "white trash" now has marked those down at the bottom of the class pyramid with a primal stain their "racial" makeup can't remove.[10]

Whatever rigor may attach to a definition of class rooted in "the relations of production" tends to become more elastic in the mercurial realms occupied by my chosen six. Cowboys were working stiffs and heroes of lone rebellion at one and the same time. Makers of the Statue of Liberty were champions of bourgeois liberal democracy, in flight from working-class insurgencies, and phobic about immigrants. Vice President Richard Nixon was a veteran anticommunist yet a herald of the classless society. Martin Luther King's speech rejected skin color as an arbiter of one's fate, but over the years that followed licensed a national amnesia about how social class continued to play that tragic role.

And when we talk about the first colonial settlements and the Constitution that turned a loose confederation of ex-dependencies into united states, the relations between the powerful and the subordinate seem categorically different than in later centuries. Within settler communities in Massachusetts and Virginia, traditional hierarchies from the Old World prevailed alongside the first intimations of modern classes. Meanwhile, outside the stockade these colonial outposts dominated aboriginal communities, an overlordship that ended in the extinction of the indigenous settlements as viable societies. Here class took on the character of imperial predation, including the racial coloration that so often rationalizes colonialism. At the same time, these settlements themselves were subjected and subordinated to the powerful institutions of global trade and finance. And as for the nation's founding document, the struggle to formulate and adopt it set off an encounter between a frontier agrarian society against the commercial momentum of a seaside one that would decide the country's future.

Class in America has always mattered, then, but not always in the same way. Lineaments of the country's classes have been reconfigured again and again. The middling classes of nineteenth-century family capitalism have only a resemblance to the suburban world of the 1950s when I was a kid. The robber barons, who by and large refused to donate money to build the Statue of Liberty, were differently motivated than the corporate CEOs who applauded Dr. King's speech on the Mall.

Moreover, the way classes have dealt with each other, the way their presence has been reflected in our imaginative as well as our political and moral life, has mutated again and again, expressing the fluidity characteristic of any capitalist society and emphatically true of the United States. Consignment to one class has always, for many, seemed temporary even if it wasn't. Immigrants reduced to *Stücke* in Carnegie's steel mills could nonetheless harbor the dream that they could flee their proletarian exile for an American paradise. Footloose cowhands were one or two lucky breaks away from a herd of their own. What persists, as shown in these essays, is the way class has figured in the disposition of power in a society that has struggled mightily to fend off the recognition that class matters.

1

East of Eden

I live in rural Manhattan. That oxymoron refers to the uppermost point of the island. There a climax forest rises above the banks of the Hudson River. A scattering of private homes still stands nearby. Apartment buildings top off at six stories, which by Manhattan reckoning may as well be the Great Plains.

As recently as the beginning of the twentieth century there were still working farms in the neighborhood where residents could get freshly laid eggs and milk. The IRT subway line didn't get to Dyckman Street, the southern border, until 1906. In the decades that followed Inwood became a haven for working-class Jewish immigrants on their way up and out of the teeming precincts of the Lower East Side and Brownsville in Brooklyn. Already living there were working-class Irish, some with lace-curtain aspirations. If they managed to get the curtains, they left. By the time I arrived in the 1970s, Inwood was overwhelmingly blue-collar Irish, plus a remnant of old Jews, some wiling away the day reading the *Jewish Daily Forward* or its Yiddish edition, the *Forverts,* on sidewalk benches, and an outpost on the east of working-class African Americans living in a housing project where Kareem Abdul-Jabbar grew up.

Studs Lonigan might have grown up there as well. It was clannish and class conscious. More people read the *Irish Times* than the *New York Times* and probably as many as read the *Daily News*. Rumor had it that guns were run out of the neighborhood to the IRA. Money certainly was. Every Irish bar and restaurant and boutique (selling plastic shamrocks, Irish flags, soda bread, Claddagh rings and mugs, Waterford crystal, green ice cream cones, and Irish Republican paraphernalia) hung signs urging support for the hunger strikers in Ulster prisons. During "the Troubles" the Irish population of the neighborhood was refreshed with young refugee/recruits from the Republic.

Although New Yorkers, they rarely left the neighborhood except to work: construction jobs, on the subways, as domestics, as cops, as firefighters. Picture an Irish and Manhattan version of *Saturday Night Fever*. Young people like Studs graduated high school or dropped out and then matriculated into a lifetime of manual labor; a smaller fragment made it into low-level white-collar jobs on Wall Street or in Midtown. While still young and fit they played ball, but drugs and drinking soon benched them. Wary of beat cops who were always hassling them about petty vandalism or booze, they deferred to the local parish priest, before whom they knew to genuflect and sanitize their language. Except at home and at church, authority was unwelcome. By their midtwenties, for most "Gotham" might as well be in a galaxy far, far away—not their hometown but an exotic amusement park for the rich and sophisticated. Unless a job took them there, only an occasional (and too often financially unapproachable) Knick or Ranger game found them mixing with a world they sensed as alien. When they voted, if they voted, that semi-underground feeling of being a class apart surfaced in loyal support for their local congressional representative, a populist-minded Democrat who still aroused the class-inflected passions of the New Deal years.

Outliers, they treated me like an outlier among outliers. Middle class and of the wrong ethnicity, I was tolerated at pickup basketball games but otherwise ignored; although they nicknamed me Woody after Woody Allen, whom they thought I looked like (short, glasses, Jewish—or short, glasses, and therefore Jewish), and/or because Woody stood as a not-hostile but not-friendly moniker for a social boundary not to be crossed. Whatever they may have felt, I winced at the estrangement for two reasons. I didn't like being stereotyped. But I fit the stereotype and lamented my own inability to cross that class divide, in part because as a young political activist I wanted to make contact with just this sort of passed-over working-class world.

Then again, being a bit of a loner myself, this treatment did not bother me all that much. And I was in graduate school becoming a historian of American labor, so I had a certain sympathy for and interest in worlds inhabited by Studs Lonigan and those like him. If my neighbors distrusted middle-class outsiders, I thought I had an inkling as to why.

Nowadays, Gotham is rapidly absorbing Inwood. Once it was the last Irish neighborhood left in Manhattan, but the Irish are greatly reduced in number. Gentrification is spreading. Many of the bars are gone. Bodegas have replaced them, along with a smattering of hookah bars, tapas cafés aimed at the newly arriving white upwardly mobile, and even a waterside nightclub for the glitterati. Class and ethnic borders are etched more visibly into the neighborhood's geography than they used to be: east of Broadway is Hispanic, black, and working class; west is white, including some Irish hangers-on as well as the city's youthful cultural precariat of film and music makers, graphic artists, theater people, and magazine writers. Residents of the paleface precincts may also struggle to get by, enjoy as little or less security than their colored neighbors, but are more subject to illusions about their class identities, thanks in part to their skin color. All in all, though, it's still down-market (by Manhattan standards), and the neighborhood remains largely working class, now Latino, mainly Dominican. I wonder how long it will retain this class character. Not long, probably, not in Manhattan. But then again, Inwood has always been a province of outsiders.

Frequently I walk through the magnificent woods separating my apartment building from the Hudson. A boulder guards the entrance to the forest. It is a memorial rock. An inscription reads: "Sharakkopoch: According to legend on this site of the principal Manhattan Indian village, Peter Minuit in 1626 purchased Manhattan Island for trinkets and beads worth 60 guilders." Nearby are the remains of a midden, the shell depository where the Lenape coined their own wampum currency.

True or not in its particulars, the story on the boulder resonates. We all know it (although the usual version prices the island at $24). It carries with it several understories. One faintly echoes a tale of lordship and submission that began back then and with many a twist and turn resurfaced in Irish Inwood and its Dominican successor. If Peter Minuit had possessed Donald Trump's flair for self-promotion, he might have called the transaction "the art of the deal." That is to say, we recognize this as a tale of commercial shrewdness. Less "out there," conveyed more by a wink and nod, the story implies how naïve those natives were, how easily conned. Even more sotto voce than that is a dimmer awareness that something more than a piece of geography was on the block. Ways of life thousands of years old would soon cease to exist. That the rock also memorializes the emergence of American capitalism out of its relationship with noncapitalist societies is not legible at all but hidden beneath the boulder, in the earth. Down there class matters. Up here as well.

A Wilderness Story

The purchase of Manhattan, although part of the lore of early America, is not a national foundational myth the way the settlements at Plymouth and Jamestown are. It is rather a quintessential New York story, and therefore familiar yet somehow alien. After all, Minuit was Dutch, not British, and it was the Dutch who first set up shop on the Hudson (although that's where the Pilgrims were headed until a storm and navigational mistakes landed them on Cape Cod). Men from the Netherlands were the merchant kings of the world in the sixteenth and seventeenth centuries, the Dutch East India Company four or five times the size of its English equivalent. The Dutch built the wall where Wall Street runs.

There can be no question that Dutch explorers like Henry Hudson and the adventurers who followed him, financed by the great banking firms of Amsterdam and Antwerp, were after the New World's "natural" resources (timber, fur, fish, and so on) to trade around the globe. This was the age of mercantile capitalism. It was dominated by vast trading monopolies that were licensed by and collaborated with their governments; the companies and their investors represented, let us say, the embryonic Wall Streets of the world. The Dutch were first among equals back then, just as New York occupies that position today. No doubt exists about their motivations.

According to the country's origin story, our true ancestral heroes occupied a more empyrean realm. Pioneering settlers at

Plymouth and Jamestown and slightly later in mainland Massachusetts were political refugees, religious dissenters, instinctive democrats, egalitarian individualists, idealists, inventors of a "new man" in a "New World." There is considerable truth in this depiction. However, it effaces other realities, kin to the earthier aspirations of the New York Dutch. Historians have written about these, but the founding tale remains essentially intact, for the average citizen a past perfect.

Plymouth and the much larger "plantation" of Massachusetts Bay established ten years later are particularly enlightening. The original settlers were in the main (although not entirely) Puritans of one sort or another. Some were what were called "Separatists" who had been living as expatriates in Holland (or more covertly in England). Their Protestant antipathies toward the Anglican Church of England and to the Crown, which they suspected was in league with the Church's heavy tincture of Catholicism, were severe enough to countenance separation: religious, territorial, even political. They were outsiders by choice and by virtue of official intimidation. Other Puritans shared their basic beliefs but were insiders. Often enough these were men of considerable wealth, usually accumulated in trade but also in land. They might even occupy positions of political influence. They weren't separatists, but they were both dissenters and people attuned to the commercial prospects of the mercantile world.[1]

When the seventeenth century began, both those economic prospects and political pressures were becoming more and more worrisome. The monarchy was asserting prerogatives offensive to parliamentary tradition and threatening to those not disposed to conform. At the same time, the economy fell into a steep decline. The collapse that began in 1620 was the steepest in six decades. Businesses of all kinds went under. Artisans lost their workshops. Tradesmen fell into insupportable

debt. Larger merchants watched world markets shrink or
get annexed by the Dutch. Something similar happened on the
land. Tenants couldn't make the rent as bad harvests and
the enclosure of common land by manorial lords aggravated
the crisis. Even larger landlords felt the pinch. "Masterless
men"—people whose traditional and deferential ties to landlords or master craftsmen or ship captains or ship builders or
merchant princes or political patrons had been severed by
the fluctuating fortunes associated with the labile rhythms
of the market—roamed country roads and urban back alleys
in growing numbers. This vagrant underclass, although regulated and punished by the Elizabethan codes of the previous
century, remained a cause for alarm. It also had potential.[2]

Plymouth and Massachusetts Bay especially, as well as
Jamestown, were born out of this miscible brew of religious
and political high-mindedness, customary deferential social
relationships, and the economic ambitions and class tensions
characteristic of the world the settlers were leaving behind.
Many migrants came from the Midlands, a region suffering
acute distress, thanks both to the enclosure movement and to
a growth in population. Pilgrims on the *Mayflower* were joined
by forty-eight "strangers" (meaning non-Separatists) from
London and elsewhere. Of those, eighteen were indentured for
a year. There were twelve sailors, a cooper, a carpenter, a master
gunner, and a professional soldier, Myles Standish. So too the
Jamestown voyagers were a mixed lot of the high and low born.
Virginia in particular soaked up some of the surplus population
of the depressed motherland, its emigrants often recruited from
that roving population of day laborers, agricultural workers,
domestics, textile operatives, and displaced tenants.[3]

On board the *Mayflower* social ranks were clearly observed, deference shown, for example, to the Carver family (its

patriarch would become the colony's first governor, although he soon died), which brought along its five servants. The majority of those who made the earliest voyage to the New World were middling sorts, not the most deprived. Still, the part of England they left behind had long been organized into well-defined hierarchies and dependencies resting on property, age, and patriarchy. Even modestly equipped households maintained servants, although in the ruder circumstances that awaited them abroad only the wealthiest—families like the Appeltons and Bradburys—were able to reestablish servants in husbandry when they disembarked. Initially, everyone worked, including John Winthrop and others in his patrician milieu, people who would have considered labor beneath them back home.[4]

Soon after the "plantation" of Massachusetts Bay was settled, subsequent ships from England carried a growing proportion of bonded servants, some captured as prisoners of war by Cromwell's New Model Army in Scotland and Ireland, then sold and indentured. Soon enough a small population of day laborers emerged, supplemented by farmers who moonlighted for wages to survive. So a social hierarchy not unlike the one back home sprouted early on, although it was a shorter one that didn't extend so far down or up.[5]

But even if its social order was less steeply terraced than the one it left behind, settler society remained subject to the cultural assumptions and expectations of the old order: that society rested on different "condicions of mankinde," and that the wealthiest among them would by the nature of things rule. With the exception of Captain John Smith, the leaders of Jamestown were credentialed members of the upper class. Edward Morris Wingfield, the colony's first president, said of Smith, "If he were in England, I would thinck scorne this man should be my companyon."

Similarly, Massachusetts Bay was the home not only of John Winthrop but of the future nabobs of Brahmin New England, including the Saltonstalls, the Endicotts, and the Higginsons. Some of these aristocrats brought their feudal retinue with them, including stewards, their own clergy, like John Cotton, and other retainers. The *Arbella* itself was named after a Puritan nobleman's sister imprisoned by the king for two years. The Earl of Lincoln, Theophilus Clinton, had also backed the earlier undertaking at Plymouth. Yet under the changed circumstances of the New World, new forms of wealth accumulation through global trade and investment would work to undo the old order. That rankings were fewer and shorter made it easier to view the top from the bottom and left the whole system more porous. Nonetheless, as those ancient orderings weakened, new stratifications arising out of the commercial flux of the New World would take their place.[6]

All of these colonial outposts were exercises, after all, in a mercantile form of venture capitalism, whether or not they were also vessels of religious or political liberty. The *Mayflower*, the *Arbella*, and the three ships sailing to Virginia had on board a heterodox group of passengers, some true believers, some not, some of middling ranks, some rather wealthier, and some "masterless." They sailed under the flags of privately owned, although publicly sanctioned, joint-stock trading companies, some of whose investors and creditors were aboard ship, some waiting for their returns on investment back in London. (The Virginia Company conducted a public offering of its stock two years after it was created.) We call them "colonies," which presumes their character as public projects, but in fact all of their assets—land, tools, houses, and, of course, profits—belonged to the joint-stock company and its shareholders. Passengers might be shareholders or not, or some might hold a greater share than others. Each settler traveling to Plymouth had at least one share worth £10, and a second share if he or she brought £10 worth of supplies. Women and children over the age of sixteen were also granted a share (a half share was given to those between ten and sixteen). During the seven-year term of the company's initial existence, food, clothing, shelter, and drink were to be paid out of the common stock.[7]

Shareholders aboard the *Arbella* were granted land, often in groups acting as proto-towns. Founding proprietors of each "town" were given collectively six square miles, which they then could dispose of as they saw fit. The grants were usually based on the extent of each person or family's existing resources to ensure that the land would be most fruitfully developed. That in turn meant people with servants and sometimes cattle.

Right away, then, a truncated but not unfamiliar pecking order emerged. Individual landholders were free to do what they wanted with their property, subject only to certain communal constraints on how the land was used, some obligation to show real improvement in three years, and other customary restrictions. A similar evolution in the direction of private ownership of land occurred in Virginia just before the Pilgrims arrived. There, property ownership was established as a requirement for voting. According to one historian, "More than anything else, it was the treatment of land and property as commodities traded at market that distinguished English conceptions of ownership from Indian ones." Putting aside for the moment how that would open up an existential and class-inflected chasm between pre-Columbian civilizations and European ones, the pursuit of accumulation through the mechanisms of the market would also cleave the world that had been transplanted across the Atlantic.[8]

Whatever their religious or political purposes, these settlements or "plantations" were intended to be not merely self-sufficient but profit making. Their promoters were hardly shy about drawing airy pictures of untold wealth there for the taking. An early dispatch from Cape Cod called it "a goodly land" and went on to describe a commercial Eden. In New England that meant the ordinary—fish, fur, timber. In Jamestown it signaled the extraordinary, the hard-to-shake conviction that gold was there somewhere, a belief that fueled a quest that nearly destroyed the outpost, as no one wanted to work. After all, half of the 105 voyagers could be classed as "gentlemen" who looked down on labor of all kinds. Captain John Smith, who is rightly credited with imposing a harsh, if life-saving, discipline on the would-be prospectors, remarked after returning to England, "Gold promises made all men their slaves in hopes of recompenses." There was, he remembered, "no talke, no hope, no worke, but dig gold, wash gold, refine gold, loade gold, such a bruit of gold, that one mad fellow desired to be buried in sands [in order that the sands] would make gold of his bones."

Smith had little regard for "gentlemen." He thought of them as people who "never did anything but devour the fruits of other men's labor" and mocked their behavior on the Virginia frontier. where they whined about the lack of "any of their accustomed dainties, with feather beds and down pillows, taverns and alehouses, in every breathing place, neither plenty of gold and silver and dissolute liberty as they expected." In his view, "A plaine souldier that can use a pick-axe and spade is better than five Knights, although they were Knights that could break a Lance; for men of great place, not inurred to those incounters; where they finde things not suitable, grow many times so discontented, they forget themselves and oft become so careless that a discontented melancholy brings them to much sorrow, and to others much miserie."[9]

Famously, Captain Smith proclaimed that "he that will not worke shall not eate . . . for the labours of thirtie or fortie honest and industrious men shall not be consumed to maintaine an hundred and fiftie idle layteres." His envisioned a land where "every man may be master and owner of his owne labour and land; or the greatest part in a small time. . . . If hee have nothing but his hands, he may set up this [his?] trade; and by industrie quickly grow rich; spending but halfe that time wel, which in England we abuse in idleness, worse or as ill." Others of higher social station saw things differently. Even after the gold craze subsided, a Virginia Company pamphlet of 1620 advertised "the rich Furres, Caviary, and Cordage which we draw from Russia with so great difficulty, are to be had in Virginia, and the ports adjoining with ease and plenty."[10]

Part of our folklore is how this too sunny view of what awaited them, their lack of preparation, meant disaster for the colonists. Only 38 of the original 108 who landed in Jamestown made it through their first winter alive. What became known as "the Starving Time" came a few years later. Staying alive meant eating rats, cats, mice, dogs, shoe leather, and finally human flesh. On Cape Cod colonists waited for a resupply ship from England and meanwhile begged from the Indians (Virginia colonists did the same in the early years, or if they felt strong enough plundered the neighboring Powhattans). And in that connection, incidentally, it is very unlikely any turkey was served at that fabled first thanksgiving dinner hosted by the Wampanoog tribe. The bird, originally imported from Turkey to North America by the Spanish, had been hunted to near extinction by both natives and Europeans by the seventeenth century. In any event, things couldn't continue down this road.[11]

If this undertaking was to serve as a "city on hill," a "light unto the nations," it would also need to function like any more earthbound city. That meant it would have to satisfy the more secular desires of its financial facilitators. Investors and creditors were known as "adventurers," a nomenclature that had more to do with risking money than life. A generation before the Pilgrims set sail, the soldier-poet and Calvinist Philip Sidney summed up the vision of a "hazardous enterprise of planting upon the main of America, an Emporium for the confluence of all nations that love or profess any kind of virtue or commerce." "Adventurers" were customarily seeking a 30 percent return on their investment. Whether these expectations were rational or not, they put enormous pressure on these enterprises. Articles of incorporation were time bound, seven years usually, at the end of which they might be dissolved and the spoils divided up. All investors had incurred debts to finance these expeditions before they hauled up anchor and would accumulate more to survive once they landed. Plymouth "plantation" had about seventy investors, some of landed wealth, others merchants or master artisans, all in it for the good works and good returns.[12]

Deference and debt, along with visions of religious and commercial liberation, comprised the baggage carried abroad and unloaded on the shores of the New World. These were rude encampments at first. Nothing quite like the steep hierarchies of power, wealth, and preferment could be reproduced on the coastlines of an unknown continent. Planted there were the seeds of a middling social order but also one whose formative years were molded by a world accustomed to acknowledging rank, the incentives and perils of the market, and the specter of "masterless men." Barely taken into account were the people who already lived there.[13]

Solvency and Salvation

Even before disembarking, the Plymouth expeditioners nearly came to blows. We think of the Mayflower Compact as a kind of democratic and constitutional premonition, a prophylactic against tyranny or milder forms of elitism. Insofar as it is thought to prefigure the Constitution, it has been considered providential. There is some truth to this, although the Constitution it is supposed to foreshadow was itself the outcome of intense social conflict, some of which got inscribed in its articles.[14]

The language of the compact is suggestive. The signers assented "to such governance and government as we should agree to make and choose." The document clarified that they were embarked on "a voyage to plant the first colony in the northern part of Virginia" (note that they sailed at first under a license accorded by the Crown to the Virginia Company) and that they had combined "into a civil body politic" that would "enact, constitute, and frame such just and equal laws, ordinances, acts, constitutions, offices from time to time, as shall be thought most meet and convenient for the general good of the colony; unto which we promise all due submission and obedience." It is tempting, for the sake of our national origin story, to interpret the compact anachronistically.

It is easy to forget that the document signed on board the *Mayflower* was a corporate, not a communal agreement. Nor was it a state document, nor did it envision anything remotely like a new nation; indeed, it paid explicit obeisance to the king. Nor was it a secular or democratic understanding in the first instance but a religious one—as it ought to have been, given who was aboard. The Pilgrims were not against monarchy as a form of government even if they had severe differences with their present monarch. They were as well colonialists who believed in their nation's suzerainty over others as much as James I did, and thought of his foreign foes, especially the Spanish, as their own enemies as well, on both religious and political grounds.[15]

What drove the voyagers to sign a compact before disembarking were the tensions that had already surfaced between the adventurers and their fellow passengers, especially the "strangers," over the division of the profits both groups were looking forward to. The adventurers were suspected of cheating, of trying to squeeze out something extra to compensate for the risk involved in supplying the wherewithal of the venture, including the ship. This is the context in which they submitted "to such governance and government as we should agree to make and choose."

Moreover, when contemplating more precisely what ideals motivated these undertakings, it is worth remembering perhaps the most famous pronouncement of their exceptional nature. John Winthrop delivered his sermon, "A Model of Christian Charitie," while still on board the *Arbella*: "Men shall say of succeeding plantacions: 'the Lord made it like those of New England': for . . . we shall be a City upon a Hill, the eyes of all people are uppon us." The sermon makes no mention of democracy or liberty, but rather fixes its attention on the new settlement's practice of its version of the Protestant faith and how well its congregants might execute its vision of charity.[16]

Christian charity no doubt moved the consciences of many a settler. Cotton Mather referred to William Bradford, the Plymouth Bay colony's governor, as the "Moses of the Puritan migration." But the settlers were also preoccupied with surviving, thriving, and doing business. Winthrop argued on behalf of colonization not only for religious purposes but because there was a good chance it would realize high returns for the labor expended. Business, however, was not good at first.

These colonies functioned within a global web of financial and trading relationships. Their life expectancy depended not only on ensuring their material subsistence but on their capacity to produce commodities for the worldwide market that could be monetized and satisfy the adventurers' thirst for profits—and, even more urgent, pay off their swelling debts to their London bankers. That wasn't happening in Plymouth in these formative years because there was precious little in the immediate vicinity that might be shipped back to England and turned into cash. At Jamestown the situation was at first even worse. Gold fever sickened efforts at any real economy.

Much of the Pilgrims' labor in those early days was done to repay debts to their financial backers. They needed to produce vendible commodities: so that, for example, the first ship sent back to England in 1621 contained two barrels of fur and a cargo of lumber for use in the homeland shipbuilding industry. That wasn't much, however. A few years later the colony was self-sufficient in food, but its debts grew relentlessly. It owed the enormous sum of £1,300 to its creditors and still relied on being resupplied from England. The situation in Virginia was more dire. By 1612 no more stock offerings were possible to refinance the settlement. A version of martial law imposed by Smith included forced labor, no right to return home, and draconian punishment for the pettiest infractions, including death by starvation for stealing from the company stores. What was to be done?[17]

The Mad Hatter

Alice of *Alice in Wonderland* attends a "Mad Tea Party" hosted by a "Mad Hatter." Actually, Lewis Carroll named him simply the Hatter, but he quickly became known far and wide as the

Mad Hatter because he was clearly crazy. When Carroll was writing, in the mid-nineteenth century, the phrase "mad as a hatter" had been in circulation for at least two hundred years, a common idiom Carroll no doubt knew and may well have had in mind. "Mad as a hatter" has a sad backstory that speaks to class and pathology.

Fur hats had been the preferred headgear for the aristocracies of Europe, Russia, and China for centuries. This was a luxury trade of mass proportions. Making a fur hat, in particular the popular beaver hat, was a complex undertaking, labor intensive and dirty. The hat passed through several stages of production, often requiring considerable skill and some chemistry. At one point the hatter had to make use of liquid mercury, which was released as fumes as the artisan steamed the hat in order to shape it. Workers in the trade soon enough began showing various physical and neurological disorders: their teeth fell out, their kidneys and endocrine systems malfunctioned. They slurred their speech, suffered hallucinations, showed signs of memory loss as well as paranoia and depression, and often were subject to uncontrollable tremors, or "hatters' shakes": "mad as a hatter" indeed.[18]

Fur workers might be driven mad from their work, but the trade was making what we might today call mad profits. It is hard to exaggerate how precious furs had become by the time the Pilgrims set off. From raw pelt to finished hat the markup was eightfold. The great state-sanctioned trading companies monopolized the business. Their markets spanned the globe. Beaver hats in particular were coveted items in wider circuits of high-end consumption by landed elites, wealthy merchants, lawyers, state bureaucrats (including the boyars who ran the czar's autocracy and China's Confucian state functionaries). In London the upper class could shop at the New Exchange, a kind of shopping mall for the elite that included haberdashers, milliners, and the like. Quality varied depending on the nature of the pelt and the complexity of the production process. The finest were sleek, silky, sometimes lined with velvet or taffeta, finished to a glossy sheen. Beaver hats were markings of social prestige, worn within prescribed social rituals that determined when exactly they were suitable, when they were to be doffed, and so on. They made their debut in Paris in the late sixteenth century. Some remarked on their extravagance. One writer noted "fashions . . . rare and straunge, so are the things whereof their Hattes be made." Soon enough they had become what one historian has called a "golden fetish." They were also quite warming during Europe's Little Ice Age and, thanks to the beaver's way of life, relatively waterproof.

In otherwise depressed times, this luxury trade kept the economy moving. And for that reason, among others, it attracted the support of the Crown. (Prince Charles indulged his appetite for high living in every conceivable way, including a spectacular collection of beaver hats and clothing.) State policy pursued colonization in order to augment the circulation of goods (both luxury items like fur and silk, and homely essentials like lumber) and taxable revenue from their sale. Conflict with other nations pursuing the same goal was inevitable and worked to raise even further the price of beaver.[19]

North America became an increasingly desirable source of supply. Western Europe had hunted out its beaver population by this time (in medieval days local beaver had been ample and so too, therefore, hats). The beaver stock east of the Urals was likewise heavily tapped out, and in any case dealing with Russia was politically difficult and entailed hazardous transit through Archangel. Another factor, however, made North America extraordinarily appealing. Native hunters could furnish the furs and they didn't have to be paid in bullion; indeed, these men and women of the forest would have had no use for it. In a mercantilist age that placed a premium on hoarding stashes of gold and silver, this was an "offer" impossible to refuse.[20]

Beaver were not plentiful where the Pilgrims landed. But they were elsewhere, especially further north along the forested coast of Maine. Before the English arrived, other Europeans had traded there for furs. It was the discovery of this "golden fetish" in its raw form that rescued Plymouth. It became as well an important support for Massachusetts Bay.

Tribes living in the vicinity of Plymouth were mobile societies whose material well-being depended on cyclical rounds of hunting, fishing, gathering fruits and herbs, and agriculture, in particular the growing of corn. They had customarily traded some of that maize with tribes living further north for furs for their own use as clothing. The colonists caught on quickly, knowing that fur was a valuable cash commodity back where they had come from. So they traded with the locals for corn, grew some themselves, and sailed to Maine. The eastern Abenaki living along the Kennebec River were already accustomed to trading with Europeans for metal tools, cooking implements, and other items. They were also highly proficient at trapping beaver, using birch bark dugout canoes as long as eighteen feet, manned by two men and capable of carrying a cargo of a thousand pounds yet able to traverse streams with depths of only five inches. In Plymouth's first venture to the Kennebec region, settlers swapped surplus corn for furs weighing seven hundred pounds. In 1630 the Pilgrims shipped two thousand beaver pelts to England, worth about £5,000, a far cry from that original shipment of two barrels of fur. Fur trading was the colony's financial salvation.[21]

Like liquid mercury, however, the fur trade, together with the implanting of distinctively European practices of private property, would have a pathological impact. This time the victims were the trade's producers of raw material, the native sons and daughters of the New World. Social antagonism erupted both within the European settler communities and between them and the indigenous worlds they settled among. Class relations were already part of the cargo en route to America and infected the atmosphere even before landfall. They were at work insidiously undermining the harmony of the city on a hill, and imperiling the survival and civil peace of Jamestown. Once the colonies took root, newer kinds of class tensions began to mutate. Those internal social hemorrhages would sicken but not kill the body politic.

Something more deadly, however, accompanied the external transactions between mercantile and Indian societies. They would eventually poison the latter, incubating behavior and motivations as well as social and political distempers that would prove fatal. Moreover, that lethal relationship would produce a different kind of racial pathogen in the collective psyche of settler society. The primitive accumulation of liquid capital in the mercantile world accomplished by absorbing the labor and resources of noncommercial societies was a kind of supra-class form of exploitation that left indelible imprints on both parties to that relationship.

Wampum lubricated the circuits of trade between natives and colonists. It was as much a European as an Indian medium. Tribes made use of the shells (whelks and quahogs) for various ceremonial and practical purposes, including as gifts to neighboring groups and to the sachems who led them, as compensation for powwow medical treatment, and so on. Western drilling instruments made it possible to mass-produce wampum, and that made it a currency of the fur trade in Maine. However, as wampum became widely available, its very prevalence overturned customary intra- and intertribal relations, upsetting traditional systems of social status by diffusing the political power that had once attached to established leaders of the tribes. The new system promoted both competition among Indians and dependence on the English.

Commerce, not technology, revolutionized the ecology and economy of Indian life. Axes and iron pots simply made it easier to reproduce life as it had always been without uprooting those ways of surviving. Frequently such items not only proved useful but were incorporated into preexisting social rituals, functioning, thanks to their exoticism or rarity, as insignia of social status. Guns made intertribal conflict more deadly, of course, but there had always been intertribal confrontations.

Relying on European guns, however, meant that the immemorial skills of making traditional weaponry were lost, intensifying indigenous dependency on the Old World. The market as a social system increasingly reconfigured who mattered and who didn't. Traditional kinship and political hierarchies were transgressed or abandoned. The market inculcated a competitive instinct that eroded communal norms. Tribes could and did become shrewd traders (the British tried to control the trade for wampum shells with the Indians of Long Island, but the tribes were too crafty to be dominated). But whether or not they could function well or poorly in this regional and ultimately global network of trade, Indian social esteem came to rest on "killing animals and exchanging their skins for wampum or high-status European goods."[22]

Societies that had rested on production for use, with trade an occasional activity tied to reciprocal obligations and tributes, became inveigled in economies given over entirely to trade and private accumulation. And because the terms of trade so disfavored these indigenous communities, they were compelled to produce for the market at a rate and in quantities that eventually came at the expense of traditional forms of labor. Ironically, the shift to fur trapping for international markets diminished the time the natives had once devoted to making their own clothing and blankets, so that they came to rely more and more on European textiles and European goods more generally. By the latter part of the century, one observer noted, local tribes had "abandoned all their own utensils."

So too, in order to meet the demand of the global marketplace, formerly mobile communities had to become more sedentary, both because the game they once tracked was vanishing and so as to be near the source of wampum shells or beaver. Permanent settlements became denser, which made them readier carriers of disease (not to mention the near-complete eradication of Indian populations by European-born microbes against which they had no immunities). Population growth intensified pressure on the land both for hunting and agricultural purposes, and tribal diets became less varied and nutritious.[23]

It wasn't long before the only asset left to these communities was the land, but by the latter part of the seventeenth century they had lost most of it either through war, by working fields to exhaustion (something unheard of under the old regime of a mobile, cyclical economy), through sale to provision themselves with the basics, or through subterfuge and seizure by the continent's "new man." Moreover, this relentless pressure to produce a surplus for trade put enormous pressure on the animal population they had long relied on (especially given the low reproductive rate of the beaver) and on the whole ecological system of which the Indians had been a part for millennia. Bear, lynx, and elk, once staples of tribal diets, also became scarce, in part because the colonists allowed their hogs and cows to roam through the woods at will, consuming much of the vegetable matter those wild animals lived on. Cows foraged the unfenced fields of tribal communities, devouring the corn, squash, and beans planted there. As beaver were hunted out, the dams and ponds they had created, which helped make the land arable, went with them. Those same aquatic structures had encouraged fish and waterfowl by slowing water flow and raising the temperature, which nurtured plankton and insect life for the fish and birds to feed on. Everything of customary tangible value was going under.[24]

Intangibles were being lost as well, a situation just as life threatening. Along with material dependency came a cultural conversion—sometimes coerced, sometimes the outcome of the silent persuasion exercised by the new character a structured market society encouraged—that insidiously eroded the tissues of communal and familial life. These were by and large societies long accustomed to elastic notions of tribal territory and personal property that treated these not as exclusive, heritable, or alienable but rather to be held for the common use and distributed to individuals as custom and need prescribed. There was no need for property accumulation in these mobile social economies. Tools and other items were used by many people. Land was farmed and then left for brush as the settlements moved on, only to be cleared again in the future. Property was often embedded in political and cultural institutions of gift exchanges rather than sold, and such transactions were enacted in order to confirm or reaffirm social position. Fisheries and hunting grounds, berry- and nut-picking areas were treated as a tribal commonweal, a notion the British either could not understand or simply ignored. Tribe members accepted as a matter of course that they all were entitled to hunt, gather wild plants, or cut birch bark for canoes. The same sense of common usufruct applied to the rivers and coasts. Villages owned not the land but what was on the land.

Now these communities were confronted by a very different conception of property, buttressed by British law, which took for granted that property of all sorts inhered in the individual, who could do with it what he wanted: pass it on to heirs, sell it, borrow against it, and so on. So, for example, settlers adopted tribal practices of clearing land through periodic burnings, but these burnings occurred within strict property boundaries that were meaningless to their neighbors. Moreover, because colonists were free to do what they wanted with their property, their burnings were much more extensive, intended not merely to clear away the undergrowth but to eliminate the forest itself—and the forest was an ecological lifeline for the tribes. Conversely, Indians conducting their cyclical, communal burnings were held liable for damages to British property.

A fur trader named William Pynchon struck a deal with an Agawan village in 1636. The Agawans assumed they were retaining their conventional rights of usufruct—to hunt, fish, and gather on the land—and granting Pynchon and his partners permission to share in doing that, in return for which they would receive various tools. The villagers considered this an act of their sovereign tribe, not as an act that transferred ownership, and as a usufruct right that applied only to specific uses of the land. Pynchon and the English law courts thought otherwise. They treated the exchange as a private transaction that granted the Indians limited rights but vested ownership in Pynchon, the "buyer." John Winthrop confected a similar arrangement with the Indian sachem Maskonomen in 1637 in which all Indian rights were cancelled and the land comprising what became Ipswich was parceled out to private owners. Native Americans were selling one thing and the British were buying something else. All of this amounted to a kind of cultural aphasia. Non-commercial societies were afflicted, sometimes mortally.[25]

And how rapidly the affliction spread. Miantonomo, sachem of the Narragansett Indians, summed up in 1642 what had already happened: "You know our father had plenty of deer and skins, our plains were full of deer, as also our woods, and of turkies, and our coves full of fish and fowl. But these English having gotten our land, they with scythes cut down the grass and with axes fell the trees; their cows and horses eat the grass, and their hogs spoil our clam banks, and we shall all be starved." Later he was assassinated by the English. A noted historian of this profound imbalance has remarked, "By integrating New England ecosystems into an ultimately global capitalist economy, colonists and Indians together began a dynamic and unstable process of ecological change which had in no way ended by 1800."[26]

A Chosen People

Settler society from the outset erected an ideological fortress of justification for what soon had become a relationship of overlord to subordinate, a set of rationales that traversed the borders of two very different worlds. In this instance, the social illness unto death that gripped the native Americans also seeped into the cultural bloodstream of their conquerors, leaving them and their heirs carriers of a warped class and race consciousness.

Despite the colonials' early dependence on Indian foodstuffs, agricultural know-how, and woodland knowledge, the New Englanders adopted the view that tribal life was largely given over to idleness, wiling away time hunting and fishing. The very mobility that characterized Indian economies as tribes moved from place to place in accord with the seasons (and

consequently with little vested interest in property accumulation) offended the conventional wisdom of the Puritans. Fran-
ces Higginson concluded, "The Indians are not able to make
use of one fourth part of the land, neither have they any settled
places as Townes to dwell in, nor any ground as they challenge
for their owne possession, but change their habitation from
place to place."

Indian laziness forfeited any legitimate claim to the land,
so the English felt entirely within their rights to take it. Because
the natives underused the land, failed to "improve" it, they didn't
deserve to possess it. Indians would "rather starve than work"
(although under normal circumstances proportionately far
fewer Indians starved than settlers). Males were especially lazy
and lived for pleasure. Captain Smith observed, "The men
bestow their times in fishing, hunting, warres, and such manlike
exercises, scorning to be seen in any woman-like exercise, which
is the cause that women be very painfull, and the men often
idle." He was describing Indian life as he saw it in Virginia, where
"women and children doe the reste of the worke. They make
mats, baskets, pots, morters, pound their corne, make their
bread, prepare their victuals, plant their corne, gather their
corne, bear all kinds of burdens and such like."

New England settlers agreed. One Puritan noted that the
tribes were not "industrious," "neither have art, science, skill,
or facility to use either the land or the commodities of it, but
all spoils, rots, and is marred for want of manuring, gardening,
etc." Their land, "spacious and voide," was there for the taking.
John Winthrop proclaimed that except for the fields planted by
Indian women, which he considered theirs, "the rest of the
country lay open to any that could and would improve it." And
when in fact the land was "all voide" because a severe epidem-
ic had emptied it soon before the Pilgrims landed, Winthrop

considered it providential: "God hath hereby cleared our title to this place." The city on a hill would be built where "God hath consumed the natives with a miraculous plague, where by a great parte of the Country is left voyde of Inhabitants." John Cotton would offer ministerial reinforcement of that view, explaining, "In a vacant soyle hee that taketh possession of it and bestoweth culture and husbandry upon it, his Right it is."²⁷

God had help in sanctioning these behaviors and attitudes. A racially inflected view of native peoples as inferior was commonplace. In the beginning that was not entirely the case. Colonists could recognize their neighbors as human, equipped with language, large-scale social organization, government, agriculture, and so on; they could even appreciate the aesthetic appeal of body decoration common among the tribes. Soon enough, however, the acquisitive disposition of these shareholders, together with imperial instincts implanted in the homeland, fostered a dimmer view. Roger Williams pronounced native people "barbarous scum and the offscourings of mankind." Puritans were prepared to do missionary work among these benighted people but called them "savages"; in the words of Plymouth's second and long-serving governor William Bradford, the settlers had found a land "devoid of all civil inhabitants, where there are only savage and brutal men which range up and down, little otherwise than the wild beasts."²⁸

Hostile encounters were inevitable under these circumstances and occurred almost immediately upon settlement (the first at a beach now known as Wellfleet). Myles Standish, who had been hired by the Pilgrims as their military leader, was a courageous man with an inflammatory temper. He had no use for Indians and would decapitate one if he thought it called for. Even before the *Mayflower* arrived, local Indians had experienced the dark side of European commerce. Captain John Smith (who sailed and mapped much of the Atlantic coast) reported on how a sea captain named Thomas Hunt had tricked a group of thirty natives to come on board, made them captives, and sold "these silly Salvages for Rials of Eight" in Malaga. Serial conflicts with native peoples (sometimes complicated by shifting alliances between colonists and some tribes who had become the strategic enemies of other tribes) culminated in the vicious Pequot War and massacre; four hundred to seven hundred Pequots were slain by a combined force of settlers and native people in 1636. Praising God for the victory, the colonists held a thanksgiving to celebrate.[29]

Relations further south in Virginia were similarly exploitative, marked by racial stigmata and blood on the ground. Thanks to the legendary friendship between Captain Smith and Pocahontas, a royal and favored daughter of the region's principal sovereign Chief Powhatan, the Jamestown fable of bitter hardship is overlaid with an aura of romantic good feelings. And indeed, Smith and Powhatan did oversee a period of relative stability between the colonials and the federation of Algonquian tribes Powhatan presided over. The captain recognized the value of the Powhatans' rich, corn-based agriculture and their deep knowledge of the environment. That hardly called into question his firm belief in English dominance, however. After all, Smith believed in the Christianizing and civilizing mission that British colonialism purported to be about. Nor did he have any objections to indentured servitude, nor doubt the essential savagery of the native population. The tribes required, in his view, a substantial dose of discipline and a conspicuous show of force.[30]

Discipline was not the strong suit of the idling gentry who comprised such a large portion of the early settlers. They preferred not to work. Instead they took to trading with—and if they ran out of tradeables, raiding—Indian villages. This became commonplace during and after "the Starving Time." Once Smith returned to England, they kidnapped Pocahontas and ransomed her back to her father. These conflicts remained sporadic until the colonists found their own way to meet the financial demands of the Virginia Company's investors and creditors.

Tobacco became Virginia's version of the fur trade. John Rolfe, the man who married Pocahontas and brought her back to England, where she died not long after, developed a strain of tobacco based on a West Indian variety. It would soon make the Virginia Company financially viable. By 1618 the colony was shipping nearly fifty thousand pounds of tobacco annually to England, and by 1628 that had grown to half a million. The rise of tobacco agriculture in turn produced an enormous demand for labor and land. Cultivating the plant was labor intensive and exhausting, especially the weeding and planting. This would lead to a substantial flow of indentured labor from England, people tempted by a promise of land of their own once their indentures expired.

Very soon tobacco production would lead to the use of slave labor, including Indians but especially Africans (although initially that enslavement did not call upon racial stereotypes for its justification). So a steeper hierarchy of social power and powerlessness than that maturing in New England was evolving quickly to the south. Moreover, a hunger for fresh land on which to grow tobacco led to seizures of tribal plots and violent confrontations culminating in the massacre of 350 colonists in 1622 followed by a decade of warfare. Back in England, Smith advocated an official policy that in effect would provide a writ to seize Indian land, impose a military occupation, and reduce native dwellers to the status of laborers, coerced or otherwise.

At the end, no Englishman doubted that the Indian was indeed a "brute savage."[31]

Paradise Lost?

Neither English settlers nor their Indian neighbors inhabited some earthly utopia, free of social and political conflict. Clearly, the relationship established between the new occupiers and the original occupants eventually rested on exploitation of the latter that verged on extinction. Tribal life before that, however, was marked by its own social stratifications and violent conflict. A priestly class, albeit a polytheistic one, ruled, lived, and died in ways not available to ordinary tribespeople, made decisions about how the collective wealth of the community was to be used, raided rival tribes and took their women and children as captives, and so on. They hardly matched those savage caricatures deployed by the colonists from the Old World to malign those they were plundering. But they grew up in complex societies thousands of years old that had constructed their own political and social hierarchies characteristically patriarchal and, in Smith's not entirely inapt word, "monarchical."

So too, when the passengers disembarked at Plymouth or at Jamestown, they brought with them their own distinct social and political pecking orders. These were long-established deferential relationships that dictated economic and political behavior, who ruled and who didn't, who worked and who didn't, who owned and who didn't, how you dressed, where and how you lived, whom you genuflected to, whether you had a good or less good chance of surviving.

Therefore, it is hardly surprising, mythic origin tales notwithstanding, that the New World was neither a classless paradise nor a paradise lost. Instead, what was truly new emerged out of that intercourse between mercantile and non-market-based political economies and strikingly different ways of life. The integrity of tribal societies dissolved, their material wherewithal transplanted and transformed into liquid capital, their human resources into "human capital," their land and animals into marketable commodities, their cultural cohesiveness and independence corroded and debased.

By virtue of this same commercially driven interaction, the traditional hierarchies of Old World Europe gave way to new ones, powered by the drive to accumulate capital through global trade. In general, the trend was to abandon traditional forms of land tenure in favor of more strictly defined individual ownership that ensured exclusivity of use and strict laws against trespassing. An "Essay on the Ordering of Townes" advised that "he that knoweth the benefit of inclosing will omit noe diligence to bringe his selfe into an inclusive condicion, well understanding that one acre inclosed, is much more beneficall than five falling to his share in Common." This supported the emergence of a middling farming class but also one oriented more to the market. In turn, that meant an intensification of work, work discipline, and the duration of work. In Virginia the emergence of a commercially minded rural world of family farmers as well as a more self-sufficient yeomanry was retarded. That was thanks to the parallel development of slave-plantation agriculture dominated by large landholders. Virginia's colonial brethren to the north, however, were hard at work birthing a class structure that would soon characterize the New World.[32]

With gathering speed in colonial New England, bigger landholders like the Bradburys, Appeltons, and Gardeners hired laborers in their quest to furnish the markets in seaport towns that were themselves tied to transatlantic trade. Acute labor shortages encouraged day labor and good wages. As landed elites grew accustomed to the new commercial practices, their relationship with their tenants was modernized, made for fixed terms (usually lasting ten years) and for fixed sums, payable in currency as well as in labor or in kind. Wealth was a prerequisite to high office as it had always been; magistrates, community offices, militia captains, and other positions of authority fell to the wealthiest, but the sources of that wealth shifted in the direction of trade.

Class mattered from the beginning. *Class* may seem an anachronism. Neither the hierarchies of old nor the ones emerging in the New World conformed to modern conceptions of class. Those rest on the division between labor and capital that define the production process and/or on levels of income and styles of consumption. The former was incipient at most. As for status distinctions, while apt enough, they nonetheless embedded income and consumption in a web of heritable, religiously sanctioned, and customary arrangements that our world of invidious, consumer-based distinction would scarcely recognize or credit.

However, if we seek to appraise the validity of a story that tends to erase matters of deep social cleavage from the map of our beginnings, then "class" must be counted back in, albeit in some more capacious definition. This is true and necessary to get at a richer story. It is true because the peculiar and in the end parasitic relationship established between the colonists, native populations, and the world economy would be repeated again and again, in different contexts, for the next two centuries, both at home and abroad. This process of primitive capital accumulation at the expense of noncapitalist economies and ways of life would help define not only the economic dynamics but also the political upheavals and the ideological predispositions and prejudices of life in the New World. Likewise, those new tensions arising within settler society between middling sorts and rising mercantile elites would continue to inflame colonial and postcolonial society for a long time and find articulation in the battle over the Constitution.

Some people were disturbed by these trends, especially those fissures surfacing internally, which could seem at odds with visions of a godly commonwealth and a spiritual "errand into the wilderness." Robert Cushman, a wealthy deacon in the Separatist church in Leiden that helped organize the expedition, warned, "Let no man seek his owne; But every man another's wealth." He denounced greed, or what he termed the "belly god" worshiped by those who sought to become country gentlemen: "Men that have taken in hand hither to come out of discontentment in regard to their estates in England; and aiming at great matters here, affecting to be Gentlemen, Landed men, or hoping for Office, Place, Dignity, or fleshy Liberty, let the show be what it will, the substance is naught and that bird of self-love ... if it not be looked to will eat out the life of all grace and goodness." The powers that be, however, welcomed the "new man." Governor Bradford recognized that the settlers "began to think how they might raise as much corn as they could not obtain a better crop than they had done that they might not still thus languish in misery. At length, after much debate of things, the Governor (with the advice of the chieftest among them) gave way that they should set corn every man for his own particular [household], and in that regard trust to themselves."[33]

"Trust to themselves" became the watchword of a whole civilization, observed as much in colonial Virginia as in colonial New England, and thereafter by the new nation. It heralded a hardy individualism of the sort Captain Smith envisioned en route to North America. Treated in the right way, the virgin continent would become a paradise of middling sorts, hard-working men and women of independent means. No fixed ranks and orders—except those ordained by nature, whether by virtue of sex or race—would undercut that prospect. Yet everything that made these colonial undertakings feasible—their corporate origins, their relationship to the global marketplace, their transactions with vulnerable and incommensurate societies and, ironically, that urge to "trust to themselves"—set in motion a logic that generated new hierarchies, new forms of inclusion and exclusion, new modes of political preferment, new relationships to the natural world, new modes of work and exploitation, and finally a propulsive individualism that would inexorably undermine the chances of its own survival.

Fleeing to the New World was imagined as a way of starting over, a flight from history. But history abides. Smith's vision, the view of America the exceptional, would turn out to be a grand ambition—and a grand illusion.

2

We the People in the City of Brotherly Love

Early one weekday evening the police came knocking at my door. I was living in West Philadelphia with two friends. It was 1969 and I was twenty-three. There were a couple of uniformed officers and another three or four men in plainclothes. They belonged to a special unit of the Philadelphia police called the Civil Disobedience Squad, more colloquially known by political activists like me as the Red Squad.

They came hunting for bombs or the makings of bombs. Minutes after the Red Squad arrived, so did a television crew from the local NBC affiliate, which had obviously been notified in advance of the raid. A search of my apartment uncovered just what they were looking for: pipes, gunpowder, wires, fuses, and the powerful military plastic explosive C-4 (recently reported stolen from a local military base). All of these materials were hidden in and around and underneath the refrigerator. That's where the police, in collaboration with the Federal Bureau of Investigation, had planted them earlier that day.

Four of us were arrested and charged with conspiracy to blow up national monuments. Our arrests as suspected terrorists were part of a larger national FBI operation later identified as COINTELPRO, designed to discredit antiwar, civil rights, and Students for a Democratic Society (SDS) activists. Raiding and arresting members of activist groups was already a well-established law enforcement tradition in Philadelphia. There the police were commanded by Frank Rizzo, who had built a career by terrifying the citizenry with fabrications of alleged plots to burn down the city or (in a particularly outlandish invention) schemes by Black Power advocates to poison the police with cyanide-laced sandwiches. A beefy six foot plus tough guy rarely seen without his billy club, Rizzo promised to show no mercy, to clear the streets, to lock up all those who disrespected the flag, moral and sexual conventions, the racial status quo, and campus decorum. (Later he would leverage this reputation into two terms as the city's mayor.)

Just a month before the raid on our apartment, we were in the midst of a mass strike centered at the University of Pennsylvania that also included students from many of the area colleges. The strike was in response to the plans of a consortium of schools that had joined together to build something called the University City Science Center, which was forecasted to invite government-sponsored war-related research. Moreover, the center was to be built on land in the West Philadelphia ghetto that abutted the Penn campus, land that would have to be cleared of its low-income, largely African American tenants. It was discovered that leading real estate and financial interests had been speculating in these properties for some time, using a legal technique called the "sheriff's sale," which permitted evictions for overdue consumer debts—a car, say, or a refrigerator. Vacated homes were then auctioned off.

So if ever a strike cum occupation was overdetermined, this one based at Penn was: war, racism, and class exploitation were in the dock together. Although those occupying the Penn administration building were largely students, members of the surrounding community were present as well. The strike lasted nearly a week and ended with some largely symbolic concessions from the university. (The science center itself went up as planned.) In its aftermath, however, a movement for jobs, housing, and education that included high school students and members of the local Black Panther Party emerged in other parts of the city. One area of activism was North Philadelphia's black ghetto, the city's largest. Nearby was Temple University. There students who had participated in the Penn strike were sniffing out sheriff's sales, evictions, auctions, and land deals tied to Temple's own expansion plans.

Rizzo sprang into action. Stories appeared in local papers and were broadcast on radio that the police had come across a pamphlet on how to make bombs and Molotov cocktails that was being distributed in the ghetto by left-wing student agitators. The stage was set. Days later I was arrested along with my friends.

Getting arrested for political crimes in 1969, while not exactly commonplace, was a frequent enough occurrence in those tumultuous times. I had been arrested before. So outwardly I was, if not calm, then not entirely shocked, even in the heat of the moment and in the heat of the TV camera klieg lights. As if already rehearsed for their appearance, I launched into a running commentary on the objectives of the Alliance for Jobs, Housing, and Education as I trailed them trailing the police in their circumnavigation of our apartment.

Underneath that surface cool, however, I was unnerved. How eerie and surreal it seemed. When the police opened the refrigerator and "discovered" a sour ball candy can full of explosive, I suddenly remembered seeing the candy can, but when and where I could not for the life of me figure out. How in the world had the agents of the law managed to squirrel away this rude arsenal without any of us being aware of it? And then came one of those eureka moments, as in: "Oh, now I realize what that large tractor trailer had been doing parked outside our house for more than a week," during which not one us grew suspicious—talk about naïve. That the whole event was so deliberately staged and coordinated with the local media made it feel less like a political happening than a grotesque form of vaudevillian comedy in which I was playing a prescribed role, including my yapping at the TV cameras.

Perhaps one reason I was less scared than I might have been was this air of unreality. Theatrics notwithstanding, could it actually be the case that the guardians of law, order, and liberty could stoop to such preposterous antics and expect anyone to fall for it? No matter how politically knowledgeable I fancied myself to be, no matter what I knew to have been the case again and again over the course of the country's history, in the moment I still retained a subsurface belief that ruling institutions had to play within their own rules. One might credit that as a form of middle-class malignant indifference to the unruly reality that so often envelopes the lives of less favored classes and races.

And then again, could it be that these praetorians were so socially ignorant that they actually thought our movement was well rooted enough to represent an imminent threat to the prevailing distribution of wealth and power? On the one hand, that was flattering. But it was also untrue. Much as we liked to believe we were in touch with the grassroots, that was only partially the case on campus, faintly so with regard to the

ghetto, and no more than a pious wish when it came to the rest
of working-class Philadelphia. We knew that. Didn't they?

According to the police and prosecutor who filed charges
of conspiracy, our real object was not to incinerate or inspire
others to incinerate North Philadelphia. Nor did jobs, housing,
and education enter into it at all. Instead we were after the
Liberty Bell. Why? Was it because liberty and social justice were
at odds? Blow up one, you get the other? But that would be a
disquieting equation for the official defenders of democracy
and equality to work with.

Housed nearby in Independence Hall, the bell is a sacred
object. It rang out freedom and the birth of a nation. It had
been used to call out Philadelphia residents to the first reading
of the Declaration of Independence. To blow it up would be a
sacrilege and a mad act. Those purportedly conspiring to do so
might thereby be stigmatized as political fiends. No need to pay
attention to their ostensible concerns about economic and
racial injustice and inequality, or their worries about the infes-
tation of the campus by the military-industrial complex or their
outrage over the mechanized slaughter in Southeast Asia. Liberty and its bell could thus function as a political prophylactic.

Liberty in 1969, like liberty in 1776, was a universal bene-
diction. It didn't matter where you happened to be located along
the spectrum of wealth and income; its blessings were a birthright. And if back in 1776 it did matter what "race" you belonged
to, by 1969 that ostensibly had been taken care of by an enlightened Establishment. If matters of class and race nonetheless
intruded into a world committed to ignoring them, then the
guardians of liberty might feel driven to commit a mad act of
their own, violating liberty on behalf of liberty: a micro-version
of destroying the village to save it. So off we went, handcuffed,
into a paddy wagon, which my grandmother watched drive

away on TV before making a hysterical phone call to my mother, her daughter, to tell her the news.

Class mattered in the "City of Brotherly Love." It always had. Devotion to the classless ideal of liberty concealed that. It always had. When the bell tolled long ago, a nation emerged, one consecrated to liberty and justice for all. That pledge was later reaffirmed in a document that opens "We the People." Our national credo reveres the Constitution the way it does the Liberty Bell. Where they reign, class privilege and exploitation go to die. But that was no more the case in Philadelphia in 1787 than it was in 1969.

Brotherly Love and Fratricide

Conceived in secrecy, the Constitution was a near-miss proposition. Both the secrecy and its perilously close ratification (only thirty-nine of the fifty-five delegates actually signed the document) had everything to do with the intensity of social antagonisms that led up to the gathering in Philadelphia. Liberty was indeed at stake. For some the document that emerged would protect their liberty; for many others it would be a story of liberty lost.

Historians have argued for well over a century about whether the Constitution was the outcome of class conflict, and if so whose interests did it articulate, whose did it squelch. Among scholars that remains an unsettled question, even if the terms of that debate have been reframed more than once. For most people the matter is simpler, not really a question at all. Those fifty-five men who assembled in the sweltering July heat (and kept the windows and doors closed and locked in the East Room of the Pennsylvania State House to ensure they wouldn't be eavesdropped on) were, after all, our "founding fathers."

There is something ageless and sacerdotal about that honorarium. It cries out virtue, guardianship, and a kind of suprawisdom ordinary people simply don't possess. They were there to save an infant nation verging on dissolution. And more than that, to "secure the blessings of liberty to ourselves and our Posterity." Missioned in that way, they put the commonweal first, submerging any instinct to line their own pockets or come to the aid of any subdivision of the body politic.[1]

To be sure, there were balances to be struck. States were jealous of their independence, wary of ceding too much authority to the newly fashioned federal government. Regional interests could clash, especially those separating the North and South. Here slavery itself wasn't at stake, however. All the states were slave states, and no one was proposing a general emancipation (in fact, hopes for emancipation born during the Revolution were buried in Philadelphia). Rather, what was bargained over was how that slave population was to be counted in the distribution of congressional representation. Perhaps the most famous bone of contention we are all familiar with was how individual rights might be jeopardized by the newly empowered national authority. The Bill of Rights, later attached to the Constitution as a set of ten amendments without which passage would have been impossible, nonetheless had virtually nothing to do with any latent or explicit forms of social or class grievance.

Yet precisely such complaints and forebodings had everything to do with why the "founding fathers" gathered together at Independence Hall and why the document they cobbled together there had such trouble winning favor enough to pass. Class mattered a great deal, even if that's not the way we remember what transpired in Philadelphia in 1787.

America was overwhelmingly rural then. Ninety percent of the population lived in villages or in the countryside. So the abrasions of class showed up in different places and in different ways than people living later on in urban, industrial, and postindustrial societies might imagine or expect. The great divide in the late eighteenth century New World had already been foreshadowed at Plymouth and Massachusetts Bay and Jamestown. Would American society face east or west; that is, would it become increasingly imbricated into the circuits of global trade and finance, or would it become a freeholder settler society whose ties to the marketplace would remain supplemental to a life of agrarian self-sufficiency on the frontiers of the new nation?[2]

The outcome of a fateful standoff of that magnitude naturally depended on who had the most artillery. During the brief years that followed the victory at Yorktown, advantage seemed to be leaning strongly in favor of the settler state. The Articles of Confederation, that loosely articulated and decentralized governing mechanism put together by the ex-colonies, afforded a great deal of leeway for local and state initiatives covering the most vital elements of public life: taxes, currency, debts, interstate trade, the judiciary, militias, property rights, law and order, and more. Over and over again, those initiatives were exercised by town councils, unicameral state legislatures, local judges, and on occasion by extralegal insurgent movements. These movements and the largely rural peoples they represented were trying to extricate themselves from the webs of taxes, credit, debt, and foreclosure, all inherent elements of the rising mercantile economy that were placing in peril their existence as independent farmers.

Friction points cropped up everywhere. All the states were burdened with debts from the Revolutionary War, as was the Confederation government. During the war (and after it), a great deal of that Continental Congress's debt had been deeply discounted, as had the "Continental" currency, given the uncertain prospects of the Revolution and what might follow it. Often ordinary farmers, artisans, village tradespeople, and soldiers had been the original holders of this paper (and the equally valueless currencies issued by the separate states' governments), notoriously "not worth a Continental." Eventually much of that debt was bought up by more well-to-do speculators and others who could afford to hold onto it in its depreciated, nearly worthless state, hoping postwar authority would redeem this debt at its original and now grossly inflated face value. "Sunshine patriots" roamed the countryside buying up paper money at a penny on the dollar. But if they were to cash out, states would have to levy taxes to generate the revenue to pay them off. Some governments tried doing that and it ignited a firestorm of protest. Here and there laws were passed to declare debt moratoria, or plans were made to pay them off in installments or to inflate the currency so that debts might be discharged more easily: good news for the debtor, not good at all for the creditor. Or state legislators simply refused to raise taxes and left the debt to fester.

Nor was official state debt the only kind that abraded, far from it. Farmers and tradespeople from the interior had intercourse with the markets nearer the coast. This could work well. But then, as they grew more reliant on urban merchants and banks to sell their goods and finance their growing and harvesting, and became more oriented to producing those crops most readily converted to cash, it worked less well or not at all. Now their self-sufficiency was jeopardized. Mortgage and other debts accumulated accordingly. Dependency, sometimes insupportable forms of dependency, haunted broad patches of rural America.

One exit ramp out of that cul-de-sac also seemed threatened. "Go west, young man" was folk wisdom long before Horace Greeley suggested it to eastern workingmen looking for a new start in life. Settlement even at the time of the Revolution was still largely confined to a narrow territorial strip running not too far back from the Atlantic. Victory, however, meant that the trans-Appalachian West was now open to all comers, thanks to the peace treaty signed with the British. True enough, but some of those "all comers" included the biggest landholders and land speculators (people like Washington, for example) in the country. They had the wherewithal to aggrandize the best acreage available, to cultivate it or hold it until prices soared. In General Washington's case, after the war he had visited the Ohio Valley, where he discovered squatters who refused to acknowledge his title to the land. This was not an uncommon predicament. Incipient social conflict was a fact of life even out on the frontier (and this does not take into account the populations living there for the previous ten thousand years).[3]

No wonder the countryside was at a boil. People worried about foreclosure for debts or taxes or both. Some judges enforced the law. Others refused to. Sheriffs and militiamen might obey a command to restore law and order—or they might not. Out on the frontier chaos reigned. To call the regions lawless is not much of an exaggeration as the Confederation government's writ was too weak to mean much even back east. Land was seized, squatted on, abandoned at a show of force, then retaken. Plus, the British, the treaty notwithstanding, were still occluding settler occupation, entrenched in the fur trade, and conspiring with Indian allies.

America's First Civil War

Rebellion was in the air. Farmers in western Massachusetts, indebted to Boston bankers and merchants and in danger of losing their ancestral homes in the economic hard times of the 1780s,

rose in arms. In those years the number of lawsuits for unpaid
debt doubled and tripled, farms were seized, and their owners
were sent off to debtors' prisons. Incensed farmers led by former
revolutionary soldier Daniel Shays closed local courts by force
and liberated debtors from jail. One historian has estimated that
one-quarter of all adult men in Massachusetts enlisted in the
rebellion. The state couldn't afford to pay the militia to quash
the rising, so a volunteer army was assembled, funded by wealthy
people in Boston. Once the revolt was put down, many of the
rebels fled to the frontier, where there was little in the way of
authority and they could start over. Similar but smaller uprisings
erupted in Maine, Connecticut, New York, and Pennsylvania,
while in New Hampshire and Vermont irate farmers surrounded government offices. Ethan Allen's "Green Mountain Boys"
and the "Regulators" of North Carolina faced off against "gran-
dees and speculators" in defense of republicanism.[4]

Alarm spread among the country's elites. They depicted
the unruly yeoman as "brutes" and their houses as "sties." An
observer of the Shays transgressions worried that "if the rebels
succeed," the situation "must end in an abolition of all public
and private debts and an equal distribution of Property may
be demanded. The Countrie is not democratic in the Opinions
of these Geniuses." In New York these class animosities and fears
were out in the open. A writer with the *New York Daily Adver-
tiser* noted: "Of all the evils which attend the republican form
of government, there are none that seem to have more perni-
cious effects than the insolence which liberty implants into the
lower orders of society." Mercantile elites were frightened as
well by state governments like Rhode Island's that were more
open to popular influence, declared debt moratoria, and issued
paper currencies to help farmers and others pay off their debts.
As the date for the Philadelphia convention neared, legislators

in Connecticut voiced reservations that the state "will send men that had been delicately bred and who were in affluent circumstances, that could not feel for the people in their day of distress."[5]

General unrest created the atmosphere in which the delegates deliberated. There is no question that those assembled in Philadelphia were, at least in part, determined to confect a prophylactic against this type of democratic excess. Liberty and democracy might or might not comport well with property and commerce. As many scholars have noted, republicanism was a persuasion whose meaning remained fluid. To those social circles oriented to a marketplace-centered society, it meant a level playing field on which all could pursue their self-interest. In the outback among folk breaking land in territories of forested and mountain wilderness without roads and houses, where a rough equality prevailed, proponents of a republicanism that rested on self-sufficiency and village-level collaboration suspected the motives of their commercial-minded cousins closer to the sea. The standoff was a version of class conflict insofar as the coexistence of these two ways of life became increasingly problematical.[6]

Those who envisioned a promising future for the new nation as a participant in a flourishing transatlantic trading economy needed to be sure that the basic institutional and legal frameworks were in place to protect and foster that commercial future. That meant, on the one hand, guarding the sanctity of private contracts, whether mortgages or other forms of private credit, and protecting public debts and the power of government to honor those debts. On the other hand, to do that might mean constraining the liberty of the populace to modify or repudiate those transactions even if attempts to do so were carried out through impeccably democratic channels.

By and large, the men who met together in Philadelphia were well to do (who else would have the time to sit around talking politics for two or three months?). However, some of the delegates were not well-off (although virtually none were small farmers). Moreover, the Constitution promulgated in Philadelphia was far more than a form of self-enrichment for the already rich. A world in which trade and commerce could flourish, one that would expand the reach of the marketplace into the outback, one that would encourage the growth of towns and cities and all the trades and handicrafts likely to find customers there, one that would invite investment in new enterprises by merchant bankers at home and from abroad was broadly appealing. Sailors; slave owners engaged in the world market for cotton; artisans in Boston, New York, Philadelphia, and Baltimore; Back Bay and Hudson River merchants holding mortgages and shipping cargoes to Europe—all were enticed. So were farmers drawn by the growing domestic and foreign demand for their food and raw materials. Canal builders and ship builders owning the means of transport, town shopkeepers and great land speculators betting on the commercial conversion of the interior, small-scale manufacturers of modest means together with "moneycrats" costumed like native nabobs could all get excited envisioning a new world in which the pursuit of happiness and the pursuit of property were conjoined.[7]

Was such a grand prospect credible? Market society is always a confidence game: that is, it rests on confidence that people can be counted on to honor otherwise impersonal contractual relations, or at least that if they fail to do so, they can be coerced into doing so. Without that confidence, who will put at risk their land or liquid capital, venturing it into an unknown future? Washington's wartime comrade Lighthorse Harry Lee wrote to his ex-commander to make precisely this point about the fatal effects on prospective foreign investment if the Congress defaulted. Worried about "violent enemys to the impost" because "part of the principal of our foreign loans is due next year," Lee knew Congress lacked even the interest due on the loan.[8]

On the eve of the Constitutional Convention that confidence was at a low ebb. The economy was faltering and had been since the Revolution, although probably less than its Philadelphia critics decried. Trade between the states was again and again interrupted by rivalries the Confederation government was powerless to subdue or override. Britain could flout peace treaty provisions on the high seas and out west without fear of reprisal because the Confederation couldn't afford to field a real army or navy. Most of all, law and order, meaning the kind of law and order that ensured the sanctity of private property, was everywhere under siege by democracy. Unless that changed, unless what many in Independence Hall and elsewhere thought of not as democracy but as "mobocracy" was put to rest, there would be a real crisis of confidence. A world organized around the market would be in peril if that happened.

Liberty was born amid class conflict. Many of the debates during the convention and especially during the long months and in the angry diatribes over ratification that followed were simultaneously about liberty and democracy and about wealth and property, about what kind of political mechanisms might allow for popular government yet insulate it from an excess of popular willfulness. Who owned what and how that should influence who should rule were entangled questions, even if in retrospect our national mythos tells a story about the salvation of liberty and democracy. As Adam Smith had already commented in *The Wealth of Nations*, "Authority, so far as it is instituted for the security of property, is in reality instituted for the defense of the rich against the poor, or of those who have some property against those who have none at all."[9]

Had the stakes been not so fraught, we might not have gotten the Constitution at all. The delegates came to Philadelphia charged with the task of amending the Articles of Confederation. That is what nearly everyone, including many of the delegates, believed to be their mission. But from the outset, it became clear that the articles were going to be scrapped for a whole new plan of government. Not only did amending the articles demand unanimity on the part of the states, the document's most basic institutions and rules of procedure seemed to the framers hopelessly inadequate to rein in the "mob," separating off its pressures from legislative, executive, and judicial deliberations. Indeed, it wasn't so much the articles that were felt to be faulty as, in Madison's view, "the evils . . . which prevail in the states individually as well as those which affect them collectively." What he pointed to was state "interferences" with "the security of private right, the steady dispensation of Justice," especially when it came to how these legislators had bailed out debtors and taxpayers by printing paper currencies or allowing debts to be discharged without cash but rather through "old Horses" or trading with pine barrens instead of hard money; or by closing courts to stop proceedings by creditors; or by refusing to burden their citizens with taxes to help discharge the Revolutionary War debt.

Delegates feared the "corruption and mutability of the Legislative Councils of the States." William Plummer, a delegate from New Hampshire, noted that "our rights and property are now the sport of ignorant, unprincipled state legislators." People were tired, as Alexander Hamilton was, "of an excess of democracy," or what some likeminded thinkers called "a republican frenzy." With emotions that high, no wonder this was part of the reason the delegates' meetings were held in secret.

Neither Hamilton nor Madison held government securities. But both feared for the future well-being of the country if it lost its credibility in the eyes of potential creditors and investors. Without robust enough assurances for the safety of capital, the post-Revolution recession would drag on indefinitely, trailing in its wake a debilitating weakness. But that selfless view was mixed in with a willful blindness on the part of bondholders like the Adams family. They complained bitterly about the Massachusetts Assembly passing debtor relief legislation, conveniently forgetting that they had purchased their bonds at rock-bottom prices but were expecting to get paid interest on their face value.[10]

What began circulating around the country as a draft Constitution in September 1787 was in many respects an economic document and one whose political inventions carried substantial economic and social implications. At the time, if not since then, this was widely taken for granted; for example, it was believed that there were two great classes: "all the holders of Public Securities" and the "substantial yeomanry" who don't own them and "whose interest it is to have the public debt discharged in the easiest manner." Guy Carelton, Lord Dorchester, a Canadian observer, noted, "Many wealthy individuals have taken a decided part in favor of the new plan from the hope that the domestic debt of the Union may be funded and that the various paper securities of which they are holders to a great amount purchased for a trifle may rise to their value."[11]

Key articles endowed the new federal government with the power to levy taxes, and prohibited states from printing paper money to bail out debtors or from in any way "impairing the obligations of contracts." This section 10 of Article 1 was praised by people like Benjamin Franklin and Virginia governor Edmund Randolph as the "soul of the Constitution." So too, the new government was granted the power to regulate interstate and foreign commerce, to issue a national currency, to uphold the sanctity of contracts, to quash domestic disorder ("to suppress insurrections"), to issue and guarantee payment of a national debt, to acquire and distribute land, to establish uniform standards and measures, and to foster internal improvements. The new nation that followed these guidelines might be virtuous or it might not be, but it was definitely open for business.[12]

Moreover, the structure of government sketched by the draft Constitution was meant to reinforce protections against the excesses Hamilton and others were scared of. We are accustomed to praising the document's shrewd system of checks and balances, but it is also a system that afforded checks by the powerful against the powerless. This was part of the explicit rationale for a lifetime federal judiciary, a six-year Senate term of office, proposals like those of Hamilton for a lifetime executive, and for sizeable enough congressional districts to insulate legislators to some degree from their constituents. In a private note regarding his famous Federalist No. 10, in which Madison talks about the virtue of diverse interests functioning to counterbalance each other's ambitions, he confided, "Divide et imperia, the reprobated axiom of tyranny, is under certain qualifications, the only policy by which a republic can be administered on just principles."[13]

Madison's pragmatic pact with the devil notwithstanding, others at the time and since recognized that the Constitution would supplant one kind of republic with another. Historians sometimes distinguish them as liberal and Spartan, the former prioritizing the liberty and self-interest of the private individual, the latter the self-sacrificing communal republicanism loosely modeled on the ancient Greek city-state. These are only heuristic devices, not to be found in their pure state on this earth: plenty of raw self-interest could be found in the ranks of those defending their local communities from mercantile predators, and much genuine patriotism among those eager to join the ranks of great trading nations. Still, the debate over ratification reached such a high temperature because whole ways of life seemed to hang in the balance.

The People versus We the People

Even before the convention disbanded to go to the country for approval of its work, a tax rebellion erupted in Virginia. It was led by a tavern keeper, Adonijah Matthews. He and his followers burned the county jail in Greenbrier, vowing not to pay the tax. Soon enough the uprising spread to other counties. The rebels were also hostile to land speculators, who in turn wanted the state government to repress the rebellion. Instead the tax was repealed.[14]

Ratification, which the framers once thought would happen speedily, instead was bitterly contested and protracted. Hamilton thought the odds for a yes vote were good because that position had the backing of powerful commercial circles, creditors, men of property who wanted a stronger government as protection against "the depredations which the democratic spirit is apt to make on property." John Quincy Adams, then still at Harvard, wrote to his mother Abigail describing the lay of the land as he saw it: "While the idle, and extravagant, and consequently the poor, complain of being oppressed, the men of property, and consideration, think the Constitution gives too much liberty to the unprincipled citizens, to the prejudices of

the honest and industrious." In his diary, however, Adams as-
sessed the Constitution as "calculated to increase the influence,
power, and wealth of those who have any already," resigned to
the fact that "a free government is inconsistent with human
nature."[15]

A Massachusetts representative to the Articles of Confederation Congress saw what Adams saw, but from the other shore.
He worried about the dangers of counterrevolution, writing
home to warn of plots to restore "baleful Aristocracies." For
people like this, soon to be known as anti-Federalists, the plan
drawn up in Philadelphia was "identical with the attempt to
solidify upper class rule." When the ratifying convention assembled in Massachusetts, one delegate, Amos Singletary, argued that "lawyers and men of learning and Moneyed men"
expected to run the new government; once having grasped
power, they would "swallow up all of us little folks." Another
partisan, Timothy Bloodworth, foresaw that under the new
dispensation "the great will struggle for power, honor, and
wealth, the poor become a prey to avarice, insolence, and oppression." Spying the same trend, a South Carolina opponent
of the Constitution sought to unearth his aristocratic family
heritage back in the British isles because, "for as our steps toward
monarchy are very obvious, I would wish my Children to have
all the Rights to rank and distinction, which is to be claimed
from Ancestry. . . . We are getting back to the system we destroyed some years ago."

For a scheme that was supposed to forge unity where there
had been none, the Philadelphia plan ignited the rawest forms
of class antagonism. A Virginia anti-Federalist warned, "They
will order you, as yet smarting under the effects of bondage, to
pay immediately all the debts due to the British enmities, yea,
even the interest during the war; and they will order you to

make good the plunder of the usurers and the speculators, the abomination of the land; and all those will rejoice exceedingly." Patrick Henry sympathized: "It sounds mighty prettily to gentlemen to curse paper money and honestly pay debts. But apply to the situation of America, and you will find there are thousands and thousands of contracts where equity forbids an exact literal performance." Even after Pennsylvania ratified and assured the Constitution's passage, a fervent anti-Federalist newspaper predicted a Congress that would consist of "lordly and high-minded men" with "a perfect indifference for and contempt of" the people, "harpies of power" who would "riot on the miseries of the community" and use standing armies to enforce their will.[16]

However, if our devotion to what was wrought in the city of brotherly love makes the anxieties and forebodings of its opponents seem hysterical, is that not a verdict equally applicable to the framers like Hamilton who prophesized anarchy or monarchy as the only options left if the Constitution failed to pass? The mad passions aroused by profound discord over how the new nation should evolve were not confined to one side of the class divide. The struggle to decide if the Constitution should pass or not amounted to America's first civil war.

Pass it did. Voting patterns varied and certainly do not display some simple split between the rich and the poor; otherwise, how could it have passed? Smallholders tended to be against, larger property holders (including such property as slaves, securities, capital on loan, goods for sale) for the new government. But that was hardly an invariant outcome. What came closer to displaying the rival social orders at stake was the tendency of all towns, not just the few larger seaport cities, to vote for the Constitution. Here was the new world in embryo: merchants especially, no matter what region they hailed from, and then the more general "mercantile interest" which, according to John Adams, included "Merchants, Mechaniks, Labourers." Here too were the ship owners, seamen, dockworkers, artisans and their apprentices, all wired into the networks of domestic and international trade. So too, the Federalists drew on the support of rural areas that were enmeshed in supplying the towns and producing for the export trade.

Farther removed from that commerce, the world seemed different. A town meeting to discuss the draft in Spencer, Massachusetts, depicted itself as one of those places "distant in Situation from the metropolis . . . Renders the profits, of farmers, Very Inconsiderable, to Those of an equal Bigness, and Quality, near the Maritime and Market Towns." A similar village get-together in New York talked about the difference between "navigating and non-navigating individuals." Navigating and non-navigating indeed! The world envisioned by the framers was a mobile one, full of promise and risk, ready to put its confidence in the free market and the free individual so long as property and its privileges were closely guarded. If that meant displacing forms of local democracy and the constraints that democracy now and then placed in the way of capital's liberty to do as it desired and the law licensed, well, that was the price of progress.[17]

Ratification soon enough paid that price. A stronger central government fully capable of suppressing future debtor insurgencies exercised its power right away. Shays' Rebellion was part of a trilogy of uprisings that continued into the 1790s. The Whiskey Rebellion of 1794 was the most serious. An excise tax ("whiskey tax") meant to generate revenue to back up the national debt threatened the livelihoods of farmers in western Pennsylvania who used whiskey as a currency in a part-barter economy. President Washington sent troops, many of them

Revolutionary War veterans, with Hamilton at their head to put down the rebels. The U.S. Constitution, at the moment of its birth, and for that matter ever after, has simultaneously functioned as a blueprint for a nation and as a chastity belt for class conflict.

Liberty and Terrorism in the City of Brotherly Love

Had I been convicted of conspiring to blow up the Liberty Bell (and of a heap of associated charges), I would be getting out of jail just about now, in time to write this book (well, actually sooner than that as the charges carried a sentence of twenty-five years in prison, still a long time). Loosely speaking, it is thanks to the Constitution that that didn't happen. When eventually the FBI refused, although under court order, to turn over its surveillance records and wiretaps of our apartment and phone to the defense, the local Philadelphia judge dismissed the charges. During the two years it took for the case to be resolved, I had dark forebodings about whether I could take being locked up. I contemplated fleeing the country. Instead, I actually ran for city council, only to discover I was too young to serve if elected, and that "the mad bomber," as one paper christened me in an article about my candidacy, stood zero chance of getting elected anyway. In the end, the rule of law prevailed.

Capitalist society depends for its stability on a uniform set of laws and rights, without which the Darwinian law of the jungle would prevail with a vengeance. Even the empowered are compelled to recognize limits, most of the time.

However, if that law-bound infrastructure set me free, it is also the case that those who created and administered it prevailed. My friends and I were free. A salute is due the anti-Federalists who, although they lost the larger battle to defeat

the Constitution, mustered enough fight-back to ensure there
would be a Bill of Rights appended to the document that would
protect dissenters like me. But the Alliance for Jobs, Housing,
and Education was dead. Accusations of terrorism tend to have
a chilling effect. One might say the alliance was at liberty to
continue its struggle. But under the circumstances that would
be jejune. The rulers of law had used their lawful authority to
undermine that liberty. Local and national police, the district
attorney and the U.S. attorney general, and Rizzo and Hoover
had conspired to thwart liberty in the name of liberty. Terrorism was the pretext. The hidden text, however, was the danger
to the liberty of established elites—real estate developers,
speculators, slumlords, banks, university mandarins, military-
industrial contractors—to pursue their own interests free of
democratic constraint.

Irony, in small bits and in large, encircles liberty. Trying
to prove the police planted the evidence of my terrorist conspiracy was a quixotic crusade. On the contrary, to this day the
Philadelphia Police Department makes an annual award to one
of its members in memory of Lieutenant George Fencl, the
leader of the Civil Disobedience Squad, who led the raid on my
apartment.

At its formation, the Constitution, revered today as the
guardian of a free society, was a promissory note already in
default. It guaranteed liberty at the expense of liberty because
the country's understructure was already riven with social
tensions that could not be resolved without someone losing
out. When I came along in the 1960s, the promise of the Constitution (and its subsequent amendments, especially those
following the Civil War) was once again failing. It had failed to
deliver on equality at home. The brutal imperial war waged
abroad proceeded under a paper-thin patina of congressional

and popular consent, itself a result of cynical manipulation by the nation's elite.

Liberty is supposed to be the realm where class becomes irrelevant. But in 1787, again in 1969, and at many other times, class surfaces, and although it is denied, it matters and drives some to mad acts. Terrorism is a ghastly form of political bankruptcy. There is the official kind: Hoover's and McNamara's. There is the pathetic, if fatal, kind, practiced by crazed sectarians unable to establish a real foothold among the oppressed and exploited. Me and the millions like me were neither. And as our weak joke at the time reminded people, the bell was already cracked.

3

Wretched Refuse

Whether seen sinking beneath the waves of a postapocalyptic planet Earth in *Planet of the Apes* or erected and then leveled in Tiananmen Square, the Statue of Liberty is the world's most universally recognized symbol. Her meaning is taken as axiomatic. She is the mother-protector of freedom, tolerance, and democracy. She has achieved a kind of secular sainthood in the eyes of the oppressed, the impoverished, and the voiceless. Above all, Lady Liberty is thought of as the patron saint of hard-pressed immigrants. So it is particularly poignant to be writing about the monument at a time when the world is overrun with millions of desperate refugees who couldn't be more wretched but are welcomed nowhere, threatened everywhere.

Every schoolchild is familiar with Emma Lazarus's poem "The New Colossus" and its stirring welcome to the "huddled masses yearning to breathe free," "the wretched refuse" of Europe's teeming shores. For them the Lady lifts her "lamp beside the golden door." Lazarus imagined the statue as the "mother of exiles."

Exiles come in various shapes. Lazarus, a well-off and long-settled Sephardic Jew (her father was a prominent sugar

manufacturer), was thinking mostly about her fellow Jews fleeing the violent pogroms of czarist Russia. Who would save them?
"The New Colossus" was not a sectarian offering, however. The
lamp was lit, according to the poet, for all those driven from
their homelands by economic calamity or political tyranny or
cultural stigma: a world of exiles. In time, this polyglot bouil-
labaisse of the despised and miserable, revived by the oxygen-
ated air of a free land, would amalgamate to form the common
citizenry of a nation without crippling social hierarchies.

However, Lazarus might not have included exiles like
Emma Goldman, the anarchist charismatic. Goldman was also
a migrant Jew from Russia (modern-day Lithuania). She had
arrived in 1885, a year before the statue's unveiling, but from
considerably more comfortable circumstances than most of her
Litvak coreligionists from eastern Europe. Passionate in her
anti-capitalism, a fearless feminist and foe of imperialism, she
was jailed at the outbreak of war in 1917 for urging men to resist
the draft. Two years later Goldman was swept up in the Palmer
raids that followed World War I and was among the hundreds
of aliens whom the attorney general deported. When she sailed
out of New York on the USAT *Buford*—dubbed by the press the
"Soviet Ark"—with 250 fellow deportees, she gazed shoreward
and noted in melancholic irony: "It was my beloved city, the
metropolis of the New World. It was America indeed, indeed
America repeating the terrible scenes of Czarist Russia! I glanced
up—the Statue of Liberty!" An exile, to be sure, but headed in
the wrong direction.

Alexandra Kollontai was a Russian revolutionary, first a
member of the Menshevik Party, later a Bolshevik and Soviet
government minister, one of the first women in the world to
hold the post of ambassador. During the tumultuous years
leading up to the 1917 revolution she made a whirlwind tour of

the United States. As the Norwegian steamship *Bergensfjord* entered the harbor, the statue was "hidden by a thick autumn fog which shrouded from our naively searching eyes that symbol which once caused the hearts of our European fathers and grandfathers to beat with triumphant happiness and exultation." Four and half months later, when her tour drew to a close, Kollontai had been disabused. As the *Bergensfjord* sailed back east, the statue was no longer hidden: "The sun illuminated every line of this bronze image. And I still refused to believe my eyes. Is that the Statue of Liberty? So tiny, lost in the noise of the harbor and framed against the soaring skyscrapers of the Wall Street banks. Was this powerless, tiny figure shrinking before the all-powerful gigantic skyscrapers, those guardians of financial deals, the Statue of Liberty we had pictured to ourselves? . . . It was then that I realized that the New World, the Statue of Liberty, is simply an old and forgotten legend, a fairy tale of pre-capitalist times which can only be recounted from the reminiscences of our grandfathers."

Grandfathers and fathers, grandmothers and mothers from the shtetls and steppes of Russia, from the desiccated fields of southern Italy, from the warred-over provinces of the Austro-Hungarian and Ottoman empires, all these "huddled masses" yearning for something as tangible as enough food and as intangible as a second chance, made up a Noah's flood of exiles for whom the Statue of Liberty was an uplifting promissory note. For people like Kollontai and Goldman, exiles of a different sort, it was a note in default.

For the *Cleveland Gazette,* an African American newspaper, Lady Liberty's debut was the unveiling of an illusion: "Shove the Bartholdi [the statue's sculptor] statue, torch and all, into the ocean, until the 'liberty' of this country is such as to make it possible for an industrious and inoffensive colored man in the

South to earn a respectable living for himself and family, without being kukluxed, perhaps murdered, his daughter and wife outraged, and his property destroyed. The idea of the 'liberty' of this country 'enlightening the world' or even Patagonia, is ridiculous in the extreme." This same voice of internal exile echoed a century later in Lou Reed's "Dirty Boulevard," an anti-song of acidic irreverence. Reed mocks Lazarus's famous poem, noting that what he calls the "Statue of Bigotry" could care less about the "huddled masses" of mid-twentieth century America.[1]

Lady Liberty and the Class Struggles in France

Naturally enough, we take for granted that the Statue of Liberty was always adored as the "mother of exiles." Less known are those instances when her reputation was called into question. But whether honored or, more rarely, criticized as the guardian of the world's "wretched refuse," the monument carried no such meaning when it was first conceived in the 1870s and then finally unveiled in 1886. Lazarus wrote her poem in 1883, but it was not inscribed on the Statue of Liberty until 1903 (and was pretty much out of sight until the 1940s). For years before that, in fact, many thought the statue was imperiled by precisely those "exiles" Lazarus invoked.

Lady Liberty had two birth mothers: one French, one American. Neither had huddled masses, immigrants, or refugees of any kind in mind when they began their collaboration. On the contrary, this was an undertaking of elites who, if anything, harbored a gnawing anxiety about the bacillus of disorder or even insurrection that might fester inside any critical mass of "wretched refuse."

Originally, of course, the idea for the monument was a French one. The notion was to present the American people with a gift to commemorate the Franco-American alliance that had been so instrumental in winning American independence in the Revolutionary War a century earlier. (Indeed, the plan was to have the statue ready for the 1876 centennial.) However, this was not to be an official offering from the French government, although numerous notables from France's political class and cultural elite were deeply involved in the project.

Although Napoleon III's empire had collapsed during the Franco-Prussian War of 1870, Americans had fresh memories of how the emperor had tried to intrude into the recently concluded Civil War by sponsoring a Mexican adventure of territorial aggrandizement under the feckless reign of his puppet emperor Ferdinand Maximilian. When the Prussians laid siege to Paris, trying and nearly succeeding in starving it to death, aid packages arrived from the United States. But during the war itself the U.S. government was more favorably disposed to the Germans. So Franco-American relations, if certainly not unfriendly, were by no means fraternal, made edgy by political suspicions and trade disputes.

Moreover, after the fall of Napoleon, France was a fractured nation. The Paris Commune faced off against a reconstituted bourgeois government of military, business, clerical, and political elites that had declared itself the Third French Republic under Adolphe Thiers. The commune, a revolutionary installation of workers, artisans, and small shopkeepers—a world of *les peus* and *les pauvres*—had committed trespasses against private property, moral and sexual conventions, and religious orthodoxy—intolerable to the haute bourgeoisie of the Thiers government. The newborn Third Republic eventually crushed the commune in a spasm of unforgiving violence.

Those who concocted the idea of Lady Liberty were men of irreproachable middle- and upper-class respectability. They loathed the aristocrats, clerics, social climbers, and men on the make who had gathered in the court of Napoleon during the Second Empire. They were liberal democrats who chafed under the repressive state apparatus the emperor depended on. Believers in constitutional democracy, they admired what they imagined to be the world's best exemplar of that system of government, the United States. They were as well staunch abolitionists gratified at the outcome of the American Civil War. They sought to duplicate in France a political persuasion and constituency that would respect individual rights, private property, law and order, and a parliamentary democracy.[2]

However, these same circles supported the Thiers government and the annihilation of the commune. If the American Constitution inspired them, the commune's communalism terrified them. Nor was this a newly born fear. Ever since the French Revolution, a bourgeois class had struggled against a still-vibrant reactionary element left over from the ancient regime—monarchists, church patriarchs, the remnants of the nobility, corrupt state bureaucrats—to its right, and an insurrectionary current of working and lower middle classes to its left. Indeed, the Second Empire had been born out of this chronically unsettled state. Fearing the worst from the working-class rebels who audaciously established "national workshops" and sent the revolution of 1848 careening to the left, the French liberal bourgeoisie lost courage, depending on the new Napoleon to restore order, not quite anticipating how their savior would bury all hopes for a constitutional republic.[3]

Lady Liberty was dreamed up in this context. With Napoleon gone and the commune destroyed, how better to inspire and memorialize their dedication to a stable, liberal, middle-class society than by fashioning a monument to the nation that had pioneered in inventing it? Lady Liberty's godfather was

Édouard de Laboulaye. He was a renowned scholar whose specialty was American history. He came from an upstanding middle-class family. During the empire he had resented the restrictions on public speech and writing but kept a low profile. It was during that period that he formed the notion of creating a memorial to American liberty. Under the guise of celebrating a long-ago military/political alliance, this would also be a covert operation, an end run around the Napoleonic prohibitions against voicing democratic sentiments. Laboulaye convened a gathering of like-thinking intellectuals, politicians, and public-spirited businessmen to promote the project. That became much easier once Napoleon exited the scene.

Soon this group included Frédéric Auguste Bartholdi, a young but already established sculptor with orthodox aesthetic views and upper-middle-class credentials. His father was a civil servant and substantial landowner. The family originally hailed from the German Rhineland but had moved to Alsace, where they served as elders of a Lutheran church. Not a great artist, Bartholdi nonetheless had fared well under the empire as a designer of public monuments. He had even been involved in planning, along with Ferdinand de Lesseps, the engineering genius responsible for the Suez Canal, a stupendous lighthouse at the entrance to the canal, meant to rival the one built by Alexander, one of the wonders of the ancient world. The project was aborted but remained lodged in Bartholdi's aesthetic memory bank.[4]

Statues of women as heroines of the homeland, as guardians of domestic tranquility, had been commonplace for as long as anyone could remember, all the way back to antiquity. And Bartholdi, as an artist schooled in the neoclassicism of the French artistic establishment, was utterly at home in conceiving a statue of liberty along those lines. There was a problem, however. Another view of "lady liberty" depicted her as more sanguinary, as a militant, sword-wielding mother of revolution. She too had deep roots in the past, and had become especially prominent since the revolution of 1789, surfacing again and again in the serial revolutions that followed decade by decade, a stirring image that reached a kind of apotheosis in the celebrated painting by Eugène Delacroix *Liberty Leading the People.* Created to celebrate the 1830 revolution that finally put an end to the Bourbon monarchy, Delacroix's "lady" storms the barricades, leading an army of determined revolutionaries against their bloodied reactionary tormentors, her classical tunic, ripped in the fray, exposing her breasts, a visual emblem of the poetry of the revolution: "Liberté, Egalité, Fraternité." This was definitely not what Laboulaye, Bartholdi, and their colleagues had in mind. Or rather, it was precisely what they had in mind and were determined to avoid. Because of their own political and social proclivities and with the commune still fresh in memory, they wanted instead a stately, decorously robed lady whose classical demeanor would impart a kind of maternal calmness. Speaking at a fund-raising gathering in Paris, Laboulaye assured his affluent listeners, "This liberty will not be the one wearing a red bonnet on her head, a pike in her hand, who walks on corpses. It will be the American Liberty, who does not hold an incendiary torch but a beacon which enlightens." He assured those business circles enamored with the achievements and promise of science and commerce, "Progress is nothing but Liberty in action."[5]

The symbolic narrative evolved so that the monument increasingly veered away from any double entendre that might attach liberty to social upheaval. The sword was replaced by a tablet of laws commemorating the Constitution. The torch was not an incendiary but a light. Together with the seven rays

radiating from the Lady's tiara, the statue conveyed enlightenment, not discord (the seven rays bathing the seven continents
in sunlight were a Masonic code for enlightenment). Indeed,
originally the gift bore the name "Liberty Enlightening the
World." The crown itself was conceived in place of the original
Phrygian cap, another borrowing from Roman days meant to
signal the liberation of the enslaved and oppressed. The Lady
herself was unsexed, made virtually motionless, becalmed. Since
its inventors were antislavery men, they had at first imagined a
prominent display of broken shackles at the statue's base. The
shackles remained but are scarcely visible for fear they might
set off sympathetic shock waves in America, where disgruntled
talk of "wage slavery" was commonplace. Much wiser to keep
the message focused on enlightenment, away from liberation,
except insofar as one could conflate the one with the other: the
truth shall make you free.[6]

How this whole undertaking might be received in America was a serious worry. That might seem implausible since
after all this was intended as a gift, an honorarium that France's
onetime ally would surely welcome with open arms. The French
needed that response in part because they couldn't foot the
entire cost of creating, transporting, and erecting the monument
themselves. So too, they needed the Americans to provide a
place to put it. More than that, however, the whole political
premise of the operation was that there was a basic simpatico
between the liberal elites of the two countries. Both cherished
learning, enterprise, peaceable commerce, and republican liberties in a unified nation-state over which they presided. This
conceit presumed these two classes, although an ocean apart,
were in essential respects identical, when in fact their historical
experiences and motivations diverged in ways that made an
altar to "Lady Liberty" more problematic.

Lady Liberty and the Class Struggles in America

Strangely, their American counterparts turned out to be less than enthusiastic. The statue's French promoters did initially succeed in assembling an American equivalent to their own grouping. It was composed of eminences from worlds of politics and business and high culture, including Peter Cooper, the manufacturer and philanthropist, Horace Greeley, Longfellow, an aged Senator Charles Sumner, and President Grant. Money was raised. But not enough. Congress seemed ready to appropriate funds and deed Bedloe's Island in New York harbor as a site, but then delayed. France and America were at odds over trade and other mundane matters. New York City appeared enthusiastic, but its ardor cooled enough to encourage other cities, Philadelphia especially, to woo the statue's French sponsors.[7]

Hesitation became chronic, one reason it took about fifteen years from conception to unveiling (the other reason being the technical complexities associated with the design, construction, assembling and disassembling, transportation, and reassembling of this gargantuan memorial). Practical considerations slowed matters. It soon became clear that there was no way the statue would be ready for the nation's centennial as originally hoped; that was disappointing. More disabling, not long after the idea took root in the United States, the country plunged into the worst economic depression of its brief history. Everybody was on short rations, first of all the mass of unemployed but also the U.S. Treasury and the private treasuries of the nouveau riche, whom the statue's advocates hoped to touch for contributions.

Depression invited insurrection. Practical matters of dollars and cents morphed into a quicksand of political and

ideological second thoughts. The embryonic life span of the
Statue of Liberty extended through a decade and a half of the
bitterest class warfare. There were hunger riots, most notably
at Tompkins Square in New York in 1874. Even before the Tompkins Square calamity, the nation's "better sort" were hysterical
about the prospect of the Paris Commune being imported to
America. Specters of Amazonian *pétroleuses* (raving, long-haired
women flinging incendiary glass bombs into the streets of
Paris) haunted the middle classes of metropolitan America.
Congressman James A. Garfield, a few years from his brief
presidency, warned, "The real fool-fury of the Seine" had been
"transplanted here, taking root in our disasters and drawing its
life only from our misfortunes."

A nationwide railroad strike in 1877, to be remembered
as the Great Insurrection, involved thousands of railroad workers, hundreds of thousands of their supporters in cities, towns,
and in rural America, armed confrontations between federal
and state militias on one side and strikers on the other, millions
of dollars in incinerated locomotives, tracks, roundhouses, and
other equipment, general strikes, and scores of dead and
wounded in cities from coast to coast. Fever rose again in the
mid-1880s. In the Midwest the country's most despised "robber
baron" Jay Gould (known far and wide as the Mephistopheles
of Wall Street) faced off in a violent battle with his own railroad
workers and their legions of irate farmer allies. By 1886 what
had become a popular resistance to free-market, Darwinian
capitalism culminated in a series of rolling strikes, the Haymarket bombing in Chicago, and a nationwide movement for the
eight-hour workday. On the eve of the statue's unveiling, New
York City was in the throes of a mayoral election campaign.
Henry George, whose best-selling book *Progress and Poverty*
was a scathing indictment of economic injustice and political

plutocracy, was the candidate of the United Labor Party. In a shocking display of how deeply divided American society really was, George finished second, well ahead of his Republican rival Theodore Roosevelt.[8]

Naturally enough, therefore, the country's business and political classes were preoccupied with the class struggle in America. Unlike their French counterparts, they weren't concerned with defeating the aristocratic, clerical, and monarchist remnants of some ancient regime. There was no such regime. This was no doubt comforting. But it was also bad preparation for the kind of political craft and self-consciousness necessary for running a society, a privilege but also an obligation expected of any nation's elect.

Democracy, when coupled with capitalism, can't run itself—laissez-faire fantasies notwithstanding—as it gives rise to too many abrasive encounters. But the upstart industrial tycoons of Gilded Age America were too self-absorbed in building their patrimonies to think consistently in a more disinterested way. Doctor Elihu Hubbard Smith observed of New York's nouveau riche that they thought of nothing but "Commerce, News, and Pleasure. . . . The history of the city of New York is the history of the eager cultivation and rapid increase in the arts of gain." When they weren't indulging their appetites in the most extravagant forms of high living for which the Gilded Age became infamous, they were erecting monuments of a different sort than the one conceived in France.

A spasm of armory building followed the Great Insurrection. These were urban fortresses financed by the wealthy, constructed in the centers of big cities, armed with Gatling guns and rifle apertures commanding all the sight lines running down the cities' major arteries. The male offspring of the haute bourgeoisie trained there, readying themselves to meet the enemy, a "rabble" of the lower orders, "offal" (or, if you will, "wretched refuse") from alien shores. These were expensive undertakings but in the eyes of many a titan of industry and finance money better spent than on a statue that might even vaguely hint at social emancipation. In the two years following the Great Insurrection of 1877, the Astors, Stewarts, Vanderbilts, Morgans, and a galaxy of big businesses, like Equitable Life, Singer Sewing Machine, and Harper Brothers, among others, raised more than $500,000 to build the Seventh Regiment Armory on Park Avenue.[9]

Rule by blunt instrument and bribery was the instinctive reaction of newly risen upper classes otherwise fixated on money making and with acquiring for cold cash the social pedigrees, genealogies, equipage, manorial homes, and savoir faire they otherwise lacked. A statue honoring liberty might elicit polite applause, but there was greater enthusiasm for plans afoot to restrict suffrage, especially among the troublesome working classes, immigrants particularly. J. P. Morgan and the editor of the *Nation* E. L. Godkin, among others, did what they could to make voting a privilege rather than a right. Whitlaw Reid, the publisher of the *New York Tribune*, editorialized that "ignorant voters" were "as dangerous to the interests of Society as the communists of France." Pinkerton detectives, private militias, court injunctions, and the brute force of police, state, and federal troopers made quick work of the discontented. It was less complicated and required no compromise, as compared to devising mechanisms of social peace that might impinge on elite prerogatives.[10]

Political affairs were time consuming and required getting down and dirty with the "wrong sorts," machine politicians and their unsavory clientele, precisely those unseemly urban masses who in an ideal world would be extruded from the body politic entirely. Better to enter into a system of mutual ransom. Party hierarchs would tithe the "upper tendom" for licenses to loot the public domain (utilities, streetcar franchises, zoning and building regulations, railroad rights of way, land grants, and so on). In return, machine bosses would make sure the lower orders didn't intrude on the prerogatives of property. No ongoing involvement in public life was necessary so long as dynastic interests were looked after. If government apparatchiks presumed too much, a Napoleon of business could always call on an armada of family lawyers and a kept congressman or senator to set things right again.

Cultivating responsible ruling-class social consciousness was not likely in such unnourishing soil. Private concerns came first. Fashioning a sense of national solidarity and tradition was a lower priority. When Bartholdi first ventured to America to raise money, he found his potential benefactors obsessively focused on "the God Dollar." A decade later, former president Grant was blunt in blaming the paltry donations of the wealthiest on precisely their money-mad self-regard, taking note of "the marked indifference of the citizens of New York to the munificent gift of the French People to the People of the United States." Far too few among the country's upper classes recognized how a cultural investment in glorifying the nation-state could work as a prophylactic against the divisiveness of class animosities, something the French had learned the hard way.[11]

To be sure, there were some among the country's elect who had been enlightened in this regard by the Civil War. Monuments were being lofted left and right in the after-war years to commemorate the war dead. The Union League, a club of the most prestigious bankers and businessmen in New York and elsewhere created to support Lincoln, formed the core of early financial and public support for the statue. Its members, including J. P. Morgan and even that inveterate sea dog capitalist Cornelius Vanderbilt ponied up initially. But as the years went by the cupboard remained half bare. These were the decades when even philanthropy, which often emerges among the super-rich as a pre-political form of social engagement, was still gestating. Jay Gould wasn't giving any money away; that would happen in the next generation. Commodore Vanderbilt donated one of his steamships to the Union navy but kept most of his wealth for his offspring. Russell Sage was a miserable miser; only after his death would his wife reverse course. Andrew Carnegie wasn't yet seeding towns and cities with libraries, too preoccupied with his castle in Scotland and driving his steelworkers into open rebellion. Only after many years of ruthless acquisitiveness would the pious Baptist John D. Rockefeller shift his attention to the ameliorative measures in public health and social welfare designed to redeem his black reputation as the monopolist ne plus ultra.

Even among the most enlightened a sense of public commitment remained underdeveloped. Morgan thought of himself as the country's unofficial central banker but insisted nonetheless, "I owe the public nothing." Mark Hanna, a Cleveland industrialist and kingmaker within the Republican Party, simplified what he understood to be the essential mechanism of democratic politics in this witty aperçu: "There are only two things that are important in politics. The first is money and I can't remember what the second one is." A larger number of the nouveau riche, industrialists, financiers, a rentier class of landlords and coupon clippers were more gun-shy about embroiling themselves. Instead, they confected a hermetically sealed-off Potemkin village in which they pretended they were aristocrats, with all the entitlements and deference and legitimacy that came with that station. This was both a way of displaying power for all to see and presumably defer to, and a form of self-delusion. All the feudal paraphernalia on display at their masquerade balls, on parade in Central Park, holed up in the reconstructed gothic monoliths looming over the coastline of Newport, constituted the infrastructure of a utopian fantasy created by a newly risen class so raw and unsure of its place and mission in the world it needed all the borrowed credentials as protective coloring.

After all, many of these first- and second-generation bourgeois potentates had just sprung from social obscurity and the homeliest economic pursuits. Their native crudity was in plain sight, mocked by many. Herman Melville remarked: "The class of wealthy people are, in aggregate, such a mob of gilded dunces, that not to be wealthy carries with it a certain distinction and nobility." Mrs. Astor, the doyenne of this world whose grandfather-in-law started out a butcher and itinerant peddler of flutes, was accused of being an admirer not of the Thiers Third Republic, but of the French royalist cause. She was described as a "walking chandelier" because so many diamonds and pearls were pinned to every available space on her body. She deployed her drawing room's huge red damask divan on a raised platform like a throne. Her relative John Jacob Astor IV, a notorious playboy, was chastised by an Episcopal minister: "Mr. Astor and his crowd of New York and Newport associates have for years not paid the slightest attention to the laws of the church and state which have seemed to contravene their personal pleasures or sensual delights. But you can't defy God all the time. The day of reckoning comes and comes in its own way." (Years later Astor went down with the *Titanic*.)

Many of the great dynastic families disported themselves in the same way. It was all, as one historian noted, a "pageant and fairy tale," an homage to the "beau ideal" by a newly hatched social universe trying but failing to "live down its mercantile origins." But this dream life was ill suited to the arts and crafts of ruling over a society that was, at best, apt to find this charade amusing, at worst an insult. Wall Street Brahmin Henry Lee Higginson, fearing the "Awful Democracy"—that whole menagerie of radicalism inflaming both urban barrios and the Great Plains—urgently appealed to his fellows to take up the task of mastery "more wisely and humanely than the kings and nobles have done. Our chance is now—before the country is full and the struggle for bread becomes intense I would have the gentlemen of the country lead the new men who are trying to become gentlemen." This appeal, like the more modest one to fund a monument to the nation's revolutionary heritage, fell mainly on deaf ears. One pair among them, however, was listening.[12]

Joseph Pulitzer's First Prize

Joseph Pulitzer was an immigrant. He came from Hungary and he came poor. What made him rich was his talent for publishing a certain kind of sensationalist journalism. He wasn't the first to do this, but he was certainly among its grandest practitioners, first in St. Louis and then, seemingly, everywhere, including New York. Sometimes overlooked about what was derided as "yellow journalism" was its populist inclinations. Such papers were full of titillating gossip, scandal mongering, conspiratorial intrigue, purple prose, and cultivated exaggeration. The stories were undersourced and often bordered on fiction. But precisely because they were aimed at a working-class readership, these tabloids catered to that audience's suspicions and resentments regarding the country's pretentious plutocracy. This had been true earlier in the century when James Gordon

Bennett made fun of the "chip-chop aristocracy" in the pages of the *New York Herald*. And it became truer still during the Gilded Age when Pulitzer, along with his chief rival William Randolph Hearst, assaulted Wall Street financiers, tycoons like Carnegie and Rockefeller (Hearst was an adamant anti-monopolist), and their political enablers.

As the Statue of Liberty lay in limbo in a Paris storage shed, its promoters were still begging for the money to construct the pedestal and undercarriage that would support the gigantic memorial. The Astors, Vanderbilts, and Samuel Tilden, asked for $10,000 each, said no. The American committee created to get the job done continued to plead, managing to squeeze out some money from the ranks of the privileged. But not enough. They hired the country's architect de jour for the "upper ten-dom," Richard Morris Hunt, to design the pedestal (it was put together by Italian workers living in barracks on Bedloe's Island, sleeping on bare wooden bunks).

Bedloe's Island, a three-acre sandbank of mud and clay, had been designated as the statue's resting place. Congress had so decreed in 1877, but appropriated no money to pay for the pedestal to be erected there. Still, the island seemed a good enough spot, its sorry history having left it not fit for much else. Since around the year 1000 it had served as a hunting ground for an Algonquin tribe that spoke the Munsee dialect. The Indians lived off the island's rich oyster beds and hunted native animals. They were long gone, as were the oysters, killed off by dredging, landfill, pollution, and overfishing as first the Dutch and then the British moved in. A Dutch patroon named Isaac Bedloo swapped "certain cargoes or parcels of goods" with the island's native fish farmers in return for the oyster fishery. In the eighteenth century the island was used as a pesthouse for carriers of contagious diseases, smallpox especially. During the

Revolution it became an asylum and way station for Tories fleeing the country. Then a merchant-farmer named Samuel Ellis acquired it (along with another island that bore his name and would become the most famous immigrant processing center in the world at the end of the nineteenth century). Ellis sold Bedloo's to the federal government, which built a modest fort there. Finally, it was ready for something far more auspicious. But only if someone would pay the bill. The Social Register, however, remained gun-shy. Its ardor for republicanism was on a very low flame.[13]

Pulitzer sensed an opportunity. He launched a campaign to raise pennies, nickels, and dimes from ordinary people, even little kids, to accomplish what the high and mighty had failed to do. And mocking the niggardliness of those upper-crust misers became a piquant point of this newspaper barrage, which went on for months. "We have more than a hundred millionaires in this city any one of whom might have drawn a cheque for the whole sum without feeling they had given away a dollar.... Any one of them would have willingly spent the amount in flunkeyism or ostentation [or on] a foreign ballet dancer or opera singer.... But do they care for a Statue of Liberty which only reminds them of the equality of all citizens of the Republic." Pulitzer singled out people like Jay Gould and William Vanderbilt, characters known to be nativist in their inclinations, accusing them of buying up Confederate bonds (Pulitzer had fought in the war). A reader responded: "A few poor fellows whose pockets are not as deep as a well but whose love for Liberty is wider than a church door ... it seems that New York rich men do not." (Along with his letter came a donation of $7.25.) A ten-year-old boy sent 10¢ with a note saying, "Please take this from a little boy who wants to set Jay Gould a good example." He signed himself "A Young Patriot."

In an age when money ruled, but only alongside the most vigorous resistance, other publications joined Pulitzer's onslaught. *Frank Leslie's Illustrated* ran a picture captioned "The Statue of Liberty One Thousand Years Later"—still waiting for her pedestal. Lady Liberty was woeful, drooping, aged, exhausted. *Life* magazine ran an image of a scrawny lady and told its readers, "Jay Gould thinks we have too much Liberty here now."

As a publisher and man of affairs, Pulitzer was no radical. He was loyal to the Democratic Party, although not to its eastern wing, dominated by August Belmont and the mercantile-financial circles centered in New York. On the contrary, because his journalistic practices made him acutely sensitive to the populist, even anti-capitalist currents coursing through the national bloodstream, he knew that upper-crust world was vulnerable, its formidable wealth and connections notwithstanding. And he was an immigrant who'd come up the hard way. Whether that made a difference and prompted him to act is not clear. But the fact of the matter is that thousands and thousands of those his multicity campaign reached were immigrants; for example, by the 1870s the majority of Chicago's population was foreign born. Waged by Pulitzer papers all over the country, the campaign was a triumph. It was incentivized by the chance to see your name in the paper alongside note of your contribution, sentimentalized by publication of the scribbled letters of small children sending in their pennies, orchestrated with rallies and parades sponsored by the publisher, and tracked daily as the collections neared and then reached their goal: well over $100,000, an enormous amount to be collected in this way from people of the most limited means. So it was thanks to Pulitzer and the People that on October 28, 1886, the Statue of Liberty, then the tallest structure in New York at 305 feet, was unveiled before a throng of dignitaries on Bedloe's Island and a million watching from the shorelines of Brooklyn and Manhattan.

Predictably, the mood was upbeat. President Cleveland delivered the anointment, noting that "a stream of light shall pierce the darkness of ignorance and man's oppression until Liberty enlightens the world." He assured his audience, "Instead of grasping in her hand the thunderbolt of terror and death, she holds aloft the light that illuminates the way to man's enfranchisement." Chauncey Depew, lawyer to the wealthy, a Republican wire-puller, and president of the Union League Club and of the New York Central and Hudson River Railroad, interpreted the statue to signal that "the problems of Labor and Capital, of prosperity and poverty, will work themselves out under the benign influence of enlightened law-making and law-abiding liberty, without the aid of kings and armies, or of anarchists and bombs." French attendees painted a glutinous picture of the statue as "some fantastic apparition of a queen of the seas, emerging all aglow from her liquid domains and advancing, mysterious and veiled to greet her visitors." Mark Twain offered a lonely dissent. He didn't much care for the statue. It seemed to him smug, "too hearty and well-fed." He would have preferred a lady "old, bent, clothed in rags, downcast, shame-faced" so as to better depict the "insults and humiliations" liberty had always been subject to. Instead it seemed a monument to the "insolence of prosperity." But the statue's "artistic banality" and the president's equally banal speechifying prevailed.[14]

In the shadow of Haymarket, the Great Uprising of the eight-hour day movement, and the Henry George electoral insurgency, no mention was made of any connection between Lady Liberty and emancipation, democracy, the brotherhood of man or, for that matter, of "huddled masses yearning to breathe free," of "wretched refuse" from foreign shores. This is noteworthy, of course, because we are so accustomed to associating the statue with all or at least some of those invocations. What is even more remarkable, however, is that quite to the contrary of what we have grown up believing, very soon after its unveiling Lady Liberty was again and again depicted as besieged by "mongrel hordes" who constituted a fearsome threat to the liberty the statue was erected to celebrate. Astonishing as that seems, more extraordinary still is that the elites who had once demurred fell in love with the statue, and some of the working people who had pinched pennies to see her be erected now turned their backs, alarmed at the growing flood of "huddled masses" sailing into New York Harbor beneath her torch.

Lady Liberty and the Enigma of Class

One perennial boast made by the stewards of our country's heritage is that we are a nation of immigrants. True. By this is meant not only that we welcome newcomers from abroad fleeing this or that kind of dilemma, but that when they get here soon enough they melt, under the heat of a vigorously growing economy, into a commons of individuals all in hot pursuit of happiness. What beckons is the liberty to chase that dream free of any entangling ties to old homelands, deferments to traditional overlords, and obeisance to ancient beliefs. To those who originate as "huddled masses," poor and subordinate, the "golden door" is a passway out of that fate. A nation of immigrants is not a nation of hierarchy, of social inferiority, of class against class. As Lincoln once envisioned, even if you began life as a wage laborer, America's boundless opportunity promised that would last only temporarily.

Yet we know this is not so. Freshets of immigrants have often set off a counter flood tide of anti-alien sentiments of great force. Immigrants may arrive dreaming, but they wake up soon enough to their lot as proletarians, a condition lasting much longer (generations even) than Lincoln believed. Staying true to old religious faiths, ancient homelands and languages, kinship networks and ethnic associations, festivals, mores, eating habits, dress and deportment, child-rearing and endogamous marriage practices was more common than not. Melting was slow and sometimes coerced.

Never had the United States experienced such a tidal wave of immigration as it did during the time the statue was being conceived and built and during the immediate decades that followed. Nearly 7 million migrated to America from Europe between 1881 and 1894. Already by 1870 the foreign born accounted for one-third of the industrial workforce. Well over a million Jewish refugees arrived in little more than a decade between 1904 and 1917. Even more Italians disembarked: 2 million in a single decade from 1900 to 1909. During the 1880s the average annual inflow of immigrants was half a million; by 1907 it was 1.3 million. And the source of this mighty human river had shifted: in 1882 three-quarters came from northern and western Europe, by 1896 half set sail from southern and eastern Europe, and by 1906 70 percent did. Today nearly 40 percent of American citizens have at least one ancestor who disembarked at Ellis Island (although this number includes those who arrived after this period until the center closed in 1954).[15]

For the business classes that initially had been so reticent about Lady Liberty's welcoming torch, this was manna from heaven. After all, this was cheap labor, malleable labor, easily cowed labor that American industry—heavy industry like steel as well as light industry like garment manufacturing—relied on to move the country with lightning speed into the front ranks of the world's economic powerhouses. Trade associations and more ecumenical business federations lobbied for unrestricted immigration, sent labor agents to the far corners of the earth to recruit, entered into relations with foreign-based labor contractors, and came out against those lobbying to restrict the flow of the foreign born, to dim the light.

Hostility to immigrants has been a subtheme of American history virtually since the beginning, even as the country more and more assumed the profile of a nation of immigrants. Some of that earlier hostility was fueled by religious (Protestant versus Catholic) differences, some by ethnic suspicions (the potato eaters from Ireland were among the country's earliest white trash), and some by racial phobias (swarthy Italians and southeastern Europeans were akin to lowlife "niggers"). Anti-Semitism wounded all Jews, but the strangely costumed Hebrews from the Pale of Settlement suffered the brunt, including hostile barbs from their uptown Ashkenazi brethren from Germany who got here before them. All of these stigmata, no matter their racial, religious, and cultural colorations, carried with them the anathema of class inferiority. And with the volcanic eruption of open class warfare during the Gilded Age, low class signified as well a political category: the dangerous classes.

Animosity toward immigrants became especially heated during the Gilded Age, the formative years of the statue's presence in American public life. Old prejudices continued to inflame. But almost as soon as the statue was unveiled, class and political fears and fixations surfaced that until then had been largely camouflaged. Some of that irrational fearmongering originated in the most urbane and sophisticated sectors of American life, as, for example, among the Boston Brahmin and

New York Knickerbocker elites—men like Henry Cabot Lodge and Henry Adams. They worried about the mongrelization of the Anglo-Saxon "race" and about their own displacement as the country's bespoken stewards. Very little of that bigotry infected the business classes, which had too much to gain via the "golden door," even though they continued to brood darkly about the "dangerous classes."

But in a tragic irony, similar cultural poisons incubated within the precincts of the native working classes. Fearing for their jobs, worried about the downward pressure on wages exerted by those "huddled masses," prey to propaganda about the alien ways of these "strangers in their midst," they mobilized to shut the door. So the Chinese were excluded by an act of Congress in 1882. While the Knights of Labor had audaciously opened its ranks to all comers, the newly hatched American Federation of Labor confined itself to the skilled and native born, and agitated to shutter the sluice gates; soon the Holy Order of the Knights of Labor also succumbed. A distinction was drawn between those fit to live in "A Nation of Free Men" and the "slavish, ignorant, and unassimilable foreigners." Even leaders of the Socialist Party, founded near the end of the century, would now and then inveigh against the human flood from abroad.

Sentiments like these echoed widely. Newspapers filled up with editorials denouncing foreign "rabble, dangerous classes, ruffians, incendiaries, malcontents, rapscallions, and brigands." Cartoons depicted the statue beleaguered by such people, clawing at her robes. One magazine, reacting to the proposal to construct an immigration processing center on Ellis Island, called the project "The Proposed Emigrant Dumping Site" and accompanied its opinion with a nasty picture of European "garbage ships" unloading their human refuse at the statue's base. A cartoon in *Puck* imagined the ruination of the statue; it was infested with immigrants. A figure representing Big Business sat in front of a Doric-columned bank. Tammany leader Boss Platt was shown running the whole show to suggest an unholy alliance of money and politics colluding to provide cheap labor and cheap voters. Lady Liberty was quickly becoming an emblem of exclusion rather than a "mother of exiles." Moreover, the great preponderance of white workers, even those subjected to the most noxious forms of discrimination and bigotry, helped man the walls against any intrusion by those internal exiles from Afro-America.[16]

If it was in the enlightened self-interest of industrialists to welcome this "wretched refuse," was it not in the enlightened self-interest of the working classes to bar the door? Do the two enlightenments cancel each other out? Was there a madness to the logic? Does enlightenment, which after all was the settled-on mission of the Statue of Liberty, have anything to do with the matter? What is at stake here rather is the parochialisms that a class-divided society is subject to, boilerplate cant about American exceptionalism notwithstanding.

Emma Lazarus's poem wasn't chiseled into the statue until 1903. Even then it got little notice, no ceremony, and virtually no press coverage. It wasn't until the Great Depression and the advent of the New Deal that the memorial's connection to the immigrant experience was firmly fixed in the public mind. Earlier it had been enlisted for patriotic purposes: during World War I people were urged to buy Liberty Bonds and the money helped finance Liberty ships. Yet the 1920s witnessed the most sweeping immigration restriction legislation ever to become law. The precipitous decline in global migration during the Depression cooled political tempers. And the folk culture deliberately nurtured by the New Deal sketched out an honored place for working people and their homeland customs and habits, once so despised. In that atmosphere, the Statue of Liberty became the symbol we have assumed it always was. Nowadays, of course, it is debatable whether that is still the case.[17]

On the Road

What did those "huddled masses" make of the statue's strange symbolic transformations? Many, no doubt, were more than ready to view Lady Liberty as the deliverer Lazarus elegized. True or not in reality, this perspective became more entrenched in the second generation as a part of the cultural arsenal available to break down barriers to their own mobility. Others of the first generation—half of all Italian migrants, for example— went back home anyway, so the statue, if they thought of it at all, faded from memory. Millions of others came and remained too wretched to notice. Substantial numbers rose from wretchedness to a modicum of civilized decency, self-respect, and dignity. For them the statue might signify in retrospect a chance at self-emancipation, if not the social emancipation carefully censored out by its original conceivers. Whether faring well or less well, immigrants certainly had to wince at the way metropolitan newspapers and public speakers went on and on about how the Lady was being despoiled by people just like them. Then again, there was a good chance they couldn't read those papers or hear those orators as they didn't read or speak English.

My maternal grandfather couldn't. He was fluent in Yiddish, German, and Polish, but when he first arrived in America he knew little if any English. He hailed from Warsaw, where at an early age he learned how to do skilled work with sheet metal. That was not what his father wanted for his eldest son.

Instead, he had in mind a loftier position as a Jewish cleric. But the czar intervened. My grandfather had been drafted into the Russian Army (there was no state of Poland at the turn of the twentieth century). When he was released after two years or so, rumors began circulating that the czar was not quite done with him. But my grandfather Max was done with the czar. He told his father he was hitting the road. But for where?

Not long after the savage slaughter of Jews in the infamous pogrom at Kishinev in 1903, torrents of panicked Jews headed west, mainly to the United States, Max among them. Their German-Jewish cousins already ensconced in New York and elsewhere were less than happy about this prospect and had been for some time. They looked down on these Litvaks as uneducated village provincials, slavish believers in obscurantist doctrine. They were indeed "huddled masses" habituated to lives of demeaning poverty, living in squalor, babbling a bastard dialect. Especially as they massed together in great cities, New York above all, they could only heighten the anti-Semitism already implanted in the Western psyche and from which German Jews, wealthy or not, also suffered. Stopping the onrush, the original desire of those already settled here, proved impossible. Instead, uptown set out to civilize downtown (the *Jewish Messenger* hoped the "immigrants might be Americanized in spite of themselves") and to disperse it when possible so it would become a less conspicuous mass. Ghettos were unseemly and attracted the wrong kind of attention.[18]

Max had a skill. And he was a young (about nineteen) single male. That profile was just what the various German-Jewish-sponsored aid societies were looking for. Either through word of mouth or by direct recruitment, Max made his way, stealthily keeping out of sight of Russian police and troops, across Poland to Bremen in Germany, where a ship awaited that was scheduled to take men like him to, of all places, Galveston, Texas. His German-Jewish benefactors, seeking to spread out their Litvak charges, had identified Galveston as a port city where ships were built and metal workers were in demand, aware that Texas had been for a long time a place where Jewish refugees from the German revolution of 1848 had established communities—thus they matched Warsaw Max with the Lone Star State. Indeed, Galveston was known as "the Ellis Island of the West"; more than two hundred thousand immigrants from Germany, Greece, Italy, and eastern Europe disembarked there between 1864 and 1924.

But Galveston had been ravaged by a great hurricane in 1900, not long before Max got there, and was still recovering (it never really did, never managing to become the "Wall Street of the Southwest," as its boosters had imagined in its salad days). So my grandfather sailed to the other side of the Gulf Coast and debarked in New Orleans, a far more thriving entrepôt. Employed, but not comfortable in the Deep South, even in a cosmopolitan city like New Orleans, Max yearned to get to New York, but he lacked money and the right papers. Then he met a guy who knew another guy who was connected to the right guy and managed to stow away on a ship to Gotham.

Now what? Lost in the city, the ghetto beckoned. The great metropolis was a vast zone of intimidating anonymity for way-farers from the American outback. Its teeming ghettos might be shunned by the uptown Ashkenazi, but it was different for immigrants, who could, like homing pigeons, hone in on densely settled neighborhood reproductions of their native villages and shtetls from the Old World. In these confraternities squirreled away amid the towering monoliths of New York's movers and shakers, the chances were strikingly good that you would find not only food and drink, languages, clothing, houses of worship, newspapers, and pastimes you were familiar with but, more remarkably, someone you knew. That's what happened to Max. He ran into a landsman on the Lower East Side. That man sent him to a factory in the Bronx that was looking for skilled sheet metal workers. Max showed up and was asked for his references. He had no idea what "references" were, and anyway he had none. When after a while he managed to piece together what his interviewer meant by "references," Max held up his two rather large hands, already weathered by a young life working metal. He made his point.

Max spent many years at this work. Early on he became involved with a group of fellow workers trying to form a union. They would meet secretly at a cheap Manhattan cafeteria (probably a Horn and Hardart) before dawn on their way to work in the Bronx, afraid to meet nearer the factory; no one even dreamed they could meet on the premises. One day they won; a union local was born; how sweet.

I never heard my grandfather (or for that matter any of my grandparents, three of whom were immigrants like Max), mention the Statue of Liberty. Whether Max thought of it at all, I don't know.

What I do know is that all through his life my grandfather was loyal to three faiths: the union, Jewish socialism as it was expressed every day in the *Jewish Daily Forward* (or in its Yiddish edition, the *Forverts*), which he continued to read until he died, and his trade. Whenever I, as a child, would visit him and my grandmother, Max, who was otherwise a rather quiet, even taciturn person, would advise me that the best life, the most secure life was to be gained by mastering a trade, the way to navigate the shoals of misfortune and economic unpredictability. He referred to a skill, something so embedded in the body it was hard to replace or do without. Moreover, that skill of the sort he meant when he displayed his knowing hands gave forth a spiritual sustenance as well, an inward confidence, mastery, and a rock-bottom sense of self-worth grounded in the tangible.

Growing up, I had no time for the Statue of Liberty and I ignored Max's advice. The statue was an obligatory site visit in elementary school that, for a suburban kid in midcentury America, was a hollowed-out symbol lacking any connection to life as I knew it. Measured against other icons of Americana—Davy Crockett, say—it didn't come close. My grandfather's wisdom seemed to me archaic (or whatever a kid who hadn't learned that word yet might have called it—"old-fashioned," maybe). His words seemed to emerge out of some other galaxy, from a past so murky and strange it could no longer be quite understood—like Harold Pinter's cribbed lines: "The past is a foreign country. They do things differently there." And yet . . .[19]

Napoleon, Max, and Me

Without Napoleon III, there might never have been a Statue of Liberty. True, such endless regressions might be posed about any historical event. Nonetheless, Bonaparte's coup provided the context in which the will and the imagination of the French liberal elite took shape, finally to be embodied in Lady Liberty. Karl Marx's *The Eighteenth Brumaire of Louis Napoleon* is widely considered one of the mountain peaks of historical and political journalism in the way it captured the triangulation of class conflicts in France. Napoleon emerged from that storm of contending social protagonists—ancient elites, rising commercial classes, middle-class champions of constitutional liberty and good order, fresh-born proletarians and the still-lively currents of artisanal rebellion, not to mention the mass of the peasantry Marx considered so shapeless and so easily manipulated. The nephew of the original emperor surfaced at the dead center of this revolutionary impasse. He leveraged its yearning for resolution into his own ascension and dictatorship. Napoleon became the default position. For liberal France, the Statue of Liberty would become one exit ramp away from that dead end.

On the American side, the history of the Statue of Liberty might be thought of as the eighteenth Brumaire of Joseph Pulitzer or as a turning point in the coming-of-age of the American bourgeoisie. Neither welcomed nor rejected, the statue turned out to be more plastic than its colossal presence suggested. Pulitzer, one of the New World's Great Men of Business and the Vox Populi, had to embarrass his compeers into taking possession of a monument to their own achievement as a class. This is comical in a way that calls to mind perhaps the most famous line from Marx's *Eighteenth Brumaire* that everyone loves to quote: his notion that history repeats, the first time as tragedy, the second as farce.

A moment came in my own life in which the austere legacy of my grandfather and so many immigrants like him returned to laugh at me. When I was still in college, during the summer I applied for a job in a garment factory, hoping to thereby get close enough to my fellow workers—most of whom turned out to be internal exiles from Afro-America and colonials from Puerto Rico—to instill in them the same opposition to the U.S. imperial intervention in Vietnam that I and my fellow students felt so deeply. Unwittingly, I applied for a job as a cutter, not knowing that that was the most skilled occupation in the "rag trade." The company was a fly-by-night firm in the bowels of Queens, so when a fresh-faced nineteen-year-old showed up claiming he had such skills and was willing to work for the going sweatshop wage, no questions were asked. None, that is, until I was given a trial run on what in the business is known as a "lay" of fabrics, in this case about a dozen layers thick. On top of the lay was placed a pattern that functioned as the template for cutting the textiles. The foreman handed me a machine (I had imagined a scissors) and gave me the green light. Away I went. Or rather, away went the cutting machine, with me hanging on for dear life as the blades slashed through the fabrics at warp speed in a pattern that had no resemblance to the template; really, there was no pattern at all, not one even as coherent as those wonderful colored photos used to illustrate chaos theory. Left behind instead was a pile of shredded, now useless material that looked exactly what we all know chaos looked like before the physicists got ahold of the term.

All this took only seconds. The foreman's reaction was in its own way extraordinary. He might have come at me with the cutting machine—after all, destroying layers of fabric at one fell swoop is not happy hour in any factory, much less in a penny-pinching sweatshop. Instead, slack-jawed, open-mouthed, eyeballs rolling, nonplussed, befuddled beyond be-fuddlement, he paused to collect himself. And then, after he carefully removed the cutter from my fiendish Scissorhands, he took me down to the warehouse and put me to work as an order picker, a task a lot more suited to my skill grade.

If only I had listened to Max.

4
There Was a Young Cowboy
Homeless on the Range

A t night, when my son and daughter were toddlers, I would sing them to sleep with a melancholy lullaby they never tired of hearing; nor, for that matter, did I ever grow weary of singing it. "There was a Young Cowboy" was its title and opening line. Most of the lyrics that followed I made up. And they changed every night as I invented the young cowboy's adventures, trials, and tribulations. But the tune and the mood and the imaginative terrain were inherited. My father had sung me to sleep to the same music. He, a second-generation immigrant Jew from New York, knew the real lyrics by heart. He was not alone. Millions, just as alien as my father from the song's heartland, had inherited as part of their cultural genotype the classic ballad known either as "The Streets of Laredo" or "The Cowboy's Lament."

Apparently, the folksong originated in an Irish ballad of the eighteenth century called "The Unfortunate Rake." Later an old-time cowboy named Frank H. Maynard turned it into a song of the Texas plains. That sounds plausible. The "poor cowboy" in Laredo lamenting his fate is indeed "unfortunate" as he tells his "sad story" while dying in the street "wrapped in white linen." And he's dying because, young and "dashing" as he was, he was a "rake" who knew he'd "done wrong," shot in the chest while gambling and brawling in a barroom. Rakish he may have been, but we mourn him nonetheless. We hear his lament through the voice of a fellow cowboy who mourns his comrade, "gone to the last round-up." He leaves us in a state of emotional ambiguity:

> We beat the drum slowly and played the fife lowly
> And bitterly wept as we bore him along
> For we loved our comrade, so brave, young, and handsome
> We all loved our comrade, although he'd done wrong.[1]

When I sang this song to my children, I had long since forgotten the lyrics my father once sang to me. He, however, knew them so well because "The Streets of Laredo" had burrowed deeply into the interior pathways of the national psyche. Over the decades, renditions have been performed by numerous artists—Burl Ives, Johnny Cash, Joan Baez, Roy Rogers, Willie Nelson, the Kingston Trio, and Pete Seeger—and featured in movies like *Bang the Drum Slowly* and *Brokeback Mountain* and TV shows from *Maverick* to *Deadwood*.

Vital elements of the original were missing from my rendition. The young cowboy, perhaps needless to say, never died. And he never "done wrong." Other touchstones of mythic memory remained, however. He was brave. He was alone. He was on a quest, but one always just out of his reach. He was virtuous, not a rake, but capable of killing evil ones when they crossed his path, which they inevitably did. His horse—in my version "a young pony"—was as faithful as the most loyal comrade. Our hero was made an orphan by violent circumstance but lived in perennial hope of recovering his loved ones. He survived in a vastness full of dangerous varmints, human and animal, as well as treacherous terrain and weather. But there was nothing he couldn't handle, relying only on himself and of course his young pony. My young cowboy, my kids' young cowboy, was a hero, a savior, an adventurer, a wanderer, a protector—free, honorable, fierce when he needed to be, very male, and very lonesome.

If I couldn't rely on my own memory, I could completely count on popular collective memory to lullaby my kids to sleep. After all, growing up in a ranch house America, I was awash in images of cowboys riding the range and holing up in ranch houses (which, by the way, only faintly resembled any of the house-raisings taking place on the great plains of suburbia). It is virtually impossible to overestimate the inundation. Hopalong Cassidy, Gene Autry, Roy Rogers, the Cisco Kid, and the Lone Ranger were only among the best known of an armada of singular heroes roaming the Great Plains, chasing bad guys, singing around campfires, facing off against Indians, rounding up stampeding cattle, going mano a mano with gunslingers, lighting out for the territories once they'd saved the town, trick-riding their horses, bedding down on moonlit mountains, protecting the womenfolk. They were fearless, chivalrous, modest, rough-hewn yet soft-spoken; sometimes gathered together in fraternal revelry, but they were often alone. Whether galloping furiously across the Plains to the strains of a Brahms symphony or the William Tell Overture or meandering down the Chisholm Trail to the plaintive strumming of a solo guitar, they were America's knights of the realm. While the cowboy romance long predated my childhood, its efflorescence in the two decades following World War II was extraordinary.

Hopalong rode the range on sixty-three TV stations, fifty-two radio stations, and appeared in 155 newspaper comic pages in 1952. So many kids wanted clothes modeled on his all-black outfit that the United States ran short of black dye. The Lone Ranger did even better and could be heard or seen on 250 radio and TV outlets; Roy Rogers showed up on 175, and his celebrity was such that his name appeared on more stuff than anyone else's except Walt Disney's. Gene Autry presided over an empire worth somewhere between $4 million and $7 million in 1948. It included his own movie company, two music publishing houses, four movie theaters in Dallas, two Phoenix newspapers, three radio stations, a flying school in California, and four sizeable ranches in Texas, California, and Arizona. There were Gene Autry comic books and royalties on hair oil, jeans, hats, and cap pistols amounting to about $100,000 a year. Autry and William Boyd (Hopalong) thought of their characters as "role models for many American boys and girls."

America was awash in cowboy culture. For example, of the 2,400 movies released in 1951, 480 were westerns. Bantam Books issued 25 million western stories between 1947 and 1951. Zane Grey novels were read by 54 million people. By 1958 11 percent of all works of fiction published in the United States were westerns. Hollywood released a cowboy movie every week. In 1959 eight of the sixteen most watched TV shows were westerns. (Bob Zimmerman, a fan of Matt Dillon of *Gunsmoke*, first came up with the pseudonym Bob Dillon; only later did it become Dylan in honor of the Welsh poet.) The lingo of the mythic Wild West permeated the national vocabulary with talk of showdowns, last stands, hired guns, and roundups. And this was true for decades, going all the way back to Owen Wister's *Virginian*, which went through fifteen reprints in its first year (1902). Westerns comprised an outsized share of silent films by 1910. Newsstands in the 1920s were already dominated by cowboy magazines selling well over a million copies a year.[2]

To paraphrase a line from William Butler Yeats, mid-twentieth-century America was fed on cowboy fantasies and grew sententious from the fare. A compacted metaphor, the cowboy became the carrier of every self-congratulatory maxim of the American credo: self-sufficiency, freedom, individualism, moral sure-footedness, manly fortitude, frontier vigor, and Anglo-Saxon destiny. No other image was as quintessentially American; hence the Marlboro Man and Ronald Reagan's cowboy hat and string tie. Perhaps only GI Joe rivaled the cowboy as an emblem of what one writer has called the triumphalism of "victory culture." One thing was clear: class did not matter. The "ranch house" housed a society given over to that delusion.

As the twentieth century drew to a close, that picture of the West would darken in movie houses and on TV in dramas like *Deadwood* or in mordant novels like *Lonesome Dove*. Virtuous violence descended into mere violence. Axiomatic racism got deconstructed and condemned. Even at the height of the love affair with all things West, novels and movies like *The Ox Bow Incident* or Oakley Hall's *Warlock* would peer beneath the sunnier surface of the cowboy idyll. But the young cowboy of my childhood and the young cowboy of my kids' bedtime were washed-out characters compared to "the poor cowboy" who told his "sad story" on the streets of Laredo.

That story and song were closer to the physical and social reality in which the fantasy was nurtured and then subjected to the recombinant mechanisms of popular culture. Echoes of the cowboy's marginality, his poverty, his restless mobility, his rootlessness, his falls from virtue, his inwardness, his malignant innocence, his social invisibility except to his compeers, and his wayward violence are still audible in "The Cowboy's Lament." But they grew more and more faint. The thousand- or two- or even three-thousand-mile trail drives, the arduous monotony of day-after-day, dawn-to-dusk cattle tending, the manipulation and plundering of youthful naïfs in the cattle towns of Texas, Kansas, and the northern Plains, the vicious range wars between cattlemen, sheepherders, and "nesters" (farm folk) receded into a sentimentalized, sepia-hued yesteryear. Telling too was that hiding in plain sight was the poignant fact of the matter that the man being eulogized was thought of as a "boy," a locution so naturalized that its affectionate condescension didn't make it to the surface of public consciousness.

A near-magical transubstantiation happened. A "boy" was metamorphosed into the all-American hero. All that was distilled from his real life to form that image suggested that he was the perfect embodiment of the country's historic rejection of the Old World's cramped and suffocating social hierarchies and dependencies. Yet this man-boy was, on the contrary, a version of the perfect proletarian, set adrift from any social anchorage, from any familial safe harbor, afloat and at the mercy of the currents of global trade. At the hidden heart of the nation's primal mythos of self-sufficient manly individualism was an invisible, proletarian "poor boy"—a wayfarer who left little trace, yet an icon exalted, redeemed, and imperishable. And because that boy was an American boy, he nourished his own indigenous hopes of escaping that fate.

Human Tumbleweeds

Andy Adams made his first trail drive—well over a two-thousand-mile trek from San Antonio in Texas to the Blackfoot Indian Agency in Montana—when he was in his early twenties. It was 1882. Andy kept a log he published years later. It begins with a word about where, socially speaking, he hailed from. "Just why my father moved, at the close of the Civil War, from

Georgia to Texas, is to this good hour a mystery to me. While we did not exactly belong to the poor whites, we classed with them in poverty, being renters; but I am inclined to think my parents were intellectually superior to that common type of the South." Andy remembered his early days in a one-room log cabin as Sherman marched to the sea. Once in West Texas, "the vagabond temperament of the range I easily assimilated." Tales told by his older brother and his friends who were cowboying on the northern Plains "set my blood on fire." Until then, this young cowboy-to-be thought, "I had had adventures, but mine paled into insignificance beside theirs." So off he set on a six-month journey full of hazard and tedium.[3]

Cowboys were a heterogeneous lot. Some were ex-Confederates or at least hailed from the old Confederacy, like Andy and his brother. In fact, one reason cowboys were called "boys" had to do with the way the Civil War disrupted life in the South. With grown men away, disabled, or dead, young boys still at home took on the tasks of herding domestic cattle and horses, work that would have been done in normal times by their father or older brothers. The nomenclature actually went all the way back to the Revolution, to Westchester County in particular, where Loyalist "cowboys" and patriot "skinners" plundered each other's cattle. (It was a small band of skinners that captured British intelligence chief John André, thus foiling Benedict Arnold's plot to surrender West Point to the redcoats.)

Confederates joined ex-Union men, northerners, Indians, itinerant peddlers, and ex-slaves fleeing the terror and vassalage of the post-Reconstruction South. Charles Siringo, whose *A Texas Cowboy; or, Fifteen Years on the Hurricane Deck of a Spanish Pony* was probably the best-known memoir of this life, was a nomad practically from birth; he became a cowboy at eighteen, working for the Texas cattle king Shanghai Pierce, and later on became a range detective in pursuit of Billy the Kid. All these men were migrating to Texas from lives disrupted by war and economic depression. Or they might be homegrown one-time Texas or Great Plains farmers. What they shared was a footloose existence and the "vagabond temperament" Andy assimilated.

If not actually boys, they were disproportionately young. They were overwhelmingly single males. They were literate, but most were without more than a short grade school education (Adams was exceptional in this regard). Family life for many had grown tenuous as they hit the road in search of work. Even before they rode the range, they were already a mobile, migratory population, in some cases dispossessed from family homesteads, in others lured west by news of gold strikes or fur trapping or by wanderlust. When together on the trail, they coalesced as all-male families, bands of brothers of unshakeable solidarity when confronted by enemy outsiders or just plain outsiders. Once the drive was over, however, they tended to go their separate ways.

During the heyday of trail driving—from the mid-1870s through the next decade and dwindling after that—there were probably no more than forty thousand working cowboys; a small grouplet that left a large footprint. They filled a particular niche in the political economy of the extractive capitalism characteristic of the western half of the country. This included ranching, mining, fur trading, hunting, agriculture, timber and, as time went by, drilling for oil and other natural resources. Like every other form of newborn capitalism, these enterprises intruded onto a landscape where other economies had already rooted.[4]

The Political Economy of Extractive Capitalism

Homesteaders, prospectors, family ranchers, and native American communal hunters and village cultivators coexisted, at times
uneasily, before the great trail drives and railhead destination
towns reconfigured the terrain. Squatters in Texas and elsewhere
early on filled these empty spaces by right of first occupation,
and treated grazing land and water and bands of wild cattle and
horses as resources available to everyone. "The Great American
Desert" was great beyond imagining. It comprised 44 percent
of the land mass of the United States, an area as big as France,
Germany, Britain, Ireland, Denmark, Holland, Belgium, Austria,
Italy, Spain, and Portugal combined: roomy enough to accom-
modate a broad spectrum of settlers not yet acclimated to the
ways of life and livelihood blowing in from the East.

Ranchers raised cattle not for the world market but as part
of self-sufficient family farms. In the antebellum years, no large-
scale market existed for meat, but rather local ones for hides
(leather), horns (fancy "Spanish combs"), hoofs (glue), and
tallow. These earlier and concurrent ways of life and livelihood
were often themselves inveigled in the marketplace; in the case
of fur trading and grain production, dense commercial circuits
wired them into a global agora. But closer to the ground they
remained outside the orbit of capitalist relations; personal and
family labor predominated, and wage labor was, if not unheard
of, infrequently used. Slaves and ex-slaves, Indians, and peons
filled the occasional need for casual labor. Before Abilene was
converted into a depot for cattle trains by Joseph McCoy, an
enterprising middleman from Missouri, it was "a small dead
place ... of about one dozen log huts" and one saloon, whose
owner moonlighted selling prairie dogs at $5 a head to tourists
passing through on the train.[5]

Establishing the preeminence of extractive industry and mass-market-oriented agriculture on the Great American Desert meant first of all absorbing and supplanting those preexisting modes of life prevailing in the American outback. This was accomplished by the impersonal dynamics of the market, by guile, by force, and always with an assist from the government, no matter how much the legend insists that this was a world that had little use or patience for official state functionaries, not to mention simple law and order.

Multiple roads all led to extinction during the decades between early white settler incursion and the great cattle drives of the 1870s and 1880s. An increasing share of Indian labor was devoted to meeting global demand for fur, so older forms of mobile agriculture and tool and clothing crafts diminished, then fell by the wayside. Indians, long involved in the fur trade of the mountains and forests of the North and Southwest, eventually became dependent on it, no longer able to maintain their immemorial self-sufficient communities. Being tethered to the world market led tribal people inexorably into debt and default. With remarkable speed the animals upon which this new commerce depended grew scarce as the kill rate far exceeded the pace of reproduction.

Alien life-forms came to the Plains in waves: not just mountain men and trading posts, but then "nesters" traveling the Oregon Trail, miners, buffalo hunters, railroad crews, and last of all cattlemen. Even powerful warrior nations like the Comanche succumbed as buffalo disappeared, transformed into winter clothing and conveyor belts for factory machinery back east. Capturing horses or humans from wartime rival Indians to use or trade as slaves became harder to carry on as Anglo settlers intruded. Far to the north, the cattle business of Wyoming, where Indians occupied two-thirds of the territory, was made feasible by the erection of federal forts in places like Laramie, eventually overwhelming the resistance of the Sioux and the Cheyenne tribes of the north.[6]

So too, as the railroads and the army spread west, both developments making mass cattle herding and distribution possible, their workers and soldiers ate buffalo meat in vast quantities. A mainstay of the Plains Indians diet was killed off rapidly. In two years alone on the southern Plains, nearly 1.5 million buffalo hides were shipped to market. The army cleared the land of human competitors, herding them onto reservations. (That's why Andy Adams was headed for the Blackfoot Agency; his "outfit" was subcontracted by the army to feed now impoverished and superannuated native tribes.) And this in turn opened up the prairies for more efficient grazing by livestock as their animal competitors for grass vanished.

Government too facilitated the building of transcontinental rail lines with enormous grants of public lands and other financial favors. Once those lines reached places like Abilene or Dodge City in Kansas or Cheyenne or Laramie in Wyoming, it became feasible, although still daunting, to conceive transporting cattle from West Texas to these railheads a thousand or more miles to the east. Building vital if less imposing infrastructure (wagon roads, for example) also depended on the federal government; agencies likes the Geological Survey, the Bureau of Indian Affairs, the Interior Department, and the U.S. Land Office created a new West into which the cowboy as hired hand fitted. One historian of the American West has concluded, "In some basic ways the federal government created itself in the West."[7]

What had once been common grazing land supporting wild longhorn cattle that anyone might use, sell, or kill became enveloped in a network of legal claims to private property in land, water, steers, and horses. Barbed wire fences sprang up in a flash, sometimes covering hundreds of miles of now private rangeland. At first the fences were resented, causing range wars, fence cutting, and killings. Eventually, however, the wire proved quite useful as it made selective breeding easier. Mavericks—both longhorn cattle and wild horses there for the taking that had made possible small-time operations—grew rarer on the Plains; hence the big business in rustling as the market value of these animals appreciated.

But the armature of private property had unwelcome consequences for ranching as well. Sheepherders and farmers moved onto the Plains; the sheep were voracious as they ate what cows ate and what they wouldn't; and the nesters up-rooted the grass to plant other vegetables and fenced in what land wasn't already enclosed. On the arid Plains a quarter section was simply too little to produce enough of a crop to make farm life viable, so "grangers" pushed for more, which further crowded ranchers, some of whom, from the old days, depend-ed on the "free range," while the biggest among them fenced off what was once a commons.

Mini civil wars broke out between competing forms of agro-economies; the cowboy was caught in the middle and the life expectancy of his "career" placed in jeopardy. Surplus labor from defunct homesteads, family ranches, and exhausted fur-trading posts made his position that much more precarious. And the mining camps that sprang up in the mountainous neighborhoods surrounding the Great Plains to the north and southwest were themselves subject to periodic collapse, either actual cave-ins and explosions or because the veins of gold, silver, copper, and coal played out; consequently, ex-miners resorted as well to riding the range.[8]

Meat to Market

Long-haul cattle drives originating first in Texas began more or less coincident with the completion of the transcontinental railroads. This made vast potential markets at home and abroad accessible. Ranchers seized the moment, and by the early 1870s the Chisholm and Santa Fe trails and other less legendary routes were nearly gridlocked with longhorns and other meatier and more docile varieties of cattle. There were enough of them consisting of two or three thousand steers or more that they ran into each other regularly; indeed, sometimes days were lost separating members of one herd from another. The business was both fiercely competitive and very lucrative, especially as, at first, there was so much common land to take advantage of. On average, expeditions made a 40 percent return. Although always a hazardous undertaking for both cowboy and animal, as the routes became better known the trade grew less risky and so more tempting to join.[9]

Quickly the logic of the market attracted the attention of larger-scale enterprises. The appetites of investors back east and in Europe were stimulated. Many in that circle were already major players in western land speculations, so ambitious and aggrandizing that they tended to make a mockery of the Homestead Act, which presumably was designed to encourage land distribution to actual cultivators. The meat business became an attractive outlet for idle pools of liquid capital. English, Scottish, German, and Yankee bankers and merchants purchased huge spreads consisting of thousands of heads of cattle and employing sizeable cowboy outfits to manage and transport them. The cattle business attracted a higher percentage of European investors than any other western enterprise. The British alone poured in $45 million to set up immense spreads like the

Prairie Cattle Company, which was actually a Scottish firm and embraced eight thousand square miles. One venture capital firm from Edinburgh offered property in Wyoming consisting of four hundred square miles, nineteen thousand head of cattle, and 150 saddle or work horses. Predictably, some of these more extravagant promotions turned out to consist of phantom livestock and land. Absentee owners might occasionally visit, not to ride the range but to hunt big game or play polo. In the Northwest, much of the pressure to push tribes out of their ancestral lands came from outside eastern and European investors. An Alien Land Law passed in 1887 in Minnesota and mimicked by other states was designed by domestic competitors to banish foreign ownership in the territories but proved toothless.

Boston and New York moneymen established 91 cattle companies in Wyoming capitalized at $51 million; Colorado exceeded that with 176 companies worth $74 million. The Sparkes-Harrell spread in Nevada and Idaho grazed 150,000 head of cattle over 3 million acres. Some ranches in the Southwest were so big they were known as "cattle empires," the most famous of which in the 1870s was the King Ranch in Texas consisting of half a million acres.

When the Union Pacific reached the borders of Wyoming in 1867, similar cattle kingdoms soon emerged in the vicinity of Cheyenne. Federal law in these territories was quite elastic, allowing for gargantuan claims to land and water. What began as rude sites consisting of a dugout on the side of a riverbank with a log roof overlaid with prairie sod or adobe, or a house made of cottonwood timber chinked with mud or moss, a dirt roof, a door of dried beef hide, and a bed of wolf skins, turned into baronies. Some claimed five hundred or even as much as thirty-two hundred square miles.

Feudal domains ruled over by these freshly minted "cattle barons" behaved like mini autocracies that recognized no law they hadn't promulgated themselves. In loosely governed territories like Montana and Wyoming this was especially the case. In Wyoming, the association of the biggest livestock operations dictated the time and place for roundups, assumed the power to impose fines or penalties, and essentially made territorial law. The Cheyenne Club, a clubby combine of big cattlemen, bankers, railroad operators, investors, and commission agents, ran Wyoming while wining, dining, socializing, and enjoying the best food, whiskey, wines, gambling tables, tennis courts, and race tracks.[10]

Perhaps the best known of these corporate undertakings was the XIT Ranch in the Texas Panhandle. It was created by investors from Chicago. Its "Cattle Reservation" was over two hundred miles in length, a vast, unbroken turf of various grazing grasses, once the feeding grounds of antelope, buffalo, mustangs, and wild Texas longhorns. It employed 150 cowboys and its remuda consisted of a thousand horses riding herd on 150,000 head of cattle. Fencing in this country-sized territory required 781 miles of barbed wire, which cost about $181,000. By 1890 the amount of fencing had doubled. On the more arid stretches, artificial reservoirs were built along with storage tanks and windmills. The rather odd brand—XIT—was alleged to signal that the ranch spread over ten counties; true or not, it was a difficult brand for rustlers to counterfeit.

Texas lawmakers patented the ranch to its Chicago real estate developers (originally two farm boy immigrant brothers from England and two other partners) in return for building the State House in Austin in 1879. An undertaking of this scope required large infusions of capital, which the partners found available from British aristocrats who then sat on the board of

directors of the newly formed Capital Freehold Land and Investment Company. As that unwestern-sounding corporate
name might suggest, the XIT worked a transformation in
the human ecology of West Texas. One observer reflected: "The
practice of eating a neighbor's beef was once general upon the
ranges of Texas. Hungry men killed a fat beef when they found
one, regardless of owner, and in those days of lax business
methods and open-handed hospitality, such actions seemed
beyond reproach. But foreign capital came, the barbed wire
fence confined each brand to its own range, the happy-go-lucky
pastoral ways of the [18]70s became a business of exacting
methods, and killing strays came to be regarded as theft."[11]

Imposing as it was, the XIT model of modern ranching
was not the inexorable wave of the future. On the northern
Plains, if not in Texas, that way of organizing the business died
out. It was a case of back to the future. In territories like Wyoming and Montana these mega-businesses and their "outside"
backers generated great resentment and resistance from family
ranchers. The class hostility directed against these financial
outsiders was intense enough that even rustlers could masquerade as Robin Hoods, social bandits challenging eastern interlop-
ers from Wall Street. If the "Wild West" was indeed wild, a big
part of the reason is that it became a terrain of violence-ridden
social animosities: mine workers against owners, cattlemen
versus sheepherders, white men facing off against Indians,
Mexicans, and Chinese, cowmen of the open range against
nesters, farmers at odds with local bankers, and big ranchers
threatening littler ones.

Cattlemen in particular were prone to violence, thanks in
part to the hazy notion of claims to land and the sketchy presence of legitimate authority; driving off rivals rather than suing
them was the preferred and readier remedy. So "big thieves"

faced off against "small thieves," according to one Wyoming newspaper. Most of the small-timers were ex-cowboys who charged their overbearing competitors with being illegal monopolists. Johnson City, Wyoming, was briefly controlled by the little fry until a lynching in 1889 and imported hired guns from Texas put an end to that in the Johnson County War of 1892. As far as the ranch hand was concerned, he might at various times work for either corporate or family enterprises.[12]

On the Line

However instinctive it might be to think of the cowboy as a throwback, he was in some respects exactly the opposite. The emergence of the transient cowboy of the Wild West was a straw in the wind, a sign that the West was "wild," perhaps, but becoming less so, even as the atmospherics of the gunslinging cowboy desperado suggested the contrary.[13]

Cowboys manned the supply chain turning out mass-produced meat for the urban markets of the East and abroad. Imagining these "hands" starring in a rural version of Charlie Chaplin's *Modern Times* is both apt and absurd. Apt because they too, like the Chaplin character whose robotic movements on the assembly line erased the distinction between human and machine, were largely interchangeable parts in a highly reticulated mechanism they neither understood nor controlled; absurd because they romanticized themselves and were romanticized while going extinct, a fate no one contemplated for the human automaton of the assembly line. To think of the Wild West's picaresque, decked out in boots, chaps, and spurs, a colorful bandanna around his neck, lariat and six-shooter at his hip, serenading the heavens as longhorns bed down for the night under a star-studded sky, is to conjure up a world about as far away as it's possible to get from the clanging cold geometry and dolorous, suffocating regimentation of the factory production line. Nonetheless, an understructure of capital accumulation lends these two alien life-forms an essential affinity.

Whether employed by a giant corporate ranch covering millions of acres or a more modestly sized one, the cowhand could reckon on a work life whose rigors were both nicely captured and grossly demeaned by his metaphorical reduction to a "hand." Wages were low, around $1 per day plus food and a bunk bed when not on the trail. He wasn't paid until the drive was over. Then he got gold because many of those ex-Confederate cowboys had been burned by worthless paper they'd received as soldiers. A cowhand was on call and on horseback most of the hours of every day, and he regularly worked for twelve hours. It was a life of work, eat, sleep. On the Chisholm Trail, it took two months to travel a thousand miles and many drives were far longer than that. Whatever the natural charms of the wide-open spaces, unexplored rivers, and breathtaking mountain ranges, as a daily experience trail herding could also entail a deadening monotony.

Andy Adams remembered spending sixteen to eighteen hours in the saddle. "We frequently saw mirages, though we were never led astray by shady groves of timber or tempting lakes of water." Those endless, parched days and nights made towns like Dodge "points of such interest to us that they were like oases in desert lands to devotees on a pilgrimage to some consecrated shrine." The dust created by the herd as it traveled was often so thick it saturated right through clothes and into the skin. On the largest ranches, cowboys often lived off by themselves in sod-covered lean-tos, doing their cooking over outdoor fires. Employment was precarious. Winter often meant layoffs, and survival depended on scaring up a job as a bartender or cook. Establishing a family under these circumstances was rare. Once the drive concluded, there was no assurance the cowhand would be hired on for the next one.

Danger lurked everywhere. Cowboy "outfits" were always at risk of life and limb from stampedes, floods, and windstorms, from fording raging rivers, dealing with unfriendly Indians, enduring blizzards and scorching heat in an arid land, evading panicked cattle wielding horns that could cut deeply. Longhorns were not overly friendly and were nervous beasts, easily stirred up by anything from thunder and lightning to a passing animal, but cowboys had to chance that because a stampeding herd might run off a cliff, a thousand at a time. Breaking a bronco was rough work and risky, requiring special skills. The cowhand was even expected to face off against rustlers. He didn't own the livestock, but it was understood that the cowboy was bound to safeguard it even if that meant gunplay. Life on the trail was a young cowboy's way of life because older ones had mainly been all used up, suffering everything from broken bones to rheumatism. There were not many, if any, occupations as dangerous.[14]

Although the cowboy often worked on his own or with a comrade, there was an implicit work discipline. It was first of all imposed by the natural rhythms of this exercise in long-distance animal husbandry: when cattle and horses needed to rest, when they needed water or grass, preventing them from wandering too far afield, bedding them down in time, keeping up a pace that assured timely arrival at this river or that trail before it closed off or got flooded, relieving each other at regular intervals to ward off exhaustion, siphoning off the sick and lame, and so on.

Hierarchies of skill and authority configured the cowboy's workplace, even if that site extended over enormous distances and he worked alone or with a single comrade much of the time. The trail boss, or drover, acted like a foreman, allotting tasks that formed a rough occupational division of labor. The drover could handle business matters as well when the outfit reached the market. On the larger ranches, the owner often settled in town, leaving day-to-day operations to the foreman. For all that he was well paid. So was the cook, who not only prepared the outfit's meals but functioned as a kind of quartermaster, managing supplies of blankets, saddles, and so on. The wrangler took care of the horses, grouped together as a remuda of fifty to a hundred ponies; he was usually a teenager. The cowboys who led the herd were also among the most highly skilled and were called pointers. They were charged with preventing the mixing together of cattle from nearby herds and with stopping stampedes. Swing riders, flank riders, and then drag riders at the rear had their own distinct tasks; although among the less skilled, they had to watch out for straying calves and sore-footed and tired adults.

"Cutting out" mature cows, ready for slaughter, from their calves was a tough and demanding job, requiring considerable talent with a rope. Branding was less skilled but rough. A line rider patrolled to make sure no predators—animal or human or bacterial—were making off with members of the herd. Once barbed wire arrived, the line rider became a fence rider. The semiannual roundup entailed a complex choreography of men and beasts that involved branding, culling diseased cattle from the herd, and a dozen other tasks performed over ranges the size of Connecticut. A cowboy of average competence had to be able to track both cattle and horses.

Each position not only carried with it a set of skills and obligations but also established an order of command. These were more or less informal arrangements sanctioned by tradition and the more natural hierarchies of age and experience. But in the most modern enterprises work rules were explicit. The XIT Ranch issued "Rules of the XIT Ranch" to each hired hand. The rules made clear no guns were allowed, no gambling, no mingling of mustangs with XIT horses, no liquor on the premises, that work was expected seven days a week for seven to eight months, and that all employees were prohibited from maintaining their own livestock or horses on the ranch; the employee was a "hand" indeed.

Yet putting yourself at risk chasing rustlers or fighting Indians or embracing the social norms of collective work or respecting the wide spectrum of skills and experience and earned authority knitting the outfit together or participating in the comradery of nighttime campfire singing and storytelling suggest that the "hand" was also a brother. As much as his experience might be compared to a life of proletarian estrangement, debased and unskilled, this was a world, on the contrary, of hard-earned knowledge learned on the fly, of multifaceted crafts and the social esteem that went with them. The trials and demands of cowboy existence nurtured both a toughened sense of self-reliance and mastery and of a kind of work group solidarity. Living a spare social life and by and large not religious, cowboys, for just those reasons, highly valued the brotherhood.[15]

Fraternal relations were particularly prevalent on the northern Plains, where these men lived a less nomadic existence gathered together on fenced-off family ranches that functioned as "home for all." Competing outfits would, under trying emergencies or even in more ordinary times, collaborate to get the work done; that was the unarticulated protocol. However, this was a distinct kind of solidarity. It spilled over that class boundary dividing ranch boss and owner from the cowhand so as to become a peculiar, if temporary, enterprise loyalty. Here workers might at one and the same time function as the cattle baron's hands while paying a voluntary fealty to the land he ran. The outfit was simultaneously a fraternity and a patriarchy.

Had the Industrial Workers of the World formed twenty years earlier than when it did in 1905, that anarcho-syndicalist revolutionary-minded group of roving, rebel proletarians manning the docks, harvesting the wheat, digging the coal and silver of the far West might have included the footloose "range bum." Yet many of those same cowhands nurtured a more traditional aspiration, not one set on revolution. Able on occasion when times were good to mix in a small number of their own steers with the ranch owner's herd, they hoped one day to run their own spread, regain the independence they had lost, to rise the way Lincoln had imagined from wage labor to self-sufficiency. They hoped to graduate, so to speak, into manhood.[16]

Recombinant Hero

In real life that was a rare occurrence. There was no more social mobility or equality out west than back east. But the alchemical transformation of the cowboy in our popular culture made for a different story. Although there too no property got redistributed in favor of the cowboy, he was endowed nonetheless with all the attributes—and then some—that were supposed to accompany that station in life: independence, self-reliance, courage, ingenuity, an appetite for risk and adventure, a readiness to draw a line in the sand, the habit of command, and a steely will to go it alone.

Marvelous about this figurative redesign was the way it took elements from the cowboy's more proletarian way of life and transmuted them into the features of its antithesis. The fantasy cowboy hero who rode the TV range of my boyhood had shed the monotony but kept the tribulations. Drama stripped away the poverty but stylized the homespun costume, redressing the cowboy cum cavalier in fancy high-heeled riding boots, his horse with a fine saddle and silver bridle, his gun handle studded with pearls, silver-buckled cartridge belt at the ready, silver too his spurs, his chaps made of leather, hatband dressed with rattlesnake skin.

Dime novels unholstered the six-shooter the real cowboy rarely fired. Dodge, Abilene, and Laramie were turned into war zones, while back in the day very few died and most guns had to be surrendered on entering town. Once viewed as "white trash," not a suitable mate for a respectable young woman, the cowhand got a makeover to become not only dashing but socially acceptable, even desirable. "Rough men with shaggy hair and wild staring eyes in butternut trousers stuffed into great rough boots," fated for failure, morphed into heroes. The cowboy might be coarse, but he was strong, inventive, and a man among men—unlettered, perhaps, but his virtue and intelligence came naturally. Long gone were the days when President Chester Arthur sent a message to Congress in 1881 asking for the military to put down bands of "armed desperados known as 'cowboys'" who were terrorizing the good citizens of Arizona. Myth retained the cowboy's juvenile delinquency, yet erased the more prosaic danger of his workaday life.[17]

The cowboy was invariably a white man; his storied legend edited out not only the substantial presence of African American cowpokes but also our hero's own axiomatic prejudices. Indians, everybody agreed, were savages, so in popular mediums like movies and comics no censorship was required, even while veteran trail hands marveled at native American horsemanship and deep knowledge of the outdoors. Hispanic vaqueros (who had pioneered the cowboy craft in the New World and from whom much of cowboy dress and lingo was borrowed, including *rancho, corral, lasso,* and *bronco,* Spanish for wild horse) were looked down on by their Americano counterparts out on the Plains. One cowhand noted to his buddies, "Speaking of Mexicans and Indians I've got more use for a good horse than I have for either of these grades of humanity." But these aliens fared far better on the silver screen, where the Cisco Kid talked a little funny but was a straight arrow and Tonto was a loyal if subordinate comrade. Where African Americans were concerned, the case was different. They were as invisible in popular culture fantasies as if they'd never ventured across the Mississippi. Andy Adams knew better. He named his favorite horse— a jet-black animal he relied on for the most trying of tasks, including night riding and stampede control—Nigger Boy.[18]

Many a movie depicted the cowboy as an existentialist, crooning to the stars and moon in a mood of contemplative melancholy and brooding, rather than engaged in the more prosaic business of lulling the cows to settle down at night, which was the practical object of his vocalizing. Stories depicted him as a solitary man but omitted the insecurity. Cinematic cowboys could still be found gathered at the campfire telling tall tales, but stretches of suffering hunger and thirst got largely erased. Our hero wasn't a wage-earning functionary or a sometime bindle stiff; rather, he lived in an empyrean realm where plainsmen became Übermensch.

Most of what connected the cowboy to the commercial mechanisms of the global marketplace receded into the background; after all, as an action figure he was a living critique of modernity. Foregrounded instead was the violence-prone loner, the self-reliant frontiersman, the manly man, a natural-born survivor, nature's husband and master. Cherished was the solitary, not the comrade, the mountain man and pathfinder, not the cowpoke who actually poked cows with a rod designed to get them moving along, either to their soon-to-be-mechanized feeding stalls as the business got more organized for mass production, or to their slaughter. If the real West was about business and real estate, the confected West was inspired by depictions of white knights and black knights dueling at high noon as in the movie of that name or in the climactic shoot-out at sundown between Owen Wister's Virginian and a horse thief.[19]

Cowboys were refashioned as voluntary exiles from an industrial-urban civilization grown culturally obese and unnatural. Life on the range was an antidote to that enervating eastern-bred routine, its effeminate lusting after creature comforts, its social affectations and nose-in-the air snobbery, its stultifying uniformity, its urban density, its alienation from the natural world. That's why once and again cowboy Theodore Roosevelt idealized that rough-riding life, rode the range, went back and forth to his ranches in North Dakota (on the Big Horn, where Custer met his fate) and Montana, hoping to export back east some of its native resilience and bravery before it was too late. The original "Rough Rider," an offspring of cosmopolitan elitism if ever there was one, affected to despise its overcivilized softness, its cold rationality, and the promiscuous undermining of those unique and uniquely male, Anglo-Saxon racial virtues.

Indeed, if much of what made up the reality of cowboy life got diluted or washed out entirely when laundered by myth, one element instead was hugely magnified. Violence! Incipient violence, acted-out violence, an inward reservoir of violent emotion supplied the atmospherics of the cowboy legend. Moreover, it was cleansed of moral reproach; on the contrary, violence practiced by the cowboy hero was reconstituted as a virtue—however much it might be regretted, it was also righteous. And glamorous.

Yet the actual incidence of violence among cowboys, however rough and tumble their lives were, however thin on the ground the basics of law and order were, was miniscule in comparison. On the Chisholm Trail encounters with Indians were common, but very few ended in combat, most that did involving the toll cattle herders had to pay to pass through what after all was Indian country. As long-haul trail herding climaxed in the 1880s, there was a simultaneous drop in violence. Partly that was due to the presence in cow towns of outside lawmen like Bear River Tom Smith in Abilene (Smith was originally from New York, where he broke up street gangs during the Civil War). The only marshal to be killed in all of the Kansas cattle towns was killed by a farmer. Dodge was the deadliest, at least by reputation, but neither Bat Masterson nor Wyatt Earp killed anyone (or Earp may have got one—nobody seems to know for sure). Sheriffs in these towns used gun-control ordinances, as in Wichita, to keep order. Town elders, including clerics, merchants, and other middle-class businessmen, exerted their own pressures as they sought to make these places fit habitats for families, schools, and churches. Lynch law and violence generally were directed far more against social crimes, especially "crimes" against property—horse theft, most fatally, but also against encroaching sheepherders or between mine owners and their workers or loggers and timber companies—than against individuals.[20]

Moreover, the metaphoric arsenal of the Wild West could be imported back east to fire at working-class insurgents and radicals. Strikers were pinioned as "savages" who needed to be dealt with the way the western hero treated Indians and bandits—that is, with no mercy, unsanctioned by law, with direct and violent action. James Gordon Bennett, a sensationalist newspaper publisher, reversed the equation and labeled the

Sioux as "communistic" and tramps as "savages." Frederic Remington, whose sketches of life on the range memorialized that
infatuation for everybody (he was the illustrator for Roosevelt's
series of articles in *Century* magazine on the West) said he
"hated" the immigrant aliens, "the rubbish of the Earth," pol-
luting the cultural atmosphere east of the Mississippi. His
drawings were meant to depict a world with backbone enough
to stand up to this spiritual mongrelization. Perhaps this alternate universe of nature's aristocrats might reinvigorate and
morally rehabilitate the Republic, saving it from the "scourings
of the Devil's leavings." Compared to that decadence, one
story writer at the beginning of the twentieth century offered
this elegy of the primitive refugee from effete civilization: "Here
was a riot of animal intensity of life, of mutiny of physical man,
the last outbreak of innate savagery. The men of that rude day
lived vehemently. They died, they escaped." Or, as Mark Twain
memorably observed, the cowboy was one who "lights out for
the Territory to escape the constraints of Civilization."[21]

Mockery of Wall Street ranchers, absentee owners from
New York or Chicago or London, was commonplace on the
Plains. And the hostility was more than a purely economic complaint about the way these investors crowded out smaller, homegrown operations. The indictment covered as well the offense
that a preoccupation with finance presented to a way of life and
a region where nonmaterial values—a rough equality, honor,
and fraternity—mattered more. Latent in this fable was a social
flight from the onrush of mass society, from its spirit-diminishing
entanglements, its worship of Mammon, and its crushing anonymity. The cowboy romance provided therapeutic relief, if not
from capitalism per se, then from the type of civilization corporate industry and finance was incubating and which threatened
to ensnare everyone, whether they liked it or not.

Inheriting a genotype that went way back long before the wild longhorn spread to Texas, the cowboy became a kind of cultural bandit admired by those who hadn't his courage. His was an amalgamated image. It condensed the knight errant, the pirate, the mountain man, the buffalo hunter, the pathfinder, the Indian fighter, the desperado, the Robin Hood of the Plains, the gunman, and the no-questions-asked, quick-on-the-draw lawman. At times he lost most or any connection with cow tending and became instead Billy the Kid (a pathological teen-ager from the Bowery in New York who was very briefly a cowboy) or Kit Carson (a bona fide fur-trapping mountain man but not a cowboy) or Wyatt Earp (who hailed from Illinois and was at one time or another a bouncer, a gambler, a teamster, a buffalo hunter, a brothel keeper, a miner, a boxing referee, and a lawman—but never a cowboy, although he ran them out of Dodge City and Tombstone, Arizona) or Doc Holliday (an al-coholic dentist from back east) or even John Fremont (the first Republican candidate for president in 1856, a military man who grew up in Georgia and became known as the Pathfinder for his daring explorations of the West before, in a fit of reckless impetuosity, he anointed himself governor of California in the wake of the Mexican-American War and was court-martialed for his trouble). Buffalo Bill, hero of dime novels and Wild West theatricals, was perhaps the greatest fabricator of all, who in his later years had so fallen in love with his own press notices that he crafted his own epitaph: "I stood between savagery and civilization most of my early days," when in fact he had been a hunter, freight hauler, army scout, and a guide of average competence and courage. All of these figures, each in his own way, encapsulated the romance extracted from a political economy of extractive capitalism. The abiding allure of these recombinant heroes was their implicit repudiation of the pedestrian, soul-crushing wave of the future rolling in from the industrial, urbanizing East.

Moreover, this seduction appealed not only to urban cowboys but to the real McCoy. In the actual, not the fanciful, life of the range bum, hard as it was, there was embedded a kind of masculine reverie. Veteran cowboy Jim McCauley recalled the pain and exaltation: "I wish I had never saw a cow ranch. ... While Ide rather be on a cow ranch and work just wages ... than anything you could name ... the wild free life where you have to feel if your closest friend is still on your hip ... and if your old horse will make it in, and to make the Mexico line and get back without any holes in your hide—that is real living, that is sport but 'tis the violent kind and lots of people love it beyond doubt."[22]

Our fantasy cowhand avoided the fate faced by most. He had managed to stay clear of the demoralizing and enervating way of life urban-industrial America was embracing. He escaped or fought against its demeaning structures of authority at work, its supercilious social distinctions based on wealth and lineage, its conformity to the rhythms of the machine, the way it emasculated free men.

Moreover, the homoeroticism that went along with the adulation of the cowboy is hard to miss as, for example, in the opening pages of Owen Wister's classic *The Virginian*. On the very first page we meet the hero as he climbs down from a corral gate "with the undulations of a tiger, smooth and easy, as if his muscles flowed beneath the skin." He is "a slim young giant, more beautiful than pictures. ... The weather-beaten bloom of his face shone through duskily, as the ripe peaches look upon their trees in a dry season. But no dinginess of travel or shabbiness of attire could tarnish the splendor that radiated from his youth and strength." The countless sketches of cowboy life by Wister's contemporary Frederic Remington conveyed a sexual magnetism radiating from the lean and muscular athleticism of the cowboy in action. Eventually he would reappear riding through the Rockies selling cigarettes for Marlboro. However, this studied machismo was at odds with the actual social and sexual awkwardness of the cowhand. He was a social naïf who lived almost exclusively among other males. He might blow off sexual steam during his brief sojourns into cow towns, but he was far more a creature of Victorian inhibitions than he was a Don Juan.[23]

Part of the proletariat of the American West, along with loggers, miners, migratory farm laborers, fur trappers, and railroad gangs, the cowboy, uniquely, escaped the proletarian condition—yet only in the nation's imaginary life. He was both the perfect proletarian and the perfect free man. He was the invisible American and the legendary American. His seductive power as an exemplar of the triumphant outsider, the naysayer to the dolorous shades of factory and office, was and has remained a spiritual aphrodisiac. After all, we love our subterfuges.

"Our Hippie Cowboy"

Jed Briscoe joined the round-up the day following Fraser's initiation. He took silent note of the Texan's popularity, of how the boys all called him "Steve" because he had become one of them, and were ready to either lark with him or work with him. He noticed, too, that the ranger did his share of work without a whimper, apparently enjoying the long, hard hours in the saddle. The hill riding was of the roughest, and the cattle were wild as

deers and as agile. But there was no breakneck in-
cline too steep for Steve Fraser to follow.

Once Jed chanced upon Steve stripped for a
bath beside a creek, and he understood the physical
reasons for his perfect poise. The wiry, sinuous
muscles packed compactly without obtrusion
played beneath the skin like those of a panther. He
walked as softly and easily as one, with something
of the rippling, unconscious grace of that jungle
lord. It was this certainty of himself that vivified
the steel-gray eyes which looked forth unafraid,
and yet amiably, upon a world primitive enough to
demand proof of every man who would hold the
respect of his fellows.[24]

The above is not a subterfuge. Nor is it about me. It is
instead a wondrous coincidence if you happen to be me writing
about the national love affair with the cowboy. Steve Fraser the
ranger appears in a book called *A Texas Ranger* published in
1911 in a chapter called "The Broncho Busters." I have never
busted broncos nor been confused with a panther. However, I
came close enough to smell the coffee.

Long ago I attended a wedding in the borderlands between
eastern Colorado and Wyoming. The ceremony was outdoors,
by which I mean it took place in the great outdoors in the steep
rust- and ochre-colored canyons and boulder-laced plains of
that territory. The wedding party was on horseback. It included besides the bride and groom a trio of guitar-strumming
cowboys serenading the couple. They rode down a ravine to
where the rest of us were sitting on rocky outcroppings that
formed a naturally terraced arena. A minister in cowboy garb
performed the nuptials. Then we feasted on the better part of

a whole steer that had been rotating all day on a spit over an open fire.

I was there to celebrate the marriage of one of my dearest friends. Richard had rented an apartment with me years earlier in Philadelphia when we were both in school, both political activists, and both arrested for a crime we didn't commit. Richard went to Swarthmore. It didn't suit him, nor probably would any college. He used to walk around campus in a cowboy hat, chaps, spurs a-jingling. What he really wanted to do is what millions of American boys grew up wanting to do: to become a cowboy. Unlike those millions, he actually did it.

Richard remembers: "I grew up in Vermont and just outside New York City and I went out West in 1972. I have a drawing (crayon) of the 'Sunny Hollow,' my mythical horse farm, done at age 8. My sister Betsy married a man whose dad had a ranch in Colorado. I spent two summers ... working on that ranch. The foreman ... was an alcoholic so he taught me to drive when he was too drunk to drive. Anyhow, I loved riding horses and moving cattle, putting up the hay."

Once political turmoil subsided and we were exonerated, Richard headed where he'd always been destined to go. Out west he found work on family ranches in the foothills of the Rockies, in northeastern Colorado and southeastern Wyoming. "My first job was on a ranch on the Laramie River at about 8000 feet. It was January and it was way cold. I didn't have cold weather clothing so I only lasted 3 or 4 days. But during that time I watched a calf being born and something about that experience really moved me. I knew then what I wanted to do. I wanted to do it on my own terms."

Now and then I would visit, even join Richard on cattle drives (when the livestock had to be moved to higher elevations in the early summer). But I was no mere summertime cowpoke.

I have photos of me hooded in a sheepskin hat with donkey-size earlaps and wearing a long sheepskin coat riding through a snowy mist like a phantom figure from *McCabe and Mrs. Miller*. In better weather my family came along, and my young son was thrilled to sit on the saddle with me as we did our best to move recalcitrant steers up the foothills. Even a single day's work was hard—but thrilling.

For Richard, this hard life was always gratifying and still is. It somehow embraced the antimonies peculiar to the cowboy experience: proletarian harshness combined with an antimodernist exaltation that made the cowboy an imperishable element of the American mythos. Richard slid down the slope of class preferment until he reached a place well away from that metric: under that radar, so to speak.

At first, Richard's life was more than hard, it was an intellectual challenge. He knew precious little about what it took to be a competent cowboy. "When I moved out West I had almost no required skills. I grew up in an upper middle class suburb." Painstakingly and painfully, he had to master a great range of skills and knowledge that had always been prerequisite even if the lingua franca of the West had minimized that repertoire, diminishing it to something a mere "hand" could do. Roping cattle and training horses were essential skills. So he went to the Livermore, Colorado, Roping Club three times a week to practice. At first he was pretty bad at it; "local kids out-roped me." But he persevered and noticed that however poorly he performed, his western neighbors admired the "try" in him. One time when Richard was competing in a roping contest a stranger watching him remarked, "Who the hell is that hippie?" (he had kept his hair nearly shoulder length, a souvenir from the 1960s). His neighbors answered: "He's our hippie." Richard had arrived.

Eventually Richard became a good "hand" with a horse and rope. And he learned many other tasks: how to help a cow calve, repair fences and irrigation equipment, do artificial inseminations, doctor sick cattle, break in a horse, grow and bale hay, build a corral, and a dozen other jobs requiring both knowledge and experience. Early on he had lived on his own far from the main ranch house, isolated by the heavy snows, where he learned to hunt for his own food and deal with the loneliness. He was truly living "off the grid," yet because he was living in the late twentieth, not the nineteenth century, he also had to master "rudimentary mechanics," to keep trucks and tractors operating, haying machines repaired, even "to replace a U-joint on a pickup truck stuck over a little creek in the snow" in the midwinter blizzard of 1979. "Most of my learning was trial and error." A glamorous life it was not.

Nor had it ever been. One observer of cowboy life in the 1950s, when I was reveling in what I supposed to be its high drama, painted a more edifying if soberer picture: "He can rope a cow out of brush patch so thick that a Hollywood cowboy couldn't crawl into on his hands and knees. He can break a horse for riding, doctor a wormy sheep, make a balky gasoline engine pump water for thirsty cattle, or punch a string of postholes across a rocky ridge. He can make out with patched gear, sorry mounts, and still get the job done. . . . On top of all this, he's got a quality common to most cowhands: a way of meeting life head-on." As a myth he was saturated in glamour. In real life he was, going all the way back and in Richard's day too, "first of all a worker with cows . . . and not a gun-totin half alligator, half-man, on a drunken spree in a red-light town."[25]

By the end of the 1970s Richard had become a foreman on the XX Ranch, "my first job running a ranch. It was remote, high altitude, and big, 25,000 acres. I had never worked as hard as I did at that job. For one it was a Wyoming ranch and if you are a cowboy nothing is better than a Wyoming one."

Wyoming was among the last of the cowboy redoubts. Even before the cowboy arrived it was home to the original mountain men who braved the forested wilderness of the Rockies. There, in places like Laramie and Cheyenne (quite close to where Richard lived), the wide-open spaces were late to get fenced in. Military outposts (particularly Fort Laramie) were staging grounds instead for hemming in native Americans. The fort was established originally by John Jacob Astor's American Fur Company with fifteen-foot-high walls surmounted by a palisade. It served as well as a supply center for migrants on the Oregon Trial. And the trail was a conduit for the mass shipment of cattle from Oregon back east.

Conflicts between cattle barons and sheep farmers erupted into open civil war in the Wyoming Territory. Confrontations were marked by ethnic prejudices; ranchers viewed sheep farmers as lower-order Hispanics, Basques, and Mormons. The Laramie County Stock Association, which grew into the Wyoming Stock Growers Association, was the most powerful in the history of the cattle trade, exercising enormous behind-the-scenes political influence; it essentially compelled the 1876 treaty with Sioux and the northern Cheyenne. Wyoming was a dangerous, semi-lawless place. The Johnson County War of 1892 between cattlemen (if you're an owner, you're a "man"; if a mere herder, you're a "boy") and homesteaders and smaller ranchers and rustlers posing as "social bandits" featured hangings and shootings and eventually the intervention of the National Guard. And the weather in the Wyoming Rockies was unforgiving. The frozen corpses of cowboys reemerged with each spring's thaw. Wyoming supplied the physical and social geography of enduring legend. This was where the Virginian left his stamp.

It was enduring enough that finding yourself working its rocky surface a century removed from its glory days could still be relished.[26]

However, by the time Richard arrived in the storied territory, its glory days had faded; his timing was off. In the 1980s the world market played havoc with the meat industry. True enough, President Ronald Reagan, code-named Rawhide by the FBI, might be vacationing on his California ranch, riding a horse and sporting a cowboy hat. And Ralph Lauren was running ads in *New York Magazine* to capture the mystique: "The West. It's not just stage-coaches and sagebrush. It's an image of men who are real proud. Of the freedom and independence we all would like to feel. Now Ralph Lauren has expressed all this in 'chaps,' his new men's cologne. 'Chaps' is a cologne a man can put on as naturally as a warm leather jacket or pair of jeans. It's the West. The West you would like to feel inside yourself."

But Richard was feeling something else. The early years of the Reagan administration were marked by the Federal Reserve's austere credit policies. The whole agricultural sector was in crisis. Exports collapsed and the demand for beef fell by 20 percent. Land values in Montana and Wyoming imploded. Nature collaborated with a prolonged drought and voracious grasshoppers. The northern Plains were pockmarked with decay. Even before that, private as opposed to corporate ranching had become a luxury for rich widows and investment bankers and oil millionaires in the Panhandle. They could afford to lose money in pursuit of pleasures. Most ranching business was conducted by even bigger businesses operating in other sectors of the economy—oil and gas, TV stations, banking, and so on. Massive mechanized feed yards were wired into global markets. "It's like being in a factory, only outdoors," noted one reporter. Could the dream abide in such circumstances?[27]

On Ranch XX Richard tried to weather the storm. "The winter of 1979–80 was an incredibly hard winter—from an historic Thanksgiving blizzard through early May it stayed snowed up. . . . There were times that winter when I was by myself." Yet trials like that were also redemptive. "Lost in a blizzard trying to feed 400 cows and 300 yearlings just trying to get equipment through the snow that winter went a long way to showing me that I could do it. I kept at it." A cowboy tradition of enterprise solidarity clicked in. "Neighboring ranches would help when they could." When a broken-down truck left Richard stranded in the drifts, he walked miles through the blizzard to get help, and between Christmas and the New Year fellow workers helped him fix the truck. First, though, he had to ride another nine miles on horseback to Ty Siding, the nearest Wyoming town, to borrow a car to get him to a Ford dealership in Laramie, and then finally another neighbor snowmobiled him back to the XX Ranch.

Being a cowboy had always been a young man's game. Notwithstanding modern technologies and conveniences, it remains so. Richard not only had to weather the elements and survive the perturbations of the economy, the toll on his body grew heavier and heavier as he aged. In the course of his work, he took numerous spills from his horse, hoofs to his midsection from irascible steers, and less visible wounds to his innards. Eventually, he had broken most bones from his ankles on up through his hips. Artificial joints replaced natural ones. Painkillers became a dietary staple. His lungs betrayed him with rheumatoid arthritis so he rode with an oxygen pack strapped to his side. But he rode on, the cowboy ethos he admired so much as a kid too resilient to die.

So he prevailed, but could not hold out against the headwinds of the world economy. Richard managed for a time to lease his own ranch, raising cattle and horses. He ran seventy cows of his own and three hundred more "on shares." Here was that old dream of the cowboy proletarian, to be his own man. But "I went broke" during a severe drought and a downturn in the meat market (both for cow and horse meat). That was a hard blow.

Still, for Richard, as for so many others, it had never been merely a business, about making money. The horses he raised and trained and sometimes sold for breeding rights were also his comrades. They meant that much. The cowboy love affair with his horse has always been part of the mystique and a well-grounded one. Today Richard rides three horses, in particular, that he raised from foals. "I have gotten older and more broken down and these three horses really take care of me. They are still very athletic and yet they let me slide on and off them, lead up to the back of a trailer so I can more easily get on them. So maybe my 'Sunny Hollow' dream did come true."

Yes and no. A cowboy named Henry Blanton lived in the Texas Panhandle when a reporter for the *New Yorker* wrote about him in the late 1970s. He longed for the heroic West but lived in the new one of agribusinesses featuring huge automated feed yards, brokers and financiers and college-educated managers—all of which left him disappointed. As a young man, he was a drifting cowhand, paid poorly, living in shacks. Blanton had moved up over time, become a foreman, and owned a prefabricated house with running water and electricity. But he felt the absentee owner continued to treat him as "an overgrown boy." Blanton went so far as to characterize the ranch owner's attitude about taking care of the cowboy as "like taking care of a good slave before the Civil War." And where he lived, traditional forms of deprecation—"just a cowboy" or "there's nothing lower than a cowboy" or "poor cowboys"—were commonplace. Sometimes the insults took on an ironic form of self-deprecation as "poor cowboys" vented their hangdog resentment of being taken advantage of by New York financiers and the whole "economics deal."[28]

Like Richard, however, Blanton, although bitter (which Richard is not), remained captured by the life, its myth as well as its reality. My friend put it like this: "When I moved out west I'm not sure what called me. Probably the myth of the Old West and the cowboy and his rugged individualism intrigued me.... It also had to do with being so influenced by nature. The rhythm and flow of the seasons . . . watching young calves and foals that I helped birth grow to be useful animals either as tools (horses) or as a product for the general public." Despite the solitary nature of cowboy life, he was surrounded and embraced by a community alien to his upbringing but one that respected and loved him for the odd hybrid he'd become. "Being part of the earth and its cycle of being, able to deal with the aloneness of the life, being able to deal with the extremes of the weather, these are the things that make me feel good about myself. Now, I'm old before my time, broke, broke down, and lonely, but I am proud of what I've done."

A neighbor of Richard's, a cowboy and songwriter, borrowed a phrase from a Larry McMurtry novel, a phrase that Richard always favored, as the title and refrain of a ballad called "My Heart's Pastureland." Through the arduousness and hardships, the loneliness and insecurity, the social devaluation and personal invisibility, a dream abides. Not the sentimental and brutal and demented dream of a nation in flight from itself, but an unassuming one in which a footloose range bum, a proletarian of the Plains, finds solace and his heart's pastureland.[29]

5
John Smith Visits Suburbia

People stocked backyard bomb shelters with survivalist essentials and their favorite comestibles, planning on a life underground. The nose cones of newly deployed intercontinental ballistic missiles pointed at great cities all over the Northern Hemisphere. Lethal submarines would soon patrol the depths with enough firepower to incinerate the planet. Endgame theorists plotted scenarios for "mutual assured destruction" (MAD). Diplomats walked on the brink of a global precipice, playing a grotesque game of chicken.

Amid all this Armageddon-like fist waving, an odd kind of domestic squabble broke out in a kitchen in, of all places, Moscow. At the American National Exhibition in that city in 1959, Vice President Richard Nixon and Soviet premier Nikita Khrushchev faced off in an argument about just who would bury whom and how. Instead of pointing to their muscle-bound arsenals, the two would challenge each other about which society was likely to produce the best stoves, washing machines, televisions, electrical appliances, and other consumer delights. The "Kitchen Debate" would become one of the more memorable chapters in the history of the Cold War. It was also the mise-en-scène in which America redeemed its IOU to the world as a paradise without classes.[1]

At the center of the exhibit the Americans had built an entire six-room ranch house they claimed everyone in the United States could afford and filled it with all the latest gadgetry. The house itself was split in half to make it easier for the enormous crowds anticipated to pass through. And enormous crowds there were. William Safire was then a young press agent working for the American company that built the house. He later remembered they decided to call it Splitnik because it was indeed a split-level and split in half, but also to draw the contrast with the Soviet's singular recent achievement: the extraordinary launching of a vehicle into outer space. And, in fact, the Sputnik satellite had been on display a month earlier at the parallel Soviet exhibit in New York. While both countries showed off their varied accomplishments in the arts and sciences, the Russian exhibit emphasized Soviet strides in production technology while the Yankee display was heavy on creature comforts.

Staged today, the debate might have erupted in a fully loaded rec room illuminated by the lime-green glow of IT devices. Back then, however, no room better epitomized the frontier of modern living than the kitchen. It was the site where technological marvels were revolutionizing space and time. More than that, this Tomorrowland kitchen promised to level the playing field between haves and have-nots. Only the well-off had previously enjoyed a distinctly separate space for cooking and serving meals. For most people the place where they cooked at a coal stove and ate at a side table was also where they usually slept and sometimes worked. The Moscow kitchen was an angular, self-contained module with squared-off appliances, unified in design, of standardized measurements, a terrain of conjoined countertops supporting mass-produced electrical and mechanical devices. There were toasters and juicers and sinks and ovens, even a color TV, that in real life were in turn hooked up to intricate power, water, and gas grids and systems. Not lime-green, but lemon-yellow, the kitchen beckoned like a sunrise. Actually, there were several kitchens on display; one offered by RCA-Whirlpool, dubbed the Miracle Kitchen, was allegedly run entirely by push buttons. General Mills presented its own version of a labor-saving wonder. But it was General Electric's ranch house model that captured the world's attention when East met West to decide who was best. As these Fortune 500 household names suggest, the American exhibit was a collaboration between corporate America and the U.S. government. The State Department invited and received substantial financing for staging the show from General Motors, Ford, IBM, GE, Disney, Westinghouse, Pepsi, and other heavyweights of America's mass-consumption economy. Gilbert Robinson, an organizer of the event for the State Department, put his finger on the deep, even historic purpose of this public-private enterprise. It was to display the stark difference between the lives of average citizens of the two countries and to draw a conclusion about which society had in fact come closer to achieving some egalitarian nirvana.[2]

Nixon and Khrushchev jousted about exactly that as they ambled through the kitchen and the rest of the exhibition. The vice president told the premier that "the United States, the world's largest capitalist country, has from the standpoint of distribution of wealth come closest to the ideal of prosperity for all in a classless society." Soon enough, Khrushchev retorted, the Soviet Union would catch up and then pass the United States, "saying Bye, Bye" as it zoomed away into the future. The dialogue was alternately chiding and angry and diplomatically polite. Nixon: "See the built-in washing machine?" Khrushchev: "We have such things." N: "What we want is to make more easy the life of our housewives." K: "We do not have the capitalist attitude toward women." When the vice president boasted that a steelworker making $3 an hour could afford to buy a $14,000 house, the premier claimed, "We have peasants who can afford to spend $14,000 for a house." All was not a matter of dollars and cents, however. The Soviet leader pointed out, "Many things you've shown us are interesting but they are not needed in life. They have no useful purpose. They are merely gadgets." Nixon had a ready and ideologically powered response: "We have many different manufacturers and many different kinds of washing machines so the housewives have a choice. . . . We hope to show our diversity and right to choose."[3]

Nixon's defense of "the right to choose" was treated back home as if he had enunciated a twentieth-century version of the Emancipation Proclamation. The debate was broadcast by all three major networks. *Time* magazine congratulated the vice president for his championing of the American way of life and the national character, "confident of its power under threat." He and the exhibition had made a potent connection between the state and its citizenry, proving that science and technology opened up a universal passway to progress and social concord. For a man already prepping to become his party's presidential nominee, it was a triumphant moment.[4]

The Kitchen Debate confirmed what had already become an all-consuming way of life. The *Journal of Retailing* (a trade magazine) reached for the injunctive. "Our enormously productive economy demands that we make consumption our way of life, that we convert the buying and using of goods into rituals, that seek our spiritual satisfactions, our ego satisfaction in consumption." *House Beautiful* plumbed the social significance of ranch house architecture: "Our houses are all on one level, like our class structure." *Life* magazine concurred, noting that "people are getting more and more on a level with each other." A Labor Department study, *How American Buying Habits Change,* issued the same year as the Moscow encounter, concluded that the automobile was "breaking down barriers of community and class." *Business Week* headlined news of the future: "Worker Loses His Class Identity." Like his vice president, Eisenhower sent a message to the Russians about just who could legitimately claim the mantle of labor's emancipator: "They [the Soviets] fail to realize that he [the American worker] is not the downtrodden, impoverished vassal of whom Karl Marx wrote. He is a self-sustaining, thriving individual living in dignity and freedom."

Before "Make love, not war" became the anthem of opposition to the bloody debacle in Vietnam, an analogous formula summed up the midcentury state of the global class struggle: "Make washing machines, not missiles" was the message conveyed by both debaters at their historic kitchen encounter, even if they didn't put things in exactly those words. What Nixon actually suggested, and the Soviet premier concurred, was: "Would it not be better to compete in the relative merits of washing machines than in the strength of rockets?" Khrushchev, blustery, witty in the fashion of a folk-wise peasant, supremely sure of himself, and proud of his nation's material accomplishments, might have passed for a corpulent American CEO. Lean, not yet bulldog jowly, quick at repartee, Nixon seemed just as confident as his Soviet interlocutor about his side's ultimate ideological superiority and might have passed for a gray-flannelled commissar. Two utopians—antagonists yet carriers of visions that seemed to converge on some class-free elysian fields of plentitude—certain, or so it seemed, of their eventual victories. Still, they were haunted by legacies of social discontent they could not shed.[5]

Who Will Bury Whom?

The Kitchen Debate is recorded as a landmark moment in a war that seemed destined either to go on forever or end in an apocalyptic flash. It might also be thought of, however, as a cease-fire. After all, both sides agreed on the fundamentals. The only issue in doubt was which nation would bury the other, as the Soviet premier would later foretell, under an avalanche of goods and services that would permanently anesthetize whatever social wounds still festered from the past. What the Chinese Communist rivals of their Russian big brother would characterize as "goulash Communism" enjoyed a kinship with the American boast that the evil days of capitalist scarcity and class inequality were already in the country's rearview mirror. Jeremiads from yesteryear about exploitation, alienation, and wage slavery from the Soviet camp, and about collectivist slavery, godless Communism, and state tyranny from the American side still echoed in the background, but more and more faintly. Both leaders had spied the future in the eyes of the other as if looking in a mirror. And the future worked, like a well-oiled machine. Such was the shared fantasy of inveterate enemies celebrating their respective golden ages.[6]

Sic transit gloria. For the Soviet Union that fate would come true with a vengeance unto extinction. Done in as much by its own internal social repressions and economic dysfunction as by the hostility of the West, goulash Communism provided neither goulash nor Communism. Yet at the time, it seemed Khrushchev had the wind at his back. Although the mainstream

media declared the American vice president the winner, at a
deeper level Nixon was playing defense. He was arguing, after
all, that the United States, a capitalist society through and
through, would be—indeed, already was—the first to make
good on the promise long ago articulated in *The Communist
Manifesto:* America was well on its way to erasing class from its
economic and political vocabulary, leveling its social terrain so
that it began to resemble the harmonious utopias once considered the wooly-headed notions of feckless radicals. The New
World, just as John Smith had prophesized, was becoming a
land where "every man may be master and owner of his owne
labour and land." Take that thought and plant it in a suburban
ranch house and you get the equivalent of the immaculate
conception: capitalism without classes.

Geopolitics, thermonuclear terror, subversion and
counter-subversion, all the grotesque paraphernalia of superpower bullying can't account for why the vice president of the
"Free World" wanted to upstage Karl Marx, to claim the arch-
enemy's inspiration as his own, to bury him, so to speak, in a
grave of his own making.

Recent history better explained Nixon's premature conversion to a class-free America. It was an odd one, to be sure.
Nixon had come of age as a fierce practitioner of anti-
Communism during the heyday of Senator Joseph McCarthy.
That's what got him elected to public office in California and
made him someone to be reckoned with in Republican Party
politics. But the very potency of that politics of fear was also a
measure of how much the politics of class still smoldered beneath the surface. The United States had only recently emerged
from the Great Depression, the New Deal, and the social turmoil
that had called into question the viability of capitalism. Nixon
operated in a political culture where memories were still fresh

of mass and general strikes, factory seizures, street demonstra-
tions of the unemployed, farmer rebellions and penny auctions,
violent confrontations between workers and private corporate
armies, farmer-labor party electoral victories—memories of a
time not so long ago when calls to "share the wealth" and ex-
communicate Wall Street were avidly listened to by millions.
Nixon's political debut coincided with the largest strike wave
in American history immediately following World War II.

By the time the vice president arrived in Moscow in 1959,
much of that upheaval had subsided (although that year also
witnessed the longest strike in American history when the steel
industry shut down for months). Still, the international rivalry
with the Soviet Union pressured the United States to make the
case that its uglier history of class warfare was over with. Instead,
in vying for the allegiance of people at home and abroad, the
nation's political elite could claim that it had solved the riddle
of history posed by Marx. Ever inventive, the country had discovered that if the history of all previously existing societies had
been one of class struggle, America had figured out a way around
that. Hence the underlying irony of the Kitchen Debate: Nixon's
victory, if that indeed was what it was, came by way of ceding
the high ground to the Communist ideal. That high ground, a
society without classes, could be found cropping up all over the
American heartland, forming its own New World: suburbia.[7]

The Class That Is No Class

Ranch houses with kitchens like the model in Moscow reconfigured landscapes. Where once there had been forests, mead-
ows, hillsides, farmland, ocean fronts, marshes, riverine villages,
and whistle-stop towns, now there were paved roads, central
shopping districts and malls, one-family homes on streets

without sidewalks, commuter lines running to and away from work—all of it laid out with a kind of geometric symmetry that resembled the uniform rectangular subdivision of the Great Plains during the era of the homesteader. Suburban settlements blanketed the country at an extraordinary rate in the decades following the end of the Second World War. They were the universally recognized site, headquarters even, of what the economist John Kenneth Galbraith called the "affluent society" in a best-selling book of that title. Galbraith's term was meant ironically as he was by no means enamored with this development. But for most people there was no ambiguity. Suburbia was the romance of everyman.

On the grasslands of well-manicured front lawns, Middle America erected a cordon sanitaire against the past. All the insignia of proletarian degradation were erased: no more dilapidated, ill-ventilated, overpopulated tenements; settlements of uniform design instead of city chaos; patios in place of back-alley squalor; refrigerators instead of iceboxes; coal soot banished by electric stoves; horizons of shrubbery, flower gardens, and sunlit expanse rather than cracked concrete and fire escapes, a shadowland of grime and rationed sunshine. Children's rooms, master bedrooms, living rooms, dining rooms, multiple bathrooms, backyards, fences, and of course the "miracle kitchen" formed the physical geography and architecture of a reborn landed yeomanry. Suburbia also constituted a kind of psychic rezoning that opened up room for private and familial preoccupations in spaces once reserved for more promiscuous social intermingling. Here the inner self could be explored, ministered to, remade, liberated. If the Soviets could boast of creating a "new man," so could suburbia.

Thomas Jefferson had once dreamed it possible to immunize the New World against the class antagonisms, the extravagance, poverty, and corruptions of the Old World, by buying Louisiana. History could be stopped dead in its tracks west of the Mississippi. That territory would become an "empire for liberty," so vast it would afford generations to come the chance to set themselves up as self-sustaining citizen-farmers, dependent on no one: neither overlords nor subjects. Suburban America was reimagined as a mid-twentieth-century facsimile of that prospect. It had about it a more or less equal quotient of the real and unreal as had Jefferson's idyll. The Kansas land rush and Levittown were self-evidently quite different anticipations of the future. What they shared was a deep commitment to protecting free individuals from whatever might jeopardize their self-reliance. Where they differed fundamentally, however, was in identifying the enemy and how to fend it off.

For generations of nineteenth-century Americans, the threat to their independence was wage slavery; land or other kinds of property ownership (workshops, stores, professional assets) could function as prophylactics against becoming proletarian. Both the danger and the way to defuse it were to be found in the realm of production. Cold War–era suburbanites, on the other hand, had long since become "wage slaves." True, some still held out the hope they might one day escape, reinvent themselves on the frontiers of entrepreneurship; white-collar workers especially weren't about to identify as working class. Most blue-collar people instead took their proletarian status for granted because, to begin with, that was just the way things were. Virtually no one any longer thought that condition was subject to overhaul on a scale that would reconfigure the social landscape. But more than that, they didn't think of themselves anymore as "wage slaves," even though they did indeed work for wages.

If in some theoretical sense they suffered a subordination in the realm of production, they found release in the realm of consumption. They had been granted the inalienable right to choose, the summa of freedom. Nixon had it right. In a thousand car dealerships, department stores, home appliance outlets, furniture emporiums, supermarket bazaars, TV and radio channels, movie theaters, and exotic locales where you could get away from it all, the right to choose could be exercised over and over again. Each time it was an affirmation of a new form of freedom, self-assertion, and, when it seemed called for, the power to try on an entirely new self.

Nor should the vice president's boast be taken lightly. The embodiment and exfoliation of human creative powers in kitchenware and jet planes, in life-saving pharmaceuticals and central heating and air-conditioning, in telecommunications and food enough to keep billions alive is, whatever else one might say about it and the way it was accomplished, stunning. The national output of goods and services doubled between 1946 and 1956 and doubled again by 1970. Between 1949 and 1973 median income and mean family income doubled. One out of every four homes standing in 1960 was built in the 1950s. In that year 62 percent of Americans owned homes, compared to 44 percent in 1940. The statistics measuring the increase in consumer durables—everything from cars to washing machines—indexed the same remarkable growth. The suburban population rose by 43 percent between 1947 and 1953. *Newsweek* anointed a new world peopled by "men of property."[8]

Still, Nixon had politics first and foremost in mind. If the material gratifications on sale were made widely accessible and alluring enough, they would temper the social resentments of the past and deliver a rough approximation of the country's egalitarian credo. And they would cultivate a sense of individual autonomy that would neuter quests for freedom aimed at dismantling the prevailing hierarchies of power and wealth.

Once the workplace had bred class resentments and yearnings for liberation. Now those passions had cooled. Or rather,
the gulf between haves and have-nots had narrowed; suburbia
promised to efface it completely. Desires for social emancipation
were privatized. The *New York Herald Tribune* put it plainly:
"The rich man smokes the same sort of cigarettes as the poor
man, shaves with the same sort of razor, uses the same sort of
telephone, vacuum cleaner, radio and TV set." In 1951 *Fortune*
published a special issue: "USA: The Permanent Revolution,"
in which it made so bold as to allude to Trotsky, the inventor
of that notion of "permanent revolution," and the classless
society it foretold.[9]

Conversely, and ironically, none of this would have happened without the exercise of the collective power of organized
proletarians in the economic and political arenas. The postwar
rise in the standard of living rested on the collective mobilization of the industrial working class during the Great Depression
into militant unions and the potent political influence they
exercised inside the Democratic Party and thereby the government. Wages rose not only in unionized companies but in many
companies that hoped to avoid unionization by matching those
increases. Vacations, cost-of-living adjustments, productivity
bonuses, pensions, medical care, and a host of other "fringe
benefits," without which the "affluent society" would have been
less a reality than an aspiration, were the fruits of class consciousness.

So too, the social welfare state, whose foundations were
laid during the New Deal years and got added onto afterward,
would never had advanced as far as it did without the sense of
social solidarity that for a season infused American political
culture. Hard to imagine now, but in the 1950s the top tax
rate on the rich stood at 91 percent. Minimum-wage and

maximum-hour laws, public works and public relief succored the down-and-out.

But while it has become commonplace to think of that welfare system as aimed at the poverty-stricken, unwed mothers, and others consigned to the social margins, actually its most generous allowances (not counting those tax breaks and subsidies incentivizing big business and financial institutions) were enjoyed by upwardly mobile working-class citizens. This was true of specific pieces of legislation like the GI Bill, which made housing and education widely affordable for veterans, housing finance laws more broadly, Social Security and, later on, Medicare for the elderly, publicly supported universities, and other innovations to eliminate the pervasive insecurities that had always before characterized life as a proletarian. Underlying that legislative infrastructure, moreover, was a commitment of fiscal and monetary policy to buoying up the purchasing power of consumers when the business cycle threatened to subvert it; Keynesianism originated as a kind of class consciousness of the political elite seeking to resecure the social foundations of modern capitalism.

As it aged, however, it became less that than a technique. The triumph—partial, to be sure—of a class-inflected politics persuaded many that a class-inflected politics had become a thing of the past, no longer called for in an "affluent society" that had transcended class. Necessary instead was a well-trained bureaucracy capable of managing the "new order," deploying an arsenal of psycho-social as well as economic therapeutics to treat whatever malfunctions might arise. Theorists of the postwar order—variously labeled post-industrial or post-capitalist—took it as axiomatic that the new liberal dispensation epitomized the rational, functioning as a finely reticulated mechanism for resolving social conflict. History, not merely the economy, seemed to have achieved some permanent plateau of social harmony and efficiency, at least inside the borders of the homeland. Class warfare had been exported abroad where it could be waged, at harrowing risk, to a successful conclusion in part precisely because it had disappeared at home.

Celebrants and more dispassionate observers noted the sea change. Onetime left-wing intellectual Daniel Bell announced the "end of ideology" in a book with that title published in 1960. While this soon turned out to be a grossly premature prediction, what Bell put his finger on was the passing away of the "proletarian metaphysic" and all that it had portended about the elimination of capitalist society. He argued, in fact, that all the grand humanistic ideologies born out of the Enlightenment were exhausted. Proletarian revolution was the last such historical romance. These dreams of transcendence had been replaced by a narrow-gauged system of technical adjustments to social dysfunction.

Bell's pronouncement was not exactly a lament, but it bore an air of lowered expectations. Similarly, Louis Hartz in *The Liberal Tradition in America* explained that precisely because the country never had to take on a real aristocracy, it had never developed the kind of class-driven, ideologically informed politics true of Europe. That America was an exception to that rule left Hartz mordant about the limits of the nation's political imagination, at a disadvantage when it came to dealing with its subsurface social tensions.

Others were more unequivocal in welcoming the new order. John Kenneth Galbraith criticized old-fashioned capitalism but looked more favorably on what he and others called post-industrial society. Mainstream social scientists and historians rediscovered the indigenous American genius for doing an end run around history. Whether thanks to providence, nature's bequest, the application of macroeconomic and social science, or a composite of all three, America was once again proving itself the exceptional nation its colonial and revolutionary forefathers had foreseen. In 1957 journalist and ex–left winger Max Lerner published *American Civilization,* which was meant as an encomium to the American zeitgeist and as an apologia for earlier heresies. The historian David Potter in *People of Plenty* argued that the abrasions of class conflict had been regularly submerged, cauterized, and healed in the bathwaters of material abundance.

Daniel Boorstin and Clinton Rossiter pointed to an innate American inventiveness, ingenuity, and individualism to account for the nation's frontier vigor and resourcefulness; the fixities of social rank could not take root in such hostile soil. Political and social scientists like Nathan Glazer, Seymour Martin Lipset, and Robert Dahl explained how class alignments dissolved into a plurality of interest groups and the demographic amorphousness of the suburban resettlement. Under these circumstances, transitory coalitions and the mechanics of compromise worked to disarm more dangerous kinds of class conflicts that could so easily get out of hand. Politics itself tended to become a branch of consumer culture, another place where glamour and charisma might work its magic on the "right to choose." Leonard Hall, the chairman of the Republican Party in 1952, spoke these words of wisdom: "You sell your candidate and your program the way business sells its products." He went on to hire the leading advertising agencies to develop messages tailored to each market segment. Economists and schools of business and industrial labor relations proved that the once overwrought arena where boss and hireling went head-to-head had become instead a meeting ground where labor and management partnered on behalf of the general corporate community.[10]

A whole new academic discipline was born to explore the distinctive national experience. American studies departments mushroomed in the postwar era. They shared a premise, if only an implicit one, with John Smith and the Puritan divines and Jefferson: that what was happening in the New World was indeed new in some profound sense. Why that was the case and what kind of society emerged from that experiment in starting over were just the sorts of questions students and professors of American studies sought to figure out. Whatever varied answers might surface, underlying the researches was a Cold War–inspired conviction that class no longer mattered in the homeland.

Specialized scholarship, however, was not required to come to this judgment. It was already in the atmosphere, the oxygen of everyday belief, the philosophy of everyday life. Professional philosophers, to be sure, offered their own elegantly formulated treatises, but so too did preachers and policy wonks, journalists and state managers. The modern corporation together with the welfare state worked to efface class. A loose consensus of intellectuals and pundits, including people like Galbraith and Clark Kerr (soon to become infamous as the target of the Free Speech Movement at the University of California at Berkeley where Kerr was president), was confident that the social order was infinitely malleable, no longer subject to the rigidities characteristic of capitalism in its formative phase when great dynastic owners treated their employees like serfs.

Neither capitalist nor socialist, this new social species fused free-market liberalism with social democracy; the future beckoned. As Marx had once prophesized, capitalism had evolved. Its modern corporate form "aims at the expropriation of the means of production from all individuals," although, he pointed out, "the conversion to the form of stock still remains ensnared in the trammels of capital." The philosopher George Lichtheim categorized this world as "post bourgeois," one where old class structures had dissolved along with private entrepreneurship, where the "idle rich" had become superfluous while the working class had been leveled up by the welfare state.

Intercourse between mass production and the mass market reproduced mass society, a disaggregated but uniform body of roughly equivalent middle-class individuals, so all-encompassing that other social classes were simply disappearing over the horizon of American life. Soon enough that would become true of the whole world (the "free" western half of it, anyway) as the United States tutored its new dependencies in Europe and Asia in the rudiments of democracy and economic growth, exporting its bureaucratic and managerial expertise along with its largesse, liquid capital, and triumphant armed forces.[11]

If there remained problems to be sorted out, they didn't involve social struggles for power but rather the power of positive thinking. Sociologist David Riesman depicted the new mass man as "other directed," engaged in a recurrent effort to reshape himself in the eyes of significant others, especially inside the anonymous warrens of the corporate bureaucracy, but also in his social life more generally. Middle-class mass man became a kind of infinitely fungible commodity, like a human form of money. This performing self was an ego in a chronic state of liquefaction, an identity at risk. This too was a form of powerlessness but one to be addressed in the realm of the psyche. Even when popular culture showed sympathy for working-class subjects, it did so insofar as they faced personal dilemmas, not ones traceable to their class origins. As one historian has pointed out, one need only contrast movies of the 1930s like *Scarface, Little Caesar, Public Enemy,* or *Grapes of Wrath* to postwar films like *They Live by Night, White Heat,* or *Death of a Salesman,* which psychologized what had once been treated as the wounds of social inequities. Alienation was made to fit inside the confines of family melodrama.[12]

Norman Vincent Peale spoke to millions about the power of positive thinking in an idiom nearly as old as the country itself. He was a Methodist minister raised in a strictly prohibitionist Ohio family. He was "plain people," or so he portrayed himself; "Everyday people of this land are my own kind." In 1957 he reached an audience of 30 million each week. Well over a hundred newspapers carried his column, "Confident Living." His radio show, *The Art of Living,* broadcast into 1 million homes. He could be seen on 140 TV stations. He made records, lectured widely, and *The Power of Positive Thinking,* published in 1952, had sold 2 million copies by 1955. Peale preached that Christianity was a practical guide to successful living. It offered self-mastery. That appealed to many who might be sensing a loss of self-control in the modern world, where anonymity loomed. Peale's message was a reaffirmation of that native belief in self-creation, revised to take account of the fact that the forested wilderness had been paved over, subdivided, and reassembled in the dolorous glass and steel monoliths of government and corporate bureaucracies. Yet even here the free individual could abide—armed with the right attitude and the right kitchen.[13]

Life on Lee Avenue

I grew up in a house with that kitchen around the time of the Moscow debate. Whether it was lemon yellow I can't recall. But it was full of those gadgets Khrushchev both admired and mocked. The kitchen was not in a ranch house, but it had been remodeled to show off just what Nixon boasted about. The house itself was actually an old colonial-style one in an affluent New York City suburb. The area was not exactly typical of the places to which the postwar exodus headed. It was older and richer, more akin to the fictional hang-out of James Gatz, otherwise known to us all as the Great Gatsby.

To a young boy this meant very little, if anything. Yet something about our social circumstances did register. I became dimly aware that we didn't quite fit. While it would be years before I heard of people like David Riesman, Nathan Glazer, or Max Lerner, their take on class-free suburbia didn't quite mesh with my own experience.

We were not rich, not rich enough, anyway, to mimic everything about the lifestyle of our friends and neighbors. My father had acquired enough cash to make the move from Brooklyn. But that didn't last long. Nonetheless, his commitment and my mother's to hanging on meant that eventually we moved into more modest housing, much more like what was on display in Moscow. I was aware, of course, that this was happening. My friends all went away to summer camp. I stayed home and played in the Police Boys Athletic League. When I went to play at friends' houses, it was fairly common that a live-in maid/domestic worker loosely monitored what we were up to. Their parents belonged to private swim and tennis clubs. I played at the public courts and swam at the public pool. As we grew a bit older and clothes became important, something that proved if you were "cool" or not, I was understocked with what was in fashion. At school I was in nonstop trouble with the authorities, banned from the cafeteria and forced to eat lunch in the vice principal's office along with "the Murphy boys," working-class toughs, brothers who scared me to death. (Luckily the vice principal scared even the Murphy boys, so lunch was nonviolent.)

None of this bothered me (well, maybe my uncouth cloth-ing rankled). I was, after all, living the childhood version of the suburban good life. I had a dog, a big backyard, a bedroom of my own, an attic hideaway on the third floor, a bike on which I was free to roam the leafy, quiet streets and parklands of our "Gatsbyville." I was a Cub Scout and a Little Leaguer. Later I would join the "Pepsi generation." My father commuted into the city to work on Madison Avenue, and I was there to meet him at the end of each day at the station as he returned home on the 5:58. My mother was a pianist; she gave private lessons at home and later, when our finances declined, taught music in the public schools. She was a wage earner, to be sure, but also a homemaker in all the ways that conformed to the profile of suburban middle-class domesticity.

Yet my parents were different (and I later learned so were some of the parents of my friends) in a way that hinted both at the unreality of the suburban myth and why it was so alluring. And I don't mean just that they were less well-off than their neighbors, although they were. The realization of their differ-ence first came to me as if from another world. Directly across the street from my spacious backyard—hardly the right word for an area spacious enough for a rock garden, flower gardens, a vegetable patch, a mulch pit, a grape arbor, peach and pear trees, and various oak, chestnut, and maple trees—was a road called Lee Avenue. Never was a street more improbably named. Lee Avenue was not an avenue or even a plain road; it was a dirt lane that turned to dust or mud depending on the weather. It wasn't even flat, but rutted and rock-strewn, dotted with hardy weeds that eked out a life from sandy soil.

On the corner lived Billy O'Brien. A bit older than I, he took me on scarifying adventures to the "clay mines" (a wood-ed area fetchingly dark and dense, watered by a stream that turned the ground into a moist clay we "mined" for treasures while fearing it might suck us in and under). Billy's house was half the size of mine, old and ramshackle, needed painting and a new roof. It didn't belong in Gatsbyville. Nor did Billy. He didn't go to my school, but instead attended a Catholic parochial school in another town. There he went in terror of the nuns, with their inflexible discipline enforced by knuckle-bruising rulers. To this day, I still shudder when I remember Billy's tales of spectral, black-hooded "sisters" who seemed not only ominous but decidedly unsisterly.

Stranger people even than Billy lived down the road from him on Lee Avenue. They were black. The structures they lived in made Billy's house seem palatial. Shacks, really, some with rickety front porches, doors half off their hinges, paint peeling like bark on a tree, perched precariously on a short rise above the "avenue" so they wouldn't get washed away when rainwater coursed down the road. Sometimes garbage floated by. Inside, the homes were dingy and ill lit. I became familiar with these dreary interiors later on when I was old enough to be a newspaper delivery boy and came by weekly to collect. But I knew what the insides were like much earlier than that because I made friends with a boy who lived there. I can't remember his name. We were buddies, but I also sensed we were different from each other. And I don't mean because he was black, but rather because he was so damn poor.

I felt sorry for him, and even now I get queasy recalling this. I asked my parents if I could invite him home to eat with us because I somehow intuited he wasn't eating right or enough. They readily agreed. Looking back, I wonder if the invitation was really their idea. They were Depression-era people who had become left-wing political activists. Their days of activism were fading, but their social conscience about class and racial inequity lived on. Moreover, it turned out that others of that same persuasion had migrated like we had from the city to this particular suburban outpost. Gatsbyville was undergoing a makeover, becoming less Jazz Age glamorous and more a haven for an upwardly mobile middle class whose more modest social origins and moral seriousness would make the town well known for its enlightened attitudes.

To suburbia they had fled, carrying with them, along with their bags and baggage, beliefs from another time and place. They were drawn, like millions of others, by the allure of a class-free affluent society, yet marked by still-fresh memories of the old world they were fleeing. Lee Avenue was an anachronism and, for my parents, an embarrassment, too close by to ignore. So, by the time I was in the fourth grade I had exported my own version of the Kitchen Debate to my classroom, where I argued with my teacher—a secular version of Billy O'Brien's sisters named Mrs. Pingree, a party-line Cold War Republican with silver-gray hair and a face as stern as Stalin's whose withering glance was as frightening as any nun armed with a ruler—that the Russians weren't so bad as she was painting them. I had learned at home what she apparently wasn't aware of: that in no time at all, a people once so poor had acquired washing machines, refrigerators, and every other convenience Mrs. Pingree said they went without. Then back home I went, now armed with the other side of the argument, and had it out with Mom and Dad. That was the setting in which one day there we were: me, my little outlier friend, and my parents, sitting around a table in a dining room nearly as big as his house.

Lee Avenue was one of several byways sprinkled here and there throughout Gatsbyville where the servant class of that bygone era were consigned. A whole micro neighborhood of this kind, tucked away on the outskirts of town (but close enough to be available when called upon) bore the picturesque name of Steamboat Road. Precincts like that were customary enough in the upper-class world Gatsby aspired to belong to. Not so in the "new world" of Nixonland, where classes and castes of all kinds supposedly went to die, especially so in the peculiarly configured left-wing version of my parents' own suburban idyll.

The Snake in the Crabgrass

Lee Avenue and Steamboat Road might be stark anomalies from another age. Yet for just that reason, they shed a lurid light on what otherwise remained a dark secret about the postwar suburban romance. Not only were most of these settlements all white, they were also the locus of intricate social hierarchies, social science word pictures notwithstanding. Some were rooted in disparities in wealth and income that distinguished one suburb from another: Levittown from Gatsbyville. Some were stratified internally by the same disparities, by the varying lifestyles they could finance, and by an inherent culture of invidious distinctions that had long been part of the American makeup at least since De Tocqueville first observed them. Egalitarian anonymity bred its opposite, a yearning for recognition fueling a chronic racing after social esteem to buoy up a fragile self-respect: "Where everybody is somebody, nobody is anybody." C. Wright Mills described "status panic" as the distinctive affliction of this world. Like the numerous mock architectural styles that were reinvented on these suburban flatlands—neo-colonial, neo-Georgian, neo-Tudor, neo-cowboy, neo-bungalow—suburbia itself was in some measure a façade. It concealed social fissures while embellishing the American Dream. Arguably that was its function.[14]

Romances of this historic magnitude are inherently over-blown. From the outset the postwar suburban phenomenon was riddled with class divisions, status anxieties, and racial exclusion. So too was it a bastion of patriarchy. For example, veterans were overwhelming male. The GI Bill opened up higher education and housing to men; moreover, it helped far more middle-class than working-class men. Demographics displayed far less social mobility than advertised. Credit agencies, banks, and mortgage brokers favored middle-class white people. A study of blue-collar workers in suburban Michigan conducted in the 1950s found them less excited by their prospects than Nixon. Anomic, uncertain about their purpose in life, not so driven by the quest for upward mobility that was supposed to be an American birthright, they weren't living the dream. In Michigan, they were more prone to vent their frustrations in wildcat strikes. The belief, widespread, that suburbia anesthetized union or class consciousness was at best a half truth.

Golden ages age. As the suburban one proceeded, it became ever more, not less, class and racially segmented. Hierarchical identities, now defined by the market and consumption patterns, became pervasive. The suburban ideal rested on a culture that had at first presumed a kind of classless uniformity. William Levitt himself was a liberal as well as builder and quite conscious about the class issues at stake in his revolutionary construction. His dream of life beyond class notwithstanding, the opposite increasingly marked real life on the crabgrass frontier.

Distinctions in housing styles and size, both conspicuous and subtle (prefabricated starter or mansard-roofed mansion), downtown architectural flourishes (strip mall or gothic façades), select country clubs or public parks, postage-sized mowed lawns or acres of exotic landscaping, tonier residential estates elbow to elbow with more down-market subdivisions within a single suburb, as well as racial and ethnic composition mapped the social terrain. Marketing departments became more attuned to and indeed helped create these newer, status-inflected identities. Identity politics, which would later erupt in a far different form, owes some of its psychological makeup to this formative experiment in consumer living.[15]

Dissonant as well was the role of the government. The native version of utopia, deeply embedded in the American grain, is an exaltation of the self-reliant individual. John Smith was fully prepared to enforce martial law over a colony verging on mayhem. But he did so in the hope that one day the land would support a society of free-standing citizens roughly equal in condition, requiring only a common moral character to cohere. Suburbia might be metamorphosed to resemble that kind of setting in the imagination of its promoters and ideologues.

In reality, however, the suburban mass migration was not born de novo. Its existence depended on an elaborate array of government facilitators. The infrastructure of roads and highways, public utilities and commuter rail lines, schools and hospitals, was constructed by local, state, and federal governments. Building this infrastructure employed capital and labor and was part of the reason the era was called "affluent." Neither Levittown, USA, nor the posh environs of Orange County would have happened without what American utopians might decry as the heavy hand of the leviathan state. Indeed, those avatars of the free market in Southern California were utterly dependent on the military-industrial complex located close by for their material wherewithal.

In Moscow, Nixon suggested that the ranch house, its model kitchen, and the techno-wonders, material pleasures, and social security that went with them were universally available. Instead a whole phalanx of government housing programs, private-sector financing, local zoning protocols, and state and federal tax subsidies and shelters guaranteed that those options were really only practicable for families of more than modest means and of the right complexion. The suburban dream, like the American Dream more generally, turned out to be part real, part hallucination: class (and race) mattered, no matter the efforts to make it go away.

The Masses and the Classes

Flaws of this magnitude did more than call into question suburbia's egalitarian prospect. They also illuminated the inner dynamics of a capitalist political economy and culture that continued to rest on distinctions of caste and class. Eventually these "imperfections" would become apparent, widen the space separating more and less well-off segments of the wage-earning population, create lifestyle envies picked apart by Madison Avenue, and now and then erupt in violent outbursts against those rash enough to try to breach the invisible walls of racial exclusion. The eminent American historian David Brion Davis observed, "We have entered another era when race has pre-empted class," but he went on to prophesy that down the road Americans will have "to confront the underlying reality of class division in America and the destructive myth of a classless society."

Suburbia's alleged virtues, however, not its failures and social underside, first commanded the attention of its earliest critics. It was precisely the apparent uniformity, the glacial surface calm of the new classless America that inflamed its most passionate early critics. On the one hand, the ranch house and its amenities were a haven of intimacy where the private life could be cultivated, secured against the dangers of the concrete jungle. But Galbraith's best seller was partly a jeremiad about the "affluent society," how it crowded out public goods and corroded social consciousness.

Abundance was a blessing. But *The Hidden Persuaders,* another blockbuster book, by Vance Packard, vividly described the black arts of the advertising industry and its remarkable ability to manipulate desire. His examination of how motivational research and other subliminal psychological tactics choreograph expectations and cravings was especially chilling as Packard demonstrated their deployment in the political arena as well. So too, men in gray flannel suits, the uniform of the new "salaritariat," seemed securely ensconced inside a white-collar world no longer vulnerable to the brutalities of their proletarian forefathers. But William Whyte in *The Organization Man* depicted them as wracked by anxiety, combatants in the cold war of preferment, climbing up and sliding down a slippery slope of corporate one-upmanship.

Consumer culture enticed everybody; it dazzled and delighted, it gratified and seemed inexhaustible. Yet, according to David Riesman, it reproduced something he called "the lonely crowd." Here was a reconfiguration of the social psyche so hollowed out and vulnerable that it needed to be confirmed in its existence by outside authority. But that authority had become so amorphous, ambiguous, and diffused it left its subjects in a chronic state of anxiety. While this "new man" was by necessity open to the world, no longer a slave to tradition, made self-conscious about his "right to choose," he was infinitely pliable, paying obeisance to taste or opinion makers in the realm of material goods as well as in moral and intellectual matters.[16]

Nixon's utopia pledged to level away the old pecking orders, snobberies, and deferential barriers that once distanced the hoi poloi from their more sophisticated betters, leaving the former feeling somehow inadequate, shut out. Mass culture ended that alienation. Among its many wonders the industrial revolution had made universal literacy possible. Everybody, more or less, had access to common forms of entertainment, knowledge, art, and literature. Parochial folk cultures were left by the wayside.

Yet people like Dwight McDonald lamented what they saw as the stupefying spread of mass culture and "mid-culture." Regarding the former, McDonald credited the "Lords of Kitsch" for reproducing "the deadening and warping effects of long exposure to movies, pulp magazines, and radio." Mid-culture was worse. A form of "sophisticated kitsch," it catered to the aspirational high-mindedness of a middlebrow audience, self-satisfied and self-deluded, integrated into mass society by a debased form of an older high culture. It invited a flight from social stratification into an encompassing zone of some education and some conversance with arts and letters, a region of perpetual aspiration satisfied by shrink-wrapped consumer intangibles. *Life* magazine was McDonald's exhibit A; he noted that it appeared "on the mahogany library tables of the rich, the glass cocktail tables of the middle class, and the oil-cloth kitchen tables of the poor." It offered up a homogenized content to its "homogenized circulation" so that the same issue might "present a serious exposition of atomic energy followed by a disquisition on Rita Hayworth's love life; photos of starving children picking garbage in Calcutta and of sleek models wearing adhesive brassieres." Yet in the same breath the critic acknowledged the enormous proliferation of genuine artistic venues in the years following the war—theaters, musical groups,

literary magazines, bookstores, records, art museums, fellow-
ships, reading salons, and art films. The deeper problem was
that "our Renaissance, unlike the original one, has been passive,
a matter of consuming rather than creating." McDonald labored
to counterbalance his cultural snobbery with the remains of his
earlier leftism—with mixed results.

Class consciousness lived a shadow life, a matter of cultural taste, varying standards of dress, food, and furniture,
audible in accents, visible now and then on the big screen, but
without purchase in the realm of power and privilege. Mass
culture and mid-culture were, for McDonald, more than a
dumbing down. Under the guise of democratizing the culture,
they insidiously undermined the capacity to criticize it. Without
that resource, democracy was a dead letter and so was any dream
of proletarian emancipation. Mass culture became an instrument of domination. Social scientists objectified this atomized
mass of solitary individuals as if they were congeries of condi-
tioned reflexes to be manipulated.[17]

Acquiescence took the place of resistance and revolt. Hannah Arendt also wrote darkly about "mass society," one me-
ticulously regulated and calibrated like some organic machine
that reproduced routinized behavior without anyone exercising
conscious control. There an atomized individual—"mass
man"—achieved a frightening form of freedom, one lacking
moral responsibility, at the mercy of impersonal forces, pacified
and passive. Something vital had been lost in the process. "The
very pathos of the labor movement in its early stages . . .
stemmed from its fight against society as a whole." It had spo-
ken for all humanity, its "force of attraction was never restricted to the ranks of the working class."

When class society became mass society, the horizon of
the possible shrank. Phillip Murray, once the head of the mili-

tant steelworkers' union, testified to the shrinkage: "We have no classes in this country; that is why the Marxist theory of class struggle has gained so few adherents. . . . In the final analysis the interests of the farmers, factory hands, business and professional people and white collar toilers prove to be the same." President Eisenhower made that point more bluntly when addressing the convention at which the country's two labor federations merged to form the AFL-CIO. He told the delegates, many of whom had fought the fiercest battles against their heavily armed corporate employers during the Depression, "The Class Struggle Doctrine of Marx was the invention of a lonely refugee scribbling in a dark recess of the British Museum. He abhorred and detested the middle class. He did not foresee that in America, labor respected and prosperous, would constitute—with the farmer and the businessman—the hated middle class."[18]

Herbert Marcuse's *One Dimensional Man* somberly observed the decline of revolutionary potential in the West generally as a sedated population became the captive of "false needs" nurtured in the emporiums of consumer society. The very aptitude for critical opposition had withered, especially on the part of a working class that no longer recognized itself as a working class. Once, its honor and mission derived from its exclusion and misery in a society that promised its elevation but degraded it instead; now, that had mutated into an endless pursuit of happiness that left behind the faint taste of endless unhappiness. "The political needs of society become individual needs and aspirations" in a world that seemed the perfect expression of "Reason" yet was "irrational as a whole." How mad a predicament, in which "the people recognized themselves in their commodities; they find their soul in their automobile, hi-fi set, split-level home, kitchen equipment."

The philosopher concluded that "the containment of social change was perhaps the most singular achievement of advanced industrial society." Class existed but had become invisible. "If the worker and his boss enjoy the same television program and visit the same resort places, if the typist is as attractively made up as the daughter of her employer, if the Negro owns a Cadillac, if they all read the same newspaper, then this assimilation indicates not the disappearance of classes, but the extent to which the needs and satisfactions that serve the preservation of the Establishment are shared by the underlying population." In that new world "the administered life became the good life." Even in the industrial workplace, where the modern class struggle was born, management no longer dominated but administered; bosses vanished, bureaucrats took their place, "the technological veil conceals the reproduction of inequality and enslavement," but the slaves of modern industry were "sublimated slaves," mere instruments of a classless rationality.

One-Dimensional Man was a tragic creature and an ironic one. In the mass, he formed "the people." But "the people," previously the fomenters of social upheaval, had "moved up" to become the vessels of social cohesion. Marcuse would inspire a young generation of "new leftists." But his book sounded a note of deep pessimism. It closed with these drear words from the Marxist social critic Walter Benjamin: "It is only for the sake of those without hope that hope is given to us."

More upbeat and just as much an intellectual hero as Marcuse, sociologist C. Wright Mills also eulogized the labor metaphysic. That made sense to an embryonic New Left in search of new "agents of social change." They shared the view that categories like capitalism and socialism were outmoded, at best merely different ways of describing a technocratic industrial order run by a state bureaucracy. Mills and his younger co-activists looked abroad to anti-imperial revolutions like the one in Cuba as a source of inspiration or back at home to America's internal colonial subjects inhabiting its urban ghettos and the rural outback of the dispossessed.

Even Marcuse saw some light ahead emanating from a world of outcasts and outsiders, "the exploited and persecuted of other races and colors, the unemployed and unemployable. They exist outside the democratic process . . . their opposition is revolutionary even if their consciousness is not. . . . It hits the system from without and is therefore not deflected by the system; it is an elementary force which violates the rules of the game." As for the mainstream, that was dead water. The gloomy if not quite dystopian pessimism of people like Bell, Marcuse, Mills, and others seemed a somber commentary on the deeper significance of Nixon's utopia.

But like Nixon's, their view too would prove ephemeral. The notion of "mass society" was a compelling intellectual conceit more than it was a full-bodied portrait of social reality. In its own way, it was the obverse of the techno-liberalism it excoriated. It conceded that underlying social fissures had been effaced and it excoriated modern liberalism for that. The accusation was a trenchant one. As an instinctive expression of unease with the way things were, it was seductive; it seduced me.[19]

Professor Billshot and the Rules of the Game

"Administered" and "contained," subterranean social discontent nonetheless found circuitous outlets to the surface among coming-of-age middle-class people like me. Those eruptions could be curious indeed.

On February 11, 1965, the *Barnard Bulletin* (the student newspaper of Barnard College) ran a story with the headline "Unknown Teacher Changes 'Shapes.'" Something very odd had happened. Students arriving for the first class of a course called The Shapes of the American Experience had "found their instructor stalking to and fro at the front of the room." He identified himself as Professor Graham A. Billshot. However, the course, otherwise catalogued as English 52, was supposed to be taught by Professor John Kazvenhaven, a well-regarded scholar of American studies. As Professor K. later observed to the *Bulletin*, "Shapes of the American Experience has been taking on a new shape."[20]

Indeed! The whole class had gone missing. Professor K. spent a week hunting for it. By the time the newspaper reported the vanishing, Professor Billshot had taught three classes and then himself vanished, never to be heard from again. The registrar had never heard of him, nor had the English department.

The case of the shifting shapes of the American experience turned out to be a college prank. It was funny, but also conceived in anger and with more than a touch of cruelty. Plotted for months by a half dozen disaffected students (some attending Columbia or Barnard, some dropouts), the plan to kidnap a class and teach it was audacious at a time when audacious was beginning to supplant acquiescent.

In its own peculiar way, the scheme was designed to deliver a poke in the eye to Arendt's Mass Society, to Marcuse's repressive sublimation, to McDonald's midcult, to the whole opaque fabric of the suburban consensus, to the closing up of the political and intellectual horizon, to the infantilizing and psychologizing of social malfunction. Something was seething beneath the deadening uniformity. Grandiose rhetoric, one might say. It is grandiose. The conspirators would most likely not have articulated their motives with such high-falutin' language. We were having too good a time, after all, not authoring a manifesto. Still, there is no question in my mind that for me and my co-conspirators, we were also after bigger fish, if in a small pond.

Marcuse's book had been published the year before. I hadn't read it (and never became a big fan of it). I don't remember if my comrades had. In any event, the kidnapping might be thought of as an attempt to implement what Marcuse's grim treatise considered close to undoable. In his typically rather ponderous prose, he put it this way: "Thus the question once again must be faced: how can the administered individuals— who have made their own mutilation into their own liberties and satisfactions, and thus reproduce it on an enlarged scale— liberate themselves from themselves as well as from their masters? How is it even thinkable that the vicious cycle can be broken?" We decided that Professor K. had provided us that chance.[21]

Sad to say, I was not Professor Billshot. I was too young looking, beardless, small in stature. We picked instead the one of us with a beard, a deep voice with an English accent he picked up from his British mother, dressed him in a de rigueur tweed jacket and tie, and equipped him with a pipe. We also christened him with that wonderful name. (To this day, I marvel at the fact that no one, no student, not the *Barnard Bulletin,* the registrar, or the English department thought his name strange or amusing or had one of those "Oh!" epiphanies.)

Everything about the kidnapping, including Professor Billshot's name, was carefully thought out. We considered the whole academic enterprise a Panglossian form of bullshit, of a piece with a society that seemed deaf, dumb, and blind to its own hypocrisies and social inequities. We had scoured the Columbia and Barnard course catalogues for days before choosing what we decided was the apt expression of that kind of academic pulp. "The Shapes of the American Experience" seemed just vaporous enough to fill that bill. What in the world did it mean? We intended to tell.

It takes a village not only to steal a class but to keep it hidden, not just from the registrar but from the student body. We all had our parts to play. One problem was how to keep Professor K. from showing up before we had a chance to spirit away the students. It turned out he was away at a conference. We didn't know that at the time, so we were prepared. One of us was missioned to show up at his office before class to delay Professor K. by pleading with him for a better grade for an earlier class. This person was a woman and she was supposed to cry because we needed to eat up time and because we were sexist. Another one of us was supposed to call him on his office phone, pretending to be a professor from another university who was calling to invite him to join a presidential commission studying "the shapes of the American experience." Meanwhile, another plotter was scouring the campus for an empty room to which we might transport the class.

Harder than these logistics, however, were the psycho-logistics. Democratic and egalitarian boilerplate notwithstanding, we knew in our bones that all the great institutions that made up the Establishment, whether in the political realm, at the workplace, in the media, or in academia, rested on an unspoken deference. This was the central deception concealed beneath the flawless exterior of the liberal consensus; that's the way we saw it, anyway. The bureaucracies that kept all these realms afloat enjoyed a kind of sacred authority. I don't know if I was familiar with it at the time, but Marx had long ago offered a relevant critique: "The bureaucratic spirit is a Jesuitical, theological spirit through and through. The bureaucrats are the Jesuits and theologians of the state." He spoke to where we lived: "Its hierarchy is a hierarchy of knowledge. The top entrusts the understanding of detail to the lower levels whilst the lower levels credit the top with understanding the general, and so all are mutually deceived."

So Professor Billshot needed something more than a beard, a tweed jacket, an English accent, and a pipe. He needed, and only he could supply it, a je ne sais quoi presence, and that he had to ad lib. What the *Barnard Bulletin* failed to report was that when the first student entered the classroom and saw somebody "stalking to and fro at the front of the room," there was no reason she should have assumed this stalking character was the professor, although no doubt the stalking helped. But there was also a brief conversation. It was a drizzly, gray day in January and this first student observed as much, out loud. Professor Billshot was silent at first, pondering her words, and then in a brilliant flash of Delphic absurdity replied, "Yes, but the pigeons will always be with us."

That sealed the deal. Only a great mind could speak like that. Act 1 of the plot was mission accomplished as the rest of the students filed in and did as the first one had done, taking their seats and looking expectantly Professor Billshot's way. Deference duly established, the structure of authority in place, things would go swimmingly from here on. The member of our team assigned to find an available classroom had succeeded and Professor Billshot marched the class across the Barnard campus to room 211 Milbank Hall, which before this had been used only by geology students. There he began to teach.

But by this point the cruelty at work in this prank must be already apparent. Our fellow students, just as much as

Professor K, the institution he worked for, and the larger network of power in which it nested, were the enemy and deserving of our contempt. We harbored not a scintilla of sympathy for their position, for their powerlessness, for the plain fact that had we been in their position we probably would have behaved as they did, docile in the face of presumed legitimate authority. They might be, in Herbert Marcuse's lingo, repressively sublimated, but that earned them no mercy from our anger.

On the contrary. Perhaps the greatest pleasure we derived from our coup was the collective writing of Professor Billshot's lectures during the days and nights leading up to the next class. These might have been written by Professor Irwin Corey, a hilarious comic of that time, known as "the world's foremost authority," whose specialty was a kind of professorial buffoonery, a profundity consisting of a torrential downpour of rain forest–dense nonsense.

Professor Billshot began by striding to the blackboard, where he drew a square, a triangle, a circle, and cube. Pausing for a pregnant moment, he turned to his students to tell them that those were "the shapes of the American experience." Our team, which had joined the class as fellow learners, watched as everyone copied those shapes into their notebooks. For us it was a moment of silent triumph and, like many a triumph, not an entirely kind one.

Three lectures followed. They made Professor Billshot's opening graphics seem a model of rational coherence by comparison. They consisted of endless run-on sentences and sentence fragments, made-up words, allusions to famous people who had never existed, and titillating descriptions of "bundling" in colonial America. So, for example, Professor Billshot might wander off into a description of the founding of the country in which settlers faced daunting challenges including the development of a mahascodene at the heart of their flabbadario. A fornescrone interrupted a hunting party in Jamestown, leaving all those who witnessed it with an indelible memory of its awful shape. And so on. There is no honey-coating the meanness of this prank.

All good and bad things come to an end. The registrar went hunting for Professor K's missing class and we were found out, but forewarned by a sympathizer in the English department in time to make our getaway.

So concluded what might be considered the high point or low point or both of my academic career, such as it's been. Comic and nasty, to be sure. But what in the world has it got to do with class? On the surface, nothing at all. But that was, after all, the point of the suburban romance, the erasure of class from the national vocabulary, its submergence in the mass society and mass culture that Nixon invoked in his own way at the kitchen in Moscow.

It is the premise of this book, however, that class will out, that it always has in configuring "the shapes of the American experience." What a group of late (arrested?) adolescents living on Manhattan's Upper West Side dimly sensed was being felt by groups just like them all over the country. We were the unanticipated and unwelcome offspring of a society in denial. Affluent and complacent, yet somehow ill at ease, sensing trouble in paradise. And far larger groups utterly un–middle class, living outside the perimeters or even within the borders of Nixon's arcadia, were becoming or long had been disabused of the consoling myth that America had turned into a classless utopia. Instead, social and racial divisions, moral hypocrisy, imperial ambition, faux democracy, and bureaucratic arrogance, like an acid bath, were corroding the innards of a society hiding from itself. The utopia embodied in my kitchen and Nixon's was already imploding.

6

Free at Last?

"I Have a Dream" and Involuntary Servitude

March 15, 1964:

> I apply as simply another Northern white college
> student, intent on assuaging his paranoid, stricken
> conscience by doing his good deed for the summer.
> I realize how justified you are in assuming that. . . .
> All I can say is that I want to work in Mississippi
> very badly. There's a limit to how long you can par-
> ticipate in a vast orgy of reconciliation. I'm aware
> of the tremendous amount of work to be done in
> education. I realize the crucial importance of uti-
> lizing the political devices particularly on a local
> level. And I'm especially concerned with striking at
> the economic roots of the most abhorrent human
> perversion, racism, by organizing and uniting black
> and white workers. At the same time, I understand
> the risk you take in allowing me to take an *active*
> part in the movement. . . . I know it's essentially

your fight, but I would like to help as fully as I can.
. . . One last thing—I don't feel especially qualified
to teach and I would rather be involved in voter
registration. Thank you.

I was eighteen when I wrote this. Along with thousands
of other middle-class college students from the North, I was
applying to participate in what would soon become known as
Mississippi Freedom Summer. I don't know how much my own
brief essay accompanying my application resembled others. I
imagine it did in its essentials: the earnestness, the barely concealed white guilt and self-effacement, the audible embarrassment about being middle class, and the sense of impending
confrontation that would lay to rest that "vast orgy of reconciliation." Uniting black and white was, as well, a hymnal shared
by the whole congregation of one thousand that ended up serving in Mississippi that summer.

However, going after the "economic roots" of racism and
targeting "workers" as the particular people to unite and organize showed up less frequently, I suspect, in these essay applica-
tions. Loaded phrases like those signaled my own left-wing
upbringing. That echo of the past was hardly unique to me.
Other "volunteers" hailed from similar backgrounds. Nonetheless, it was not the universal civil religion that all of us subscribed
to. Achieving equality before the law was our common objective;
after all, we were traveling to Mississippi to register people to
vote. "Economic roots" would for the most part remain buried.

Far more dissonant to modern ears might be the phrase
"orgy of reconciliation." Beside the fact that I can't help wincing
when I read it now—its adolescent straining for effect is cringe
producing; then again, I *was* an adolescent—it also hits on
something that might seem mystifying now. What "orgy of

reconciliation"? Why the eager anticipation of ending it? Why did I see it as a way of winning over whoever it was judging the merits of my application?

Less than a year earlier I had marched with hundreds of thousands of others on the Mall in Washington, DC. Was the March on Washington a moment of combat, a moment of reconciliation, perhaps both? When Martin Luther King Jr. revealed his dream from the steps of the Lincoln Memorial, was it a call to arms, a reverie of brotherhood, perhaps both? For me and, I would guess, for most or even all my fellow "volunteers," the answer was not in doubt. We were embarked on a second civil war. Enough with reconciliation!

A loosely adhered to philosophy of nonviolence might suggest otherwise, might offer up the prospect of penetrating hostile hearts and minds. But we were headed to Mississippi, where it was prudent to heavily discount such illusions. When we gathered first early in June for a week's training at the Western College for Women in southern Ohio (surely the oddest college orientation session on record) Bob Moses, a remarkable Student Non-Violent Coordinating Committee (SNCC) leader from Mississippi (via New York, where he'd been a math teacher at the Bronx High School of Science), delivered a grim forewarning: "When you're not in Mississippi, it's not real, and when you're there, the rest of the world isn't real." I remember well, although at the time barely understood, the late-night dialogues between Moses and Mario Savio (later to become the leader of the Free Speech Movement at Berkeley) that drew on Camus and what was then a campus fascination with existentialism. Back and forth, they pondered the choice each of us faced as we set our minds on Mississippi: "If for any reason you're hesitant about what you're getting into, it's better you leave." Moses was practically begging us not to go (three civil rights workers had just disappeared in Philadelphia, Mississippi), a plea not likely to register with an eighteen-year-old who anyway thought he would live forever.[1]

When they were happening, the March on Washington, King's speech, and Mississippi Freedom Summer were all understood as sites of battle in a long-fought war that appeared to be climaxing. For all the chords of mystic memory about the nation's consecration to equality sounded in King's sermon, the dream remained unredeemed, the speech an anthem of the second civil war. Listeners could only expect more conflict ahead, the marshalling of armies on both sides, despoilers of the dream gathering above and below the Mason-Dixon Line, on the alluvial plains of the Delta, in the hollows and mountains of Appalachia, along the corridors of power in Washington and the state capitols of the old Confederacy. Just a month after King's oration, four black children were slaughtered in a Birmingham church. Reconciliation someday, perhaps, but not yet.

Indeed, these moments even carried with them faint echoes of past confrontations. If I felt it wise to allude to the "economic roots" of racism, the conveners of the March on Washington were likewise motivated. The march was for "Jobs and Freedom." That must seem an odd locution nowadays. What did one have to do with the other? For that matter, were they linked at all, or rather merely two good causes worth fighting for? Could you have a job and not be free? Could you be free and not have a job? Why mix them together? Was there a time not so long before all this when it had been more or less axiomatic that the race question and the labor question signaled interrelated pathologies afflicting the same social organism?

Today these legendary moments no longer give off the acrid aroma, the smoke and heat of battle. They have become legendary, part of American mythic memory, mainly as the stepping-stones to reconciliation. Perhaps not an orgy of reconciliation, but still the soothing bathwater saturating what had once been a painful bad conscience. Those events and those words redeemed the dream in law, at the polling place, at work, in neighborhoods, all across the public landscape of everyday life from barrooms to bathrooms, at eating places and water fountains, and most of all deep in the interior where personal humiliation and indignity once festered.

Numerous poisonous violations of this idyll disfigure our common life even now; racial and homophobic outbursts are commonplace. But these can't obscure what was a historic transformation. "I Have a Dream" is a sacrosanct, essential part of the American credo. In some sense, it outdoes virtually every other literary reliquary lodged in the national dictionary, perhaps with the sole exception of the Declaration of Independence. The writer Garry Wills has called it "the greatest speech given since Abraham Lincoln's time." The March on Washington long ago shed whatever combative reputation it once bore. No public assemblage, conceived originally as an act of defiance, retains anything remotely like the exalted esteem in which the march is remembered. When King's birthday became a national holiday, Ronald Reagan was president. The "Great Communicator" quoted the celebrated line about being judged by "the content of your character" to confirm his dedication to the dream (quite a feat of verbal gymnastics for someone who had opened his 1980 presidential campaign in Philadelphia, Mississippi, the site of Freedom Summer's chilling murder of three civil rights workers). Apple deploys the image of King along with Gandhi, Picasso, and Einstein to pump up its "think different" sales pitch. An astonishing 97 percent of all teenagers recognized the speech in 2008. In 1996, the California Republican Party used an image of King at the march to lend legitimacy to its campaign against affirmative action. Every public figure, no matter otherwise impeccable conservative credentials, honors the dream and the march, at least in public pronouncements. Even William Bennett and Rush Limbaugh sing its praises. Glenn Beck went so far as to stage a reenactment of the March on Washington to promote his own ascendancy. If Beck's was a kind of political pornography, for most the rediscovery of the march and the speech as all-American is genuine. Who, after all, could object any longer to the universal bathos of the speech's dream "that one day on the red hills of Georgia, the sons of former slaves and the sons of former slave-owners will be able to sit down together at the table of brotherhood."[2]

How could that consensus be genuine, though, in a society so infested with the most noxious forms of inequality, much of it racially inflected, even if no longer prescribed by law? The dream, the march, the summer signaled the triumph of formal equality, equality before the law: "free at last." They also turned out to be way stations on the road to a great loss. Largely hidden from view, what was abandoned still hurt, more and more as decades of neglect deepened the pain. If the "economic roots" of racism were still visible in Washington in 1963 and in Mississippi in 1964, then in the years that followed they would be buried alive. New hierarchies emerged that kept them interred. On the one hand, this season of emancipation led on to a recurring national celebration of moral accomplishment. On the other hand, it left behind an unsatisfied yearning to be "free at last." So it is that what has become a shrine to our national unity and virtue conceals within an unresolved dilemma. There the hidden injuries of class and race intermix and abrade.

Parting the Waters

Not even a single generation separates the class upheavals of the New Deal and World War II from the racial revolution of the 1960s. Hardly a decade passed between President Roosevelt's promulgation of the Fair Employment Practices Committee in 1941 and the *Brown vs. Board of Education* decision of 1954. The March on Washington we memorialize happened a mere twenty-odd years after another planned March on Washington aimed at ending racial discrimination in defense employment was called off because FDR felt its pressure and created the FEPC.

Yet our collective memory bank files away these two historic epochs as if they had virtually nothing to do with each other. The first might have taken place in some Dickensian dark age, the latter just yesterday. The first was about white people, the second about colored people. The first spoke the class-inflected language of our long-dead ancestors, the second deployed the metaphors of identity that consume us to this day. The first in one way or another interrogated capitalism, the second found that irrelevant. The first dreamed a new dream, the second recalled to mind an ancient one first articulated by the founding fathers. While the new dream faded away, the old one prevailed. Both eras promised deliverance and emancipation. But the formidable enemies of the first freedom crusade—big business—often became the allies of the second. Both aspired to be "free at last." Still, the freedom struggled for in the first epoch seems different in kind from the freedom from the burdens of ascribed racial (or other) identities that electrified the last half of the twentieth century. Their felt sensibilities seem utterly alien, one from the other, as if the nineteenth century ended in 1945 and the twentieth began in 1960. In between America fell down the rabbit hole.

Looking back, the liberation promised (if unfulfilled) by the New Deal and its aftermath seems to live in a galaxy far, far away from the liberation (itself still unfulfilled) that the Washington marchers and Mississippi volunteers hoped to see so soon.

Can this be so? It defies common sense and historical reason to think of events and movements happening practically elbow to elbow yet somehow free of any organic connection. And as it turns out, that was not true. Nor is this simply a matter of seeking out the roots, economic or otherwise, of the civil rights revolution. That is a worthy undertaking. It is important and edifying to follow the footprints the New Deal left on the trail leading to the second American civil war. Some scholars have done that and we are richer for it, even if their insights don't ring loudly enough on the public register.

What might be more intriguing is to explore why those footprints became so obscured, so lost from sight that they ceased to be part of our common sense. Arguably, for the triumph of the second civil war to be hailed by all Americans, of whatever political persuasion, it was necessary to erase those original footprints. Left in plain sight they might serve as a disquieting reminder that "free at last" still only happened in the bosom of Abraham.

The march, the speech, and the summer, unlike the other iconic Americana touched on in this book, start their story when their telltale signs of class still mattered, were still visible, if growing fainter. Like a rapidly receding star in an expanding universe, those insignia grew ever dimmer until class no longer mattered. And this is surpassingly strange. Because from the country's beginnings racial and class subordination had always and everywhere formed a Gordian knot no one could untie. Class mattered, with a vengeance.

Midnight's Children

African American slavery and capitalism grew up together in
the New World. Precisely how we should understand their relationship has long been a subject of debate. Did American
capitalism depend on slave labor in its takeoff phase, drawing
on the rich harvest of cotton plantation production to provide
the seed capital for mercantile and eventually industrial fortunes? Or did indigenous capitalism enjoy its own momentum,
one that drew on free wage labor and did not depend on (even
if it profited from) the capital originating in southern slave
agriculture? Was the assignment of African Americans to the
status of chattel a function of a preexisting set of racist presump-
tions? Perhaps, yet various kinds of unfree labor preceded black
bondage (including Indian enslavement), and slavery was an
ancient institution without any necessary connection to race or
other ascribed human qualities, and certainly not to capitalism.

Whether or not racism deserves the status of the nation's
original sin, the "peculiar institution" that defined the South
established a caste system that lasted long after the Confederacy died and the link to slavery had been severed. Is that post-
bellum system best treated as a form of racial exclusion? Or is
it best seen, like apartheid, as simultaneously a form of labor
and racial control run in the interests of what was becoming a
thoroughly capitalist society from coast to coast, above and
below the Mason-Dixon Line?

Resistance to the entwined mechanisms of racial and class
subordination marked the tumultuous decades prior to the
March on Washington. Moreover, that resistance showed itself
in the North and in the South. It arose just when and because
the distinct political economy of labor-intensive plantation
agriculture that had rested on this caste system of labor disci-

pline was falling apart. That tectonic social disruption led to both mass dispossession and mass migration. The mudsills of the American Southland struggled to survive as the detritus of an agrarian economy in which their labor was increasingly superannuated but in which racial stigmata, legal and otherwise, remained intact. Or instead they set out for the North and its promise of industrial salvation. Once there, they had to mobilize to resist the worst ravages of wage slavery.

Dixieland

Marching down the Mall that day in August 1963 were people from all over the country. Most visible and audible, however, were southern blacks. Not because they made up most of those hundreds of thousands; they probably didn't. Rather because the movement that propelled them there was most conspicuously associated with the South: the Jim Crow codes, the sickening incidences of legal and vigilante violence, the churches that headquartered the organized protests, the preachers whose dignity and passion and unmistakable southern vocalizing inspired multitudes, the bus stations, restaurants, thoroughfares, and state capitols where defiance and counter-defiance made their presences felt were southern in the bone. Something had been happening in the Southland in the run-up to the march that had turned acquiescence—the normal state of affairs even under the most appalling circumstances—into rebellion.

Rebellion against what, precisely? Before the guns of the Civil War had time to cool, peonage had replaced slavery. Sharecropping and tenant farming comprised a complex network of economic and social dependencies, one not restricted to African Americans but in which they were disproportionately enmeshed and with fewer escape routes than those available to their white counterparts. They were indebted to planters and merchants for everything from seed and tools and essential livestock to shelter and clothing.

Signatories to year-long or longer "leases" that severely curtailed moving on, sharecroppers and tenants lacked even the freedom to quit, with which mere wage laborers were ironically blessed. People were confined by their isolation to the captive markets for goods and services owned by their landlords and furnishing agents. They often were without the basic literacy and numeracy to know when they were being chiseled by their planter overlords, storekeepers, or loan sharks.

Education was a sometime thing, constantly interrupted when kids were needed in the fields, and rarely lasted as long as the eighth grade. Mississippi senator James K. Vardaman explained what really mattered. Educating the black man "simply renders him unfit for the work which the white man has prescribed, and which he will be forced to perform.... The only effect is to spoil a good field hand and make an insolent black cook." The peonage class was so mired in myriad forms of contractual obligation and subordination that the prospect of moving on was virtually a chimera. That was the point. Now that slavery was dead, the master class of the new South could rely on that immobilized workforce to sustain the southern economy. More than incidentally, this half-free labor pool also functioned to suppress the income and wage level of the Southland's "white trash."[3]

Just in case someone seriously did entertain springing free of this economic gulag (and of course many did), an intricate system of legal and extralegal coercion made that virtually impossible. This is what Jim Crow was in the first instance all about, whatever its racist rationales helped justify. It was meant to lock this system of caste peonage in place.

"Color-blind" laws turned fraudulent "contracts" into enforceable ones. Quit your leased land, walk away from your crop commitments or your job, fail to pay the usurer, demand that the landlord pay you for your "share" of the crop at the rate agreed to, even question the amount you were due from or owed to your landlord, and sheriffs would arrest you as a vagrant or defaulter or for something more trivial or entirely made up on the spot. Judges would sentence you to prison labor camps as deadly as anything dreamed of by the most sadistic slave masters or Stalinist commissars.

Debt slavery became itself a lucrative system of public finance and an ordinary business as planters and turpentine extractors and coal mine owners and even southern steel mills contracted with southern states for prison labor. In a rudimentary way, there formed a kind of informal market in collateralized debt obligations trafficking in the buying and selling of the rights to indebted prisoners, or rather to their labor. The Thirteenth Amendment may have outlawed involuntary servitude, but the redeemers who saved the South from Yankee Reconstruction effectively outlawed the Thirteenth Amendment.[4]

Jim Crow closed off all political channels of redress. The voting booth was shuttered. The Republican Party was neutered once Reconstruction was overturned. The Democratic Party was racially cleansed. Constitutional protections were worthless in a region where juries, prosecutors, and judges were all white. In 1960, .5 percent of black kids went to integrated schools in the South. As late as 1962–63, there were no black students in integrated public schools in Mississippi, South Carolina, and Alabama. In the one hundred southern counties with the highest percentage of black residents, only 8.3 percent were registered to vote. As of 1963 in Mitchell City, Georgia, not one of the city's nine thousand African Americans had ever served on a jury.[5]

Even those unofficial arteries of democratic life and resistance—newspapers, public forums, and religious assem-
blies—were hemmed in, censored by fear of what they could
say, why and where they could congregate. The black middle
class, rural and urban, that ran these institutions and accounted for the sliver of professionals, teachers, and small-business
people with some access to education beyond the most elemen-
tal found its influence and zone of freedom ghettoized. A
truncated black "elite" enjoyed a meager ration of privileges in
return for keeping the peace.[6]

Should all of this economic and political hardwiring
short-circuit, Jim Crow always could make resort to the extralegal blunt instrument: vigilante beating, terror bombing,
lynching. Often enough it was hard to draw a clear boundary
between the legal and illegal. That too was the point, as much
because it instilled a permanent preemptive atmosphere of fear
as because, when actually deployed, it worked. So it was that
caste-based peonage was frozen in place, its labor and racial
protocols forming a singular and coherent social organism.

Long after the southern Populist movement, which had
briefly challenged this state of affairs, had been killed off at the
end of the nineteenth century, this intermingling of class and
racial exploitation and disempowerment prevailed. Organizing
among tenant farmers (white and black) during the Great Depression put up some resistance. New Deal federal agricultural
programs offering aid to distressed farmers through price sup-
ports and subsidized acreage restrictions helped a bit, but only
a bit. These government agencies were supposed to be color-blind,
but in real life the old southern oligarchy ran the programs locally and made sure Jim Crow defined the rules. New Deal job
creation and welfare programs also loosened the confinement,
opening up alternative sources of income. But here too program

administrators in the South made sure those alternatives didn't disturb the ready availability or subsistence wage level of the black labor force. Moreover, thanks to the substantial political clout of the South in Washington, national legislation like the Fair Labor Standards Act excluded precisely those most critical and vulnerable sectors of work—agriculture and domestic labor, especially—from its wage, hour, and other protections.

The Machine in the Garden

Racial peonage still defined the southern status quo up to 1945. Around that time, however, the fundamentals began to shift. Nicholas Lemann's book *The Promised Land* explored the sea change. He argued that the introduction of the mechanical cotton picker eliminated, though not all at once, the underlying economic need for that system of labor. Cotton was the most labor intensive and least mechanized branch of southern agriculture. An average field hand could pick twenty pounds of cotton in an hour; the mechanical picker could harvest a thousand pounds. The introduction of chemical weed killers after World War II further reduced the need for stoop labor. New technology did not, however, sweep away the whole apparatus of Jim Crow legal, political, and social exclusion that had kept class and racial hierarchies stable for generations.

Arguably, the fate of the freedmen had always been dispossession once the party of Lincoln abandoned the incendiary idea of redistributing land in order to create an independent landowning class of small farmers out of the population of ex-slaves. What happened first during the Great Depression and then in the wake of postwar mechanization amounted to a second dispossession. In a population already suffering immiseration, now even the means of cobbling together a bare livelihood might be beyond reach. Or if rural African Americans managed to hang on, their conditions of work grew more brutal, their conditions of life more abject. For African Americans living under those circumstances, the sting of Jim Crow grew sharper still as it accentuated their isolation and impotence.[7]

Isolation and impotence are not necessarily the breeding grounds of social upheaval. On the contrary, despair is as likely an outcome. But locked-away rural enclosures were at the same time being opened up to other possibilities, both tangible ones and ones born of a new national zeitgeist.

Migration, beginning just before and during World War I and proceeding at an accelerated rate during and after World War II, offered a way out of the southern gulag: an escape from peonage, poverty, and dispossession as well as from social and political pariahdom. Some stayed in the South but moved from the countryside to the cities. One million black people made that trek. The overwhelming majority found jobs as cooks, common laborers, machine operators, janitors, and in other kinds of unskilled labor. More than half of black women in the cities worked as domestics. As late as 1890, four out of five African Americans lived in the rural South; by 1950, somewhere between 30 and 40 percent lived in southern cities.

While Jim Crow naturally prevailed there as well, opportunities for work were more plentiful both before and after the Great Depression, especially in steel towns like Birmingham or commercial entrepôts like New Orleans, in business centers like Atlanta or in the textile towns of the Piedmont. Middle-class African Americans likewise found more elbow room in these urban spaces, larger terrain on which to cultivate their professional and business aspirations, and here their social status and political influence grew weightier, albeit still within the confines of the ghetto.

A southern tributary of the great river of moral outrage and political determination that inundated Washington, DC, in 1963 formed out of this rural/urban convergence of African American desire and despair. If the southern city could speak for the countryside, it was in part because the leadership class of preachers and teachers and trade unionists in the South were often not even a generation removed from the alluvial lands of the black belt, the red clays of Georgia, and the uplands of the Carolinas. Migration to the region's cities was not only driven by the desperation of dispossession from the land; migration carried with it a promise of release. Marching for jobs and freedom in this world would always entail liberation from involuntary servitude and from social extinction as much as it would relief from the humiliations and disabilities of second-class citizenship.[8]

North Star

A second tributary rushing toward the Mall in Washington had its headwaters in the South as well. It too was fed by dispossession from the land. It too was a recombinant freedom movement struggling to throw off the irons of class and racial servitude all at once. It too was great migration away from agricultural peonage. But it headed instead to the industrial North in numbers that dwarfed the exodus to the urban South. And once there, it established a distinctive profile. In the memory of one woman, "Chicago was a real place for colored people," but not quite the promised land. "No, indeed, I'll never work in anybody's kitchen but my own, any more," she happily reported, but "that's the one thing that makes me stick to this job." More free, but not yet free.[9]

What historians have called the Great Migration happened in two stages. First came the exodus to the North during and after the First World War. Defense industries, industries converted to defense, and all those contiguous industries that sprang to life to feed the war machine or that were fed by it hungered after labor. Southern planters and other regional commercial interests did what they could to staunch the flow of cheap black labor out of Dixie. So southern economic and political elites tightened the noose when and where they could, using every available means—legal coercion and violence—to keep the labor pool frozen in place. Nonetheless, hundreds of thousands of African Americans flooded the mills and plants and packing houses of the industrial heartland.[10]

Greater in scope was the second phase of migration north that happened during and after the Second World War. Beginning in the early 1940s and continuing into the 1960s, more than 5 million African Americans left the South. While the movement was driven by the same insatiable demand for labor, it was also portentously different.

Mechanization of cotton agribusiness made the old racial peonage arrangements increasingly superfluous. Rather than keep sharecroppers, tenants, and field hands on the premises, southern oligarchs and politicians wanted them gone. They preferred that rather than to have to pay even the meanest sum for their upkeep. Now the dispossessed threatened to become a burden rather than a blessing. If once rural African Americans were pulled north by the lure of escape, now they were pushed there as well. And by the mid-1950s the push exceeded the pull as the demand for industrial labor up north began to slacken. By the time of the March on Washington, it was becoming clearer day by day that the prospects of economic opportunity up north, once so alluring, were drying up. You might say de-agriculturalization in the South (at least as a labor-intensive system of production) preceded the deindustrialization that would eventually await the region's dispossessed in the North.[11]

The Footsteps of the Deliverer

Before that reality began to bite, however, the experience of industrial insurgency and New Deal reform in the 1930s and 1940s left a permanent imprint. The trade union establishment had long been lily white. But the uprising of the industrial working class during the New Deal years upset many encrusted ways of doing things. It called into question, for example, the absolute sanctity of private property. It interrogated the viability of capitalism. Instead of warding off government intrusions into the labor market, it invited them. Once itself a hierarchy defined, first of all, by craft and skill, one that excluded millions of the less lettered, the new labor movement of the 1930s downgraded those divisions in favor of a more ecumenical embrace of all working people.

Accustomed to behaving on behalf of its own parochial interests, the insurgency appeared on the stage of public life as the champion of all those exploited, abused, and discarded by the collapse of the market system. In a nation that had always assumed that rights inhered in the individual—a bedrock principle of constitutional dogma and jurisprudence—the new labor movement helped author a strikingly original notion of collective rights that commanded the attention of lawmakers, judges, and constitutional scholars. Indeed, the labor rebellion along with the New Deal made rights where there had been none before; collective economic rights entered that pantheon of sacred national obligations once solely occupied by those civil liberties and civil rights that inhered in the individual.[12]

But what about race, that ageless and obsidian barrier to freedom? Here too the emancipatory desires that enflamed the labor movement disturbed the ancien régime. Those universalist yearnings and the ground-level social solidarity characteristic of the new industrial unions broke through to the other side. Black workers not only flooded into the auto industry and meatpacking plants, into the rubber and electrical factories, into the steel mills and coal mines, but also into the United Auto Workers, United Packinghouse Workers, United Rubber Workers, United Steel Workers, United Mine Workers, United Electrical Workers, and dozens of other organizations. And this was before they were even organizations, while they were still combat formations in a countrywide series of class conflicts, fluid social creations where old identities, including race-based ones, could dissolve and liquefy.

But not entirely. Segregated unions remained, especially in the older skilled trades. Barriers to membership remained. Even the most audacious of the new unions, often led by radicals, were tainted by racial privilege. Hierarchies of wages, opportunities for promotion, degrees of security all remained pockmarked by racist accommodations and inequities. The flood tide of black migrants was met by race riots in cities like Detroit. As for the New Deal administration, it was of course premised on not disturbing its relations with the entrenched racial order in the South. No frontal assault on Jim Crow was contemplated in those quarters, especially once the attempt to purge southern Democrats in the 1938 primaries failed.

Nonetheless, it is hard to exaggerate the transformation in African American working-class life ushered in by the economic democracy of the Congress of Industrial Organizations (CIO) and the New Deal. The CIO reconfigured the country's economic and political landscape by unionizing the unorganized who comprised the core of the labor force in American industry. Half a million African Americans joined the CIO. In the South, the new labor movement was "the lamp of democracy," a beacon of class-based rights consciousness. Talk of an economic bill of rights (assurances of a job, housing, health care, education, security in old age, a living wage), of the "Four Freedoms," including freedom from want, and of the collective right to organize unions became part of the lingua franca of the new order. Where once "employment at will" and the absolute rights that attached to private property had prevailed, now the protocols of industrial democracy penetrated the black box of the workplace, curtailing the powers of the old industrial autocracy.

A letter from Colonel Elton D. Wright VI written in 1943 to the Justice Department conveys the convergence: "I am only asking for my rights the above named men violated the citizens rights bill of the constitution of the U.S.A. by compelling me to work for them at low wages, unfair and inhuman treatment, and threatened me with death." Letters like this from cotton pickers, sugarcane choppers, workers in turpentine stills and lumberyards filled up the files of the Justice Department and the NAACP. "Slavery," "involuntary servitude," and "peonage" made up their common vocabulary.[13]

Social justice, economic democracy, collective rights and obligations established a remarkable new way of life and belief, a fresh way of reacting to the inequities and iniquities of modern life. This was true not only for the nation as a whole but for the ex-peons and dispossessed fleeing the American gulag. For a time, the struggle for civil rights was conducted within that context. A journalist observed the way the ground was shifting: "The crucial struggle for civil liberties today is among tenant farmers and industrial workers, fighting for economic emancipation and security." *Fortune* magazine called civil rights "the irrepressible conflict of the 20th century." When FDR ordered the creation of the FEPC, the *Amsterdam News* commented, "If President Lincoln's proclamation was designed to end physical slavery, it would seem that the recent order of President Roosevelt is designed to end, or at least to curb, economic slavery." Civil rights had to be simultaneously economic rights, collective rights, the rights belonging to the working class tout court, or they would fail at freedom. During the Second World War, black protest movements combined "claims to racial equality with still-robust claims of labor and economic rights."

Case law reflected the sea change. The Justice Department prosecuted civil rights complaints from the standpoint of economic as well as racial justice. This amounted to a deliberate repudiation of the individualist foundations of previous racial and workplace jurisprudence. Where judge-made law once nullified efforts to regulate wages and hours or undermined union organizing and strikes on the grounds that they interfered with the freedom of contract between employer and employee, the new dispensation established a fresh foundation upon which lawmaking might recognize collective rights.

With respect to civil rights grievances especially, the Justice Department now excavated the long-buried Thirteenth Amendment against involuntary servitude (and with frequent backup references to the Emancipation Proclamation) as a legitimate basis for adjudicating these accusations. This was particularly the case in litigation involving agricultural workers subjected to what amounted to debt slavery. Under Francis Biddle as attorney general (and onetime head of the National Labor Relations Board), the Justice Department welcomed this convergence of labor and civil rights principles. Strange as it may seem now, this was the common sense of mid-twentieth-century jurisprudence.

Even the NAACP, which for many years had rested its case against segregation on the "equal protection" clause of the Fourteenth Amendment, adopted this new approach. Questioning of racial injustice had for a long time targeted individual attitudes—in a word, white prejudice. Inequality was presumed to root in individual psychology, not in society's social structure. And violations could therefore be educated or litigated away. But now that industrial individualism (the singular relationship between an employer and employee) had become suspect, so too had racial individualism, no more a matter of settled law. But this new state of affairs would not endure. While the Justice Department persisted longer than did the NAACP, by the early 1950s this unorthodox way of addressing racial injustice as a matter of economic and collective injustice had begun to fade away. Why?[14]

The Empire Strikes Back

Cold War America was a study in intolerance. Ironically, the nation's legendary faith in American exceptionalism—the notion that the New World had afforded humankind a second chance at freedom—provided the rationale. As the American government went about consolidating its victory after World War II, as it laid down the rules and erected the institutions that would entrench U.S. political and economic dominance in the West and across broad stretches of what soon became known as the "third world," it offered a distinctive justification for that empire building. It was to be a heroic project having nothing to do with material self-interest or the antimonies of class conflict. Instead, it was undertaken to stop the onrush of

Communist tyranny, to create a fortress of freedom and democracy, a transatlantic society where class no longer mattered,
where the very language of class conflict made no sense.
America, not the Soviet Union, had achieved a classless nirvana, Richard Nixon reminded Nikita Khrushchev in that
Moscow kitchen. The rest of the Free World would follow.

One consequence of this ideological legerdemain was to
sever the race question from the labor question since the latter
was no longer to be asked. Blunt instruments could be used to
drive the point home. McCarthyism was a political plague
(laboratory tested in the highest circles of the Truman administration before being released into the general population by
the senator from Wisconsin). It infected every facet of social
justice movements, legislative reforms, government agencies,
ideological convictions, constitutional protections, civil liberties, civic organizations, school curricula, and channels of
popular culture, including especially Hollywood; all had been
in one way or another touched by the egalitarian zeitgeist of
the New Deal era. Once again, the fear and denial about class
indigenous to the American makeup worked its black magic,
turning a defense of democracy into its mad undoing.

Whether mad or crazy like a fox, the lions of the Cold War
knew the enemy: the root of the problem was this lingering
preoccupation with class, that hidden tumor that had suddenly surfaced and metastasized during the Great Depression
and that had to be excised. Symptoms appeared everywhere
across the body politic: here in union demands for universal
medical care, there in the talk in legislative chambers about
government economic planning, popping up in classrooms
where syllabi included *The Grapes of Wrath*. And the tumor was
also infiltrating organizations ostensibly committed to racial
equality.

Civil rights groups and their allies had to contend with this suffocating atmosphere, the relentless assault by innuendo, rumor, lie, and congressional witch hunt. To challenge the racial status quo had always been risky. Now it risked a deadly association. One group after another, some leaning further left than others, felt the sting and looked for cover. Walter Reuther, for example, had earned his bona fides in part by his record as a committed enemy of the Communist faction within his own union. In that connection, he explained his advocacy of civil rights as the best way to fight the red menace abroad: "We can't defend freedom in Berlin so long as we deny freedom in Birmingham" was the way he put it that day at the Lincoln Memorial. Even the NAACP, which had grown distinctly more moderate and respectable since its founding at the beginning of the century, made haste to disassociate itself from anything, however remote, that carried the curse of class consciousness. Indeed, the organization engaged in a purging of its own ranks to get free of the stigma.

It became unwise, under these circumstances, to pursue a legal strategy against segregation that pointed out its connection to the labor question and to the collective rights Jim Crow violated. A return to racial individualism was in deep harmony with the bromides of a classless America that were quickly being born again and broadcast around the world. The formal equality with which every individual was alleged to be endowed was far safer ground upon which to carry on the fight. When King later argued on behalf of what soon would be known as affirmative action, he remained mindful of Cold War atmospherics, suggesting that it would be a good idea to take "affirmative action ... to remove the conditions of poverty, insecurity, and injustice which are the fertile soil in which the seed of Communism grows and develops."[15]

Ideological genuflections like this could also, by the way, win the allegiance of Washington Cold Warriors. These mandarins confronted the global revolt against colonialism that followed the war. Housing apartheid within their own borders was an embarrassment for State Department bureaucrats. They might win over third world hearts and minds by applauding a crusade whose goal—the free and equal individual—was as American as could be. That might work, but only so long as the crusaders could not be confused with carriers of the red menace. (Before I left for Mississippi early in summer of 1964, I was sent as one member of a delegation of volunteers on a side trip to Washington, there to lobby members of Congress about the need for federal marshals to monitor what was happening in the Magnolia State. Three COFO [the Council of Federated Organizations, which sponsored Freedom Summer, consisted of SNCC, CORE (the Congress of Racial Equality), the NAACP, and the SCLC (Southern Christian Leadership Council)] workers—James Chaney, Michael Schwerner, and Andrew Goodman—had disappeared under mysterious and ominous circumstances from a jailhouse in Philadelphia, Mississippi. Among other lawmakers, we visited with Illinois senator Paul Douglas, a New Deal Democrat with impeccable liberal credentials. The senator applauded our general intentions in venturing south but warned us to be wary of the "Commies." I was stunned, embarrassed for him.)

Debate inside the legal profession about "rights" had never come to a stop, even in the halcyon days when "collective rights" were in the forefront. But now the momentum shifted back in the direction of racial individualism. Sober choices about what might be most palatable to justices without factoring in their political views was standard practice even in less incendiary times. The basic desire to achieve something tangible in whatever way always carried weight. The class biases of organizations staffed and run by upwardly mobile African Americans mattered too. Those for whom it was clear that their own self-improvement might be achieved apart from a general uplift of their racial brethren, if only certain legal barriers were eliminated, could find that strategic approach compatible with their own experience and without feeling qualms about abandoning the cause.

In any event, the NAACP's great triumph in *Brown vs. Board of Education* marked a decisive change in the weather. The case turned not on whether structures of economic and social power, both in the public and the private spheres, embedded inequality systemically. Instead, up for decision was whether government-sanctioned segregation took an unfair psychological and cultural toll on its victims, leaving behind a permanent wound to their individual self-esteem. It marked a return to the middle-class roots of the organization whose legal strategies during most of its existence focused on gaining access to schools, railroad dining cars, and middle-class neighborhoods, to the terrain on which a classless modern civil rights struggle played out.

Working people bringing their complaints to the NAACP had most often emphasized the dire economic consequences of Jim Crow. The lawyers and activists who manned the organization, on the other hand, focused more heavily on the legal category of segregation itself. The African American worker began to disappear "as a relevant legal character."

In general, the Cold War entailed a flight away from the class dimensions of social dilemmas and their material foundations. It was therefore also congruent with the effort to psychologize away any disturbing allusions to the Emancipation Proclamation or the Thirteenth Amendment or other memories of a just then bygone era.[16]

Alive in the Afterlife

Memorials to the Emancipation Proclamation and the amendment that finally abolished slavery had been a staple of American public life for decades after the Civil War. Frederick Douglass believed that Emancipation Day would outlast July 4th as
the best-remembered national holiday because it commemo-
rated a more fundamental realization of the freedom promised
in the Declaration of Independence. In Douglass's view "what
is the slave to the Fourth of July" but "a thin veil to cover up
crimes which would disgrace a nation of savages." For decades
prior to the march, black agricultural and industrial workers
had invoked the Thirteenth Amendment against involuntary
servitude in their legal battles against exploitation. When its
conceivers first planned the March on Washington, they thought
of it as "the climax to the peoples' commemoration of the
Emancipation Proclamation of 1863." Indeed, A. Philip Randolph, who was the godfather of the march, first thought of
calling it the Emancipation March for Jobs. Lincoln's executive
order and the constitutional amendment did get mentioned
at the march itself. King alluded to Leviticus and its command-
ment to redeem the indebted bondsman, to restore his
alienated land. All this, however, was more metaphor than
program.

Already by the time of the march popular celebrations of
these historic landmarks of labor emancipation had largely
ceased to be. No one brought them up—not much, anyway.
Still, it might have been expected that in 1963, the one hundredth
anniversary of the proclamation, that historic moment would
command center stage. Arguably, the proclamation and the
amendment are the most profound testaments to the quest for
human freedom ever produced by the American political genius,

far surpassing in significance the declaration of national independence of 1776.

In 1963, however, these emancipatory landmarks didn't measure up. The public eye was no longer trained on the problem of labor exploitation, no longer concerned itself with unfree labor, "involuntary servitude," half-free labor, or the "free labor" frequently referred to by earlier generations of Americans as "wage slavery." Instead, race, Christianity, the nation, the "beloved community," and the South as the land of Nod made up the moral framework of the freedom struggle in this new era.

Less lofty than these but more portentous about the logic of King's speech was its fraternizing with another metaphor: the "race of life" fit well within the imaginative comfort zone of bourgeois America. It presumed class stratification and would become, a half century later, the axiomatic assumption of the nation's first African American president when he urged all to join "the race to the top." That was and still is what people mean, what King meant, when he famously cried out, "I have a dream. It is rooted in the American dream." Its emancipatory yearnings notwithstanding, it is a dream that, without thinking about it, takes for granted class hierarchy; otherwise, what's the point of the race?[17]

Still, the past, so recent, still smoldering, could not be extinguished entirely. The oratory at the Lincoln Memorial now and then wandered into verboten territory. This was true particularly of the controversial (and censored) speech of John Lewis, representing the Student Non-Violent Coordinating Committee. Lewis struck a more militant note. Referring to hundreds of thousands not there that day, Lewis cried out, "They are receiving starvation wages . . . or no wages at all. While we stand here, there are sharecroppers in the Delta of Mississippi who are out in the fields working for less than $3/day, 12 hours a day." Criticizing the Kennedy administration's civil rights legislation then making its way through Congress, Lewis called instead for a "a bill that will provide for the homeless and starving people of this nation. We need a bill that will ensure the equality of a maid who earns $5 a week in the home of a family whose total income is $100,000 a year."

More telling than that, however, was the young student activist's call for "a serious social revolution." In what he said and how he said it—the lack of verbal polish, the drawl liquefying his vowels, the perpetual scowl—the visage of the Georgia sharecropper showed through. Red clay still figuratively clinging to the put-upon field hand, up from peonage as a student seminarian, Lewis was not about to forget where he hailed from. Nor did he fail to remind his audience that beneath all the hallelujahs for the freedom and equality promised by the nation's founders, a harsher, more intractable economic reality festered, one if left unchallenged would subvert the most exalted aspirations, turn them into hollowed-out abstractions.[18]

Martin Luther King's "I Have a Dream" speech largely consisted of those homilies and abstractions. It was delivered, however, with eloquence. And at the end it took flight with an unscripted but well-rehearsed peroration into a realm familiar to the world Lewis was still attached to, that spiritual mountain landscape where the black dispossessed of the cotton plantation and the northern ghetto communed. This was the common ground of traditional millennial release from racial bondage. An exalted vision, to be sure, but one so airborne it lost sight of the down below.

Yet even in King's speech, with which nearly everyone outside Dixie could shout amen to, there were the occasional hints of something else. The line between a version of Christian theology and secular leftism could be a fluid one. King's book

Stride toward Freedom: The Montgomery Story acknowledged the insights of Marx about the great divide separating wealth and poverty arising from capitalism's Mammon worship. Would equality before the law do much for those left hopeless in the ghettos of the North, where eating where you wanted to or voting if you wanted to might leave the status quo intact, the Man still the Man, the powers still with the power?[19]

Black leaders standing at some distance from the civil rights establishment echoed or enhanced these views. Julius Lester, Amairi Baraka, and even James Farmer, the head of the Congress of Racial Equality, noted that the speech mainly elided the plight of the urban poor of the North. For this omission, Malcolm X likened King to a "house negro." Claude Brown, the author of *Manchild in the Promised Land,* noted that no milk and honey awaited black migrants in the North, only poverty and despair: "For who does one run to when he's already in the promised land?"

Malcolm's fiery denunciations notwithstanding, King himself flirted with these same insights, a flirtation that grew more serious over time. For years before the march, King had been importuned by Randolph and Bayard Rustin to speak about the labor problem, to reach out to the labor movement. Rustin had always believed the long-range objectives of the march should focus on economic justice: "What is the value of winning access to public accommodations for those lacking the money to use them?" Those pleas registered. King's remarks devoted to employment discrimination and poverty observed that while some progress was visible in the South, in the North all he could see was "retrogression." The speech itself called out, "We cannot be satisfied as long as a Negro in Mississippi cannot vote and a Negro in New York believes he has nothing for which to vote." Just a month before people gathered on the Mall, King described for reporters the two purposes of the march: "to arouse the conscience of the nation on the economic plight of the Negro one hundred years after the Emancipation Proclamation and to demand strong forthright civil rights legislation." Addressing a demonstration in Albany, Georgia, well before the march, King compared the civil rights sit-ins to the CIO sit-down strikes of the 1930s.[20]

Practically since its founding, the CIO had pressured the Democratic Party to embrace the cause of racial justice. Many trade unions endorsed the march (even though the AFL-CIO did not). They did more than offer a go-with-god verbal piety; they went themselves in enormous numbers. Unions chartered buses and trains, bringing thousands of their own members and others to the Mall. The bodyguards protecting the speakers at the podium were union members. Posters announcing, "We march for minimum wage coverage for all" lined the walkway. Much of the music that inspired the movement derived from earlier labor conflicts, including Bob Dylan's "Power Is Their Game," Woody Guthrie and Pete Seeger's "If I Had a Hammer," "We Shall Not Be Moved," "Which Side Are You On?" and of course "We Shall Overcome"—all were adaptations of old labor songs.

Most important among these labor organizers was the conceptual godfather of the march, A. Philip Randolph. Randolph was then the head of the Negro American Labor Council (NALC), which had formed rather recently to carry on the fight to desegregate the labor movement. He was also a socialist and founder of the Sleeping Car Porters Union. And it was Randolph who threatened to mobilize a march on Washington in 1941 to desegregate defense employment until President Roosevelt hurriedly created the FEPC. For Randolph and his colleagues, the intermixing of the race and labor questions was a given. The NALC under his leadership issued the first call for a new March on Washington that we now treat with reverence. In its early incarnations, the march was to include as well massive civil disobedience around the country.

And it was to be a march for "Jobs and Freedom." On the one hand, that demand for jobs is a straightforward reminder that the march conceivers and organizers retained a living connection to an era just gone by when racial and economic freedom were consciously conjoined. This would hardly be worth mentioning were it not the case that popular memory has largely erased that from the event's genesis and purpose.

Not only jobs but other proposals were included in the call to the march that reflected the same outlook. Thus, there was talk of raising the minimum wage, about initiating public works and building low-cost housing, of establishing a permanent Fair Employment Practices Commission whose reach would extend into the private sector, of extending the jurisdiction of the Fair Labor Standards Act to embrace those occupations in which black workers predominated, in agriculture, domestic work, retail services, and so on. These demands were the stock-in-trade of the New Deal's achievements, or at least of its aspirations. Their presence on the Mall, even if uttered sotto voce, was familiar enough. Yet they also signaled that something had changed.[21]

Demanding jobs in this context was as much new as it was old. When the two great migrations unfolded, finding work was not the burning issue. (Of course, during the Great Depression work was scarce but for just that reason migration north slowed considerably.) During and after both world wars jobs were plentiful, which is why migrating was enticing at all. By the 1960s, however, the economic fate of northern ghetto dwellers had deteriorated. King noted this and so too did others, including people like Malcolm X who mocked the march. The

national economy was operating at a high voltage, but the first
signs of what over the ensuing decades would become a more
general malfunctioning that would afflict the white as well as
the black working class was taking its toll especially on those
always first to feel the hurt. It was as if the Great Depression
had returned or threatened to return and settle down permanently in Harlem, South Chicago, North Philadelphia, Watts,
and so on.

Creating jobs could address this, of course. But this demand—and the other proposals about minimum wages and
labor standards and universal protections—was now normal-
ized. Such propositions had lost their once insurgent energy.
When the labor uprising first detonated, the question was less
about getting a job than about what happened to you on the
job once you had one. At the work site humiliation and fear
were daily fare. This was the land of the voiceless, a world of
invisibles compelled to move to the rhythms of the labor market, featureless machine tenders, there to conform to an alien
discipline designed for purposes indifferent to their material
or spiritual well-being. Behind each aggrieved complaint about
wages or the speed of the line or the favoritism and insults of
the foreman or compulsory overtime or the surveillance by
company spies or the bullying by company thugs lay a deeper
determination to be free of all that and thereby create a new
definition of what it meant to be human.

A quarter century later, that metaphysics had vanished;
only the physics remained. Interrogating the justice and viability of capitalism per se was no longer part of the agenda, even
implicitly, as it once had been. The new postwar order of state-
managed Keynesian capitalism had put those kinds of questions
to bed, or it thought it had. Keynesian economists and social
engineers would make sure jobs and income were available.

What else mattered? The labor movement had made that accommodation along with others. If jobs and income were not available in the ghetto, then that would be seen to but without seriously disrupting the functioning of what was otherwise perceived as a well-lubricated machine.

An afterlife of the "labor question" nonetheless continued to haunt the proceedings in Washington. The spectral presence of the marginalized ghetto and the abused remains of the southern peon looked on and wondered.

Starkville

Lomax's Café was a one-room dilapidated wood shack—probably put up not long after the Civil War—set down in a sandy depression off the main paved road running through Starkville, Mississippi. It was nestled in the town's poorest black neighborhood, a wooded enclave traversed by dirt roads featuring houses just as frail and just as aged as Lomax's place, some with backyard vegetable gardens and a pig or chicken or two, and here and there a plain style, rickety church. Some homes had indoor plumbing; many did not. This was the left-behind world of a peonage system already in an advanced state of disintegration. Outwardly it reminded me of the Lee Avenue of my childhood, a drab poverty barely softened by its more natural surroundings. There were dozens and dozens of Lomax Cafés throughout the black Mississippi South: inviting places where people drifted in and out during the day and gathered at night to eat fresh-made pork rinds saturated in hot sauce, drink corn liquor from countryside stills (Mississippi was a dry state back then), and be together.

The café was a natural place for our fledgling local freedom movement to assemble that summer of 1964 to plan efforts to register people to vote and to discuss putting together a Starkville branch of the Mississippi Freedom Democratic Party, which at the end of the summer would challenge the legitimacy of the all-white state delegation to the Democratic Party presidential nominating convention in Atlantic City. Or we would go over "smaller" matters like what to do about the daily harassment (insults, firings, threats, false arrests) that trailed after anybody bold enough to associate with me and my fellow northern student volunteer assigned to Starkville, an African American undergrad from California. Or we just gathered at Lomax's because for some strange reason its lopsided front door, the savory aroma of coffee, moonshine, and hot sauce, the shack's makeshift counter put together from nearby logs, the cool darkness inside on even the most broiling summer days, made it feel like a haven, a sanctuary, its fragile walls somehow capable of protecting us against a very hostile white world just across Route 82.

Above all we gathered at Lomax's Café because Frank Lomax let us. Not just let us, he welcomed us, despite all the completely self-evident risks he was taking. I can still see Frank's face: very dark and round, a scar across his forehead, small boned, smiling in a sardonic sort of way, gentle beneath its weathering. Frank knew the risks, far better than I and my comrade; how could he not, growing up black in Mississippi and now hanging out with meddling Yankee "Freedom Riders"? An atmosphere of danger and powerlessness made up the oxygen of everyday life. Lomax knew the risks but took them, made himself a target.

Plenty of others were not prepared to do likewise. The African American community was as riven by social divisions as any other. There were black preachers who were friendly and those we were told would be but weren't. There were doctors and lawyers and storekeepers who also drew back, guarding what little they had, not wanting to endanger their already precarious tightrope-walking acrobatics with white elite Starkville.

All during the era of segregation the politics of racial advancement had expressed the aspirations and anxieties of this precariously positioned black middle class. Lomax's neighborhood was a study in rural poverty, but other black areas were faring better. There the roads were paved, diets included more than pork rinds, corn bread, and chitlins, including on a good day locally caught catfish. Yet local activists were more likely to be recruited there than from among the most down-and-out whose fear and abject dependency shaped a coffin of passivity.[22]

Outside of town, the African American countryside formed yet another world entirely. If there was work, it was casual—a bit of sharecropping but mainly stoop labor for wages. Corn liquor stills ("white lightning" captured well the way it hit your brain pan if you weren't used to it) cropped up here and there, hidden in the woods. There I visited Pentecostal churches with dirt floors, where congregants spoke in tongues, where swooning into unconsciousness or supra-consciousness was common, and where "freedom" had little or nothing to do with voting. I trembled with the strangeness of it all. Yet I was more than welcomed; I was treated as a hero. I don't know why—a mixture of traditional racial deference and belief in deliverance, maybe. My reward included sex offered on fallow farm fields under a vast black but starlit sky, an offering so startling it left me shaken, unable to accept . . . and mortified.

Jim Crow notwithstanding, African American Starkville, like every other black settlement in the South, did not make up a unified social organism. It was not some categorical expression of racial apartheid, an identity not chosen but imposed. Under normal circumstances, black Starkville, whatever its shared experience of exclusion, did not constitute, even metaphorically, a tribe. Instead it lived its life enmeshed in a complex if stunted hierarchy left behind by a bygone moment in southern political and racial economy. Yet under extraordinary conditions it could re-create itself.

One twilight we collected together at Lomax's. The occasion was special but not so special. It was fairly late in the summer and we had convened a meeting of our embryonic Mississippi Freedom Democratic Party (MFDP) group—as we had many times before—this time to plan for the Atlantic City convention. We had made enough progress in Starkville that sending a delegation to a statewide meeting of our new party seemed possible. For that reason, fellow COFO workers had come down from Columbus (where I had worked earlier in the summer—a bigger town, a bigger project, and only about half an hour away). They joined the two of us and about fifteen people from the black community of Starkville.

And then the police joined us as well. That wasn't unusual. Just a few days earlier my buddy and I had arrived home late at night to be greeted by a police car, lights flashing in the rural pitch black (there were no street lights in the black bottoms of Starkville), filled to overflowing with one officer and a half dozen vigilantes. Not pausing to inquire, we jumped out of our car, dashed into the surrounding woods—I fell into a pig bog along the way, which everybody but me thought was very funny—and finally holed up in a friendly house where every window and door had someone stationed at it with a gun, waiting for the officers of the law and their "deputies" to attack, which they didn't. Nonviolent resistance was suspended for the evening (it had always been for most more a tactic than a philosophy; even King kept guns). I was scared that night, as on other nights, and my first and last thought was flight, not fight.[23]

When the police showed up a few nights later at Lomax's Café, we were therefore not surprised. And we had all grown accustomed to an omnipresent undercurrent of menace from a summer's worth of jailing, beatings, being followed or chased, everyday nastiness, even one or two shootings that missed. But on this occasion the police had turned out in unusual force. Two carloads of local and state highway patrol officers pulled up outside Lomax's. They had dogs, clubs, and guns. We were in a wooded cul-de-sac. No one would witness whatever they did next. Flight or fight?

Well, we did neither. We were outside the café when they came at us, looking nasty, the dogs growling, crowding around our knees and thighs. I knew the police chief. He'd locked me up earlier in the summer and had his brother, the town tax assessor, come by the underground all-white cell to yell to my fellow inmates that I was a "nigger lover" from the North and they should beat the hell out of me. Luckily, my cell mates were not particularly fans of the sheriff's so they demurred and I, acquiescing with every bone in my body, denied what the sheriff's brother had said and claimed my own ardent hatred of "niggers." That day they left me alone. Now, at Lomax's Café, Chief Josey bellowed at us to disperse pronto. The dogs, circling us hungrily, echoed his bellow. The sheriff's posse catcalled and pounded their clubs into their palms.

Without forethought, we arranged ourselves in a large circle, clasped hands, and sang—also not an uncommon thing to do in those uncommon times. We sang the soulful lyrics of spirituals that had become the combative anthems of the movement, Jesus at the barricades. Two things happened. Like an electric current running around our charmed circle, the fear that I think I can safely say possessed us all at that moment was alchemized, rechanneled, and became instead a power in all of us to prevail—and to prevail together. This was not something ethereal, otherworldly; on the contrary, the feeling was positively tactile, sensual, even erotic. The world—this darkening, abandoned mote in time, humid with menace—suddenly looked different because our collective eyesight had improved, giving us X-ray vision. We could see and act inside the body of fear, confront it, peer into a more civilized world beyond it, only because each of us found that strange superpower in our living relationship to each other.

Long ago Robert Burns named this "social love." An autoworker occupying a GM plant in Flint, Michigan, in 1937, remembered the exaltation he experienced when he and his fellows managed to subdue all the anxieties, the inner terrors, that had disabled them until then: "It was the CIO speaking in me." Marx spoke of "species consciousness," not as an idea but as a way of life. In Starkville at that moment outside Lomax's Café, something like that was created. It was not race consciousness. Nor did it "forget" the deep social divisions that had always configured black Starkville, dissolving them into a form of Christian universalism. It was much too earthbound to be that, and too combative; agape was not our message.

So we sang and we waited. Then the second thing happened: nothing. The police left. That was truly uncommon, and a lesson in the psychodynamics of resistance and acquiescence. Tyranny, whether industrial or racial or grounded in some other form of subordination, often enough resorts to blunt instruments when challenged. But it doesn't rest on that. It depends instead—unless autocracy is prepared to live in a chronic state of civil war, which is really not feasible—on an anterior atmosphere of intimidation and a fatalistic resignation that this is the way life is, there are no alternatives. Dread and awe in the face of power, obedience to its obsidian mystery, even when it's out of sight, become the custom of the country. In Mississippi people on both sides of the racial divide breathed that belief, their cultural oxygen, so to speak, day in and day out. The Starkville Police had every right, every long-standing reason to anticipate we would back down—that had almost always been the way things were. To suddenly be faced in the flesh with the repudiation of those axioms of everyday life can be so shocking, so disarming, if only for a moment, that it may impair the will to act. Through that fractured will can slip the new world. Just for an instant, that's what happened at Lomax's Café on that August night.

How does that experience converge on the ostensible reason we were all there? Mississippi Freedom Summer was an attempt, in the first instance, to resurrect the Fifteenth Amendment (the one assuring the right to vote) from its Jim Crow burial ground. Written into the Constitution, it was a primal right. Exercising it, moreover, was not only a fundamental expression of formal equality before the law. In theory, it might open a pathway to power and social change. In other words, struggling against the farrago of reasons, excuses, traps, hurdles, fictions, and humiliations devised to stop black people from registering in Mississippi could be perceived as an assault on the entire racial and class order of southern peonage. Doing so, like our little confrontation outside Lomax's, called upon hidden resources of courage by people who had decided that asserting the right to vote, although far from a guarantee that it would remedy the misery of their material circumstances or the routine exploitation of their punishing labor, nonetheless carried with it the highest moral-existential as well as social significance.

Voting may well be the weakest expression of democracy, often enough next to useless, merely a pacifier at times. Not then and there, however. And so we tried to uphold voting rights, usually without success, often lucky just to escape without injury. One day we set out to register some people at the courthouse in Columbus—me, a few would-be voters, and a volunteer lawyer just arrived from the North that day. We made it as far as a parking space across the street when a pickup truck carrying two young white men parked about fifty yards in front of us, just for a second. Then the driver floored the truck in reverse and smashed into the front of our car. The windshield shattered, glass and shrapnel from the hood flew everywhere. No one was registering that day. We went back to our COFO house and the lawyer back to New Jersey that same night. We would try again another day. Because it was important.

Still, as one local Alabama activist observed some years later when the revolutionary temper of the civil rights movement had cooled: "A ballot is not to be confused with a dollar bill"—as true in Starkville as in Harlem. Freedom may sustain you but, according to this veteran organizer, "you can't eat freedom." What then?[24]

The Great Deletion

Up north as well as throughout Starkville, USA, those "economic roots" I'd wondered about in my plea to become a summer volunteer kept showing themselves. But then they got reinterred.

Ghetto rebellions flamed up everywhere as the decade wore on. Malcolm X likened the dilemma to a kind of internal colonialism whose purposes were as much about exploitation as racial domination. The Black Panther Party (the one started in Oakland, not in Alabama), its theatrics and posturing not-withstanding, upped the ante. Its Marxist-inflected street lingo and martial parade dress confronted the "Man" about the de-spoiling of the inner city. Meanwhile, the party's "soldiers" fed kids free breakfasts. Was that a "freedom" you could eat? Black autoworkers faced off against the UAW leadership to compel that bureaucracy to proceed with the unfinished business of democracy and equality on the shop floor and in the wider world. Roy Wilkins of the NAACP, a man of much milder tem-perament than the Black Panthers, would later note that "grim clocks were ticking in the wretched ghettos of the North where nothing was changing." During the riot in Watts, one resident's sardonic take summed up the views of many: "I had a dream, I had a dream. Hell, we don't need no dream. We need jobs."[25]

Martin Luther King's dream, even to the reverend himself, began to seem more and more improbable unless the "labor question" was addressed head-on. As the times continued to darken, he looked to other sources of the country's original sin; in particular, the failure of Reconstruction to deliver on its promise of land to the freeman meant that "the oldest peas-antry, the Negro, was denied everything but a legal status he could not use, could not consolidate, and could not even de-fend." He explicitly described white workers as "the derivative victims" of slavery, and when raising the demand for reparations for past injustices, he noted that "millions of the white poor will also benefit." Desegregating lunch counters had been a worthy undertaking, but "now we are grappling with basic class issues between the privileged and the under-privileged . . . now we are saying everybody ought to have a job and everybody ought to have a guaranteed annual income and everybody ought to have the right to live in a decent house wherever he wants to live and everybody ought to have an adequate education. This is the problem. There are those who are not willing to have this come about."

Echoes of the collective rights demanded two decades earlier increasingly sounded in King's rhetoric. He took up the call for a "GI Bill for the Disadvantaged," arguing that it "must give greater emphasis to the alleviation of economic and cultural backwardness on the part of the so-called 'poor whites.'" "It is my opinion that many white workers whose economic condition is not far removed from that of his black brother, will find it difficult to accept a 'Negro Bill of Rights' which seeks to give special consideration to the Negro in the context of unemployment, joblessness . . . and does not take into sufficient account their plight."

After the outburst in Watts in 1965, King grimly commented, "Northern ghettos are the prisons of the forgotten man." And the reverend had this to say: "A riot is the language of the unheard." A year later he concluded that the civil rights movement "had not gotten down to the lower levels of Negro deprivation" and talked about the need to "put an end to the internal colonialism" that best captured the dilemma of Africa America. Change ushered in by the civil rights acts was "limited mainly to the Negro middle class." To probe deeper than that meant "messing with the captains of industry. . . . Now this means we are treading in difficult waters, because it really means that we are saying something is wrong with capitalism . . . maybe America must move toward a Democratic Socialism." Addressing an SCLC convention not too long before his assassination, King insisted to his compatriots that the movement must reorient, must address "restructuring the whole of American society," a scheme that meant "raising questions about the economic system, about the broader redistribution of wealth" and therefore "questioning the capitalist economy." His dream had turned into a "nightmare" he depicted as "an air-tight cage of poverty amidst an affluent society."

A warrior, King inaugurated a "Poor People's Campaign." It was conceived as an answer to the economic subordination afflicting millions north and south and explicitly embraced both black and white. Plans were to include Mexicans, Puerto Ricans, Appalachian whites, and Indians. King called it his "last, greatest dream." Sunnier yesterdays were fading. "I'm not only concerned about streets flowing with milk and honey. I'm also concerned about the fact that about two-thirds of the peoples of the world go to bed hungry at night. . . . It's a nice thing to talk about long white robes over yonder, but I want some clothes to wear right down here." Hard to endure as the earlier struggle for "freedom" had been, this one would be harder still. "It is much easier to integrate a lunch counter . . . than it is to eradicate slums. It is much easier to integrate buses than it is to create jobs." The task would require a "radical redistribution of political and economic power," and "many of the allies who were with us during the first phase will not be with us now."

How true that was he hardly knew. While visions of the "beloved community" continued to resonate for some, for others the focus was on power, as much about which class had it as about which race, and how best to challenge that "ruling class." King's assassination amid a bitterly fought sanitation workers' strike in Memphis that he helped champion suggests one road traveled following the march on the Mall.[26]

But it was the road less traveled. It's impossible to grasp today, but by the time of King's death his reputation had darkened so deeply that the speech had largely vanished from public memory. Then the ghetto uprisings spent themselves, leaving little in the way of enduring organized resistance. Malcolm X was killed, and anyway it was far from clear where his fledgling movement was headed. The Panthers were run to ground by the police, their rhetoric often exceeded the party's reach, and free breakfasts were also on offer from the welfare department. Radical caucuses of African American autoworkers and others (whose membership sometimes overlapped with the Black Panthers as, for example, in Detroit) operated with more leverage than enjoyed by people on welfare but not enough to dislodge an entrenched bureaucracy that could still summon up considerable political power. King's Poor People's Campaign rested on an impoverished population with little organizational experience or resources. And the campaign was at best only halfheartedly supported by higher-ups who once treated the reverend like a saint. Indeed, like many a saint, King found his credentials airbrushed clean of the muck and mire, in this case of the detritus of southern cotton fields and northern street squalor. All these people and movements comprised a left-behind remnant giving off a dimming afterglow from the March for Jobs and Freedom.[27]

Anyone predicting at the time of the great march which of those two objectives—jobs or freedom—was more likely to be achieved might reasonably have chosen jobs. Freedom, after all, is always a long time coming, far off, never quite at hand. Jobs, on the other hand, are, well, just jobs. As it turned out, however, that forecast would have been wrong. Freedom arrived, but the jobs didn't. Or if the jobs did, they were not the ones expected, nor were they suited for most of those who made up the ranks of the dispossessed.

The Paradox of Freedom

Passage of the historic civil rights bills of that era and the various pieces of enabling legislation and court and executive orders that gave them teeth left equal rights closer to legal reality than had once seemed imaginable. In that regard, King's dream came true. Yet that was certainly not so as part of the warp and woof of everyday life; spotting the kind of kumbaya moment of white and black children embracing in brotherly love invoked by the speech remained a very sometime thing: certainly not when it came to where you actually lived or went to school as opposed to where you had the right to live or go to school; certainly not measured in jail time served or trips to the electric chair; certainly not when you toted up your paychecks or estimated how long you were likely to live.

These were the interstitial zones where formal freedom bled out. Here prejudice ceded pride of place to the impersonal dynamics of empowered wealth as an explanation for how subordination got reproduced. Discrimination lived on where it was useful and died away where it no longer served to buoy up the bottom line, or it festered among white working and lower middle classes whose own ways of life were also jeopardized by the machinations of the power elite. "Freedom" was weightless in black precincts or felt like an affront across town.

But the answer to whether freedom had finally arrived was a lot closer to emphatically yes in the voting booth, at the lunch counter, in the department store, riding on the train or bus, sitting on a jury, testifying in court, marrying whom you wanted to, being buried where you wanted to, holding public office, and so on. True enough, in these arenas the new freedom was constantly resisted, evaded, or violated. Ingenious ways were devised to circumvent the law at school, in the neighborhood, on the job. The big difference, however, was that now what was once lawful had been outlawed. There is no way to minimize that accomplishment. "Freedom now!" indeed. It had come true, so long as what was meant was honoring the rights of the individual as our founding fathers had suggested was an immanent possibility (even if they didn't intend or enjoin such equality).

Winning jobs, however prosaic, turned out to be a different matter entirely. That issue wasn't abandoned, but underwent translation. Not long after the march disbanded, a "War on Poverty" began. Hardly a shock, given the chronic turmoil in northern cities. However, the war turned out to be a distinctive one in ways that would further erode the connections between the labor and race questions. And its relationship to jobs was at best a problematical one.

Poverty was once treated as a function of exploitation at work—say, in the sweatshops, coal mines, iron forges, strawberry fields, and logging camps of old. Now it was reconceived as originating in the exclusion from work. That was a real distinction, but one that also exonerated those commanding the capital resources of the country; poverty was something that happened outside the black box of the workplace.

The enemy was reconceived as well. As the Kerner Commission investigating the ghetto riots of the period concluded, the root of the problem was "white racism." This was in some sense true, but it was also a grand evasion. Off the hook were those circles of power and wealth with the wherewithal to direct the flows of income, wealth, and liquid capital that everyone else depended on. Instead the whole tribe of whites, from bottom-dwelling "trash" to "privileged" blue-collar "aristocrats" and on upward into the guilt-ridden ranks of the well-off suburban middle class, was to wear the hair shirt. "The basic cause of Negro poverty is discrimination," declared *Business Week* in 1964. Policy memos advised that for political reasons any legislative assault on poverty should avoid "any use of the term 'inequality' or the term 'redistribution of income or wealth.'"

Secretary of Labor W. Willard Wirtz hadn't seen the memo. He proposed a jobs program costing way, way beyond what LBJ was prepared to spend waging war. So it never surfaced again.[28]

A spiritual makeover of the country's soul was alleged to be the first and, given the legal triumphs of the era, perhaps the last and surely indispensable step necessary for remediation. That became the conventional wisdom.

Furthermore, the War on Poverty was peculiar insofar as it reimagined poverty's victims as their own victimizers. Poverty was a pathogen lodging in the collective DNA of the ghetto, where it multiplied into a set of cancerous behavioral growths— idleness, chemical and other forms of dependency, familial dysfunction, learning aversions, aborted capacity to think beyond the moment, atrophy of the disciplined will, instincts for the predatory run amuck. Although a socialist and the country's most prominent rediscoverer of poverty in America, Michael Harrington made use of this thesis about a "culture of poverty" (first introduced by Oscar Lewis in 1959) in his own best seller *The Other America,* published not long thereafter.

Medicalized and psychologized just so, and immersed in the oddly consoling moralizing of "white guilt," poverty and its racial manifestations sprang free of their origins in the political economy of midcentury capitalism. This up-to-date ideology banished from consciousness the grittier social and economic realities so apparent just yesterday. Part founding credo, part vanguard social and psychological science, this new view defanged the outrage before it ventured too far. It comprised a kind of intellectual dark matter. That is to say, its purveyors could recognize neither in their "science" nor in the universal truths of their political morality the hidden hand of their own class outlook on life. As an ideology, it was the thought performance of a liberal bourgeoisie imagining itself free of any tincture of class interest or bias even as it beat itself up about "white skin privilege." It worked simultaneously as an expiation and a purgative.[29]

With this diagnosis in hand, the weapons with which to fight the war followed suit. The arsenal consisted largely of educational ventures, vocational training for jobs (either not there or disappearing), job counseling (for those same phantom jobs), welfare counseling on how to get with the program of upward bound, free food, although with humbling caveats, and a multitude of projects promising grassroots community control (that when they were implemented left the ghetto virtually intact). Vital exceptions included Medicare and Medicaid which, if they didn't go after the sources of indigence, nonetheless lightened the burden.

By and large, however, this was a war conducted by social and psychological engineers. Class animosities would subside in a carefully choreographed economy whose steady growth had become a matter of applied technique. Social adjustments made by experts along with a commitment to full equality before the law would together weaponize the War on Poverty. Social malfunctioning generally was now susceptible to dispassionate management. Class conflict need not intrude.

Nor should it, because to enter that force field instead might lead into the unknown. The white-collar armies of the War on Poverty weren't about to engage with the raw social unrest of the ghetto (except to find inventive ways of deflecting it), or mix in with the mud-encrusted tent dwellers in King's Resurrection City, or seek out some improbable common ground with shop-floor black militants with access to their own sources of power, or edit their view of young ghetto youth dressed in guerilla regalia into something less exotic and fearsome than their fevered imagination allowed. Even more bizarre and unthinkable would have been finding a way to embrace the simmering hostility of white working-class people experiencing their own material decline and social insults. None of that was about to happen.

Jobs at Last

Nor were jobs going to happen. Poverty rates fell for a time. That was a victory. Jobs, however, remained scarce, especially what we now call decent, well-paying jobs. Here and there jobs appeared. Some people qualified for work after job training. Union apprenticeship programs were on occasion forced open. In the main, however, the landscape remained bare. People worked, to be sure, in the ghetto's underground economies, at a vast array of low-wage sweatshops, in the interstices of black commercial life, as the urban servant class, at nonunion work sites. But the Great Migration and the early symptoms of deindustrialization produced a deficit only a major overhaul of the distribution of wealth and power could address. At the outset of the War on Poverty black unemployment was about 10 percent; by 1971 it was basically the same. As for inequality, the median income of blacks relative to whites over this same period remained stationary.[30]

Ironically, however, the achievement of "freedom" did generate "jobs" of unexpected kinds in unexpected places. Someone had to man this rapidly expanding social engineering bureaucracy. This was true in Washington as well as in a thousand town and cities. Openings for civil servants of all types— clerks and technicians, administrators and managers, case workers and psychologists, economists and schoolteachers, lawyers and mediators, policy creators and policy assessors— were now accessible to a sliver of upwardly mobile African

Americans (among others). Freedom had made that mobility possible by eliminating those legal barriers that had once fenced African Americans off; especially, it pried open the schoolroom doors from kindergarten to graduate school. King's dream come true for some meant a wider (if still rocky) road leading to lives as doctors, journalists, house builders, electricians, middle managers, and nurses in both the public and private sector. Great Society programs generated in the neighborhood of 2 million government jobs manning federal programs in education, health, and housing. Here was the raw material quickly forming itself into a new black middle class.

Moreover, because the War on Poverty made a commitment to community participation and governance, many of the new agencies charged with running the war were staffed or even run by blacks. Semi-independent, these community groups also enjoyed ties with established political circles (local Democratic Party machinery, for the most part) and with the world of non-profits (most conspicuously the Ford Foundation). Entrenched Democratic Party apparatchiks at first resisted this incursion. They had relied for generations on their ties to white ethnic bailiwicks to keep them in office. Black constituents were either ignored or patronized while the walls of the ghetto were preserved (public housing projects reinforced patterns of residential segregation, for example). Now challenged by a rising generation of black political activists with their own machinery, the old guard was compelled to adapt and recarve the political terrain.[31]

No conclusive evidence exists that the community action agencies of that era accomplished either their original goal of reducing juvenile delinquency or their subsequent goal of reducing poverty. But around vehicles like Mobilization of Youth (a Ford Foundation favorite) or the Model Cities program more widely, there gathered the raw material of a new black political class. For some it served as another exit ramp out of the ghetto. The number of black officeholders exploded. In 1964 about three hundred African Americans held elective office. By 1970 nearly fifteen hundred did and by 1989 over seven thousand. (Yet at the end of the 1960s three-quarters of black men were working, but only 57 percent were employed by the end of the 1980s).

Hardly a ruling class, to be sure. But African Americans began to exercise real influence within local and even national political circles that their forebears—the preachers and teachers, lawyers and doctors and storekeepers from Jim Crow days—could only dream of. One might view the young college-bound activists who ignited the sit-ins at Winston-Salem lunch counters and all through the Deep South as the vanguard of this new class, taking up the torch left behind by the decimated ranks of the black industrial working class of the New Deal era. Aspirations forged in the crucible of class struggle of that earlier time were now to be realized by a new generation. That would happen, however, not by opening up new terrain of class conflict but by shying away from it.

More portentous still, members of this new political milieu (together with the black clergy, which retained much of its potency from the past) not only assumed leadership of the emerging black middle class but, as "race men," they presumed or were presumed by others to represent as well the mudsills of Afro-America, however far removed these risen men and women otherwise were from those gulags of exploitation and dispossession. In the view of one scholar, the "singular class vision" of this newly empowered upward-bound world was "projected as the organic and transparent sensibility" of the whole race.

Naturally enough, those in this milieu partly identified with, enjoyed innumerable ties to, and shared an ideological outlook with the state-managed liberal capitalism run by the Democratic Party that had marched alongside them in the march and made war on poverty. Liberals all, they held in common a meritocratic worldview of social justice. Establishing the right to compete in the "race of life" would usher in precisely the kind of freedom King's speech pined for.

If it took affirmative action, as Lyndon Johnson and even Richard Nixon noted it would, to overcome the crippling legacies of slavery and Jim Crow to achieve that realm of true freedom, then so be it. Meanwhile, from the standpoint of the Fortune 500, segregation not only unsettled political stability but erected obstacles to the smooth functioning of the labor market and access to its nether regions. Whatever differences separated this newly empowered African American world from the inner circles in Washington and from corporate executive suites where ultimate power resided, this expanded and desegregated welfare state was their common creation.[32]

The March on Washington and the War on Poverty it helped mobilize might be considered, then, both triumphs and tragedies. Together, they opened many doors to the excluded. They made the everyday struggle to get by more manageable. They altered the nation's cultural atmosphere so that no matter how many racist-inspired outrages continue they are perceived as ignominies rather than business as usual. They elected a president.

Since the march and the speech and the summer, however, and in part because of the logic set in motion then, attention to the class dimensions of black oppression has been driven further and further underground.

Identity politics, the ideology of the new Afro-American middle class, was first formed on the battlefronts of that era. At times its atmospherics suggested something different: defiant, more militant, an opening to the left of "Da Lord." However, its most fundamental cry for equality before the law was completely compatible with the predominant message of the speech and its dream. Black power, whatever emotional intensity drove it, no matter its talk of controlling the institutions of the ghetto or carving out space for black businesses, was only a power so long as it fit within the wider sphere of a color-blind, state-administered capitalism.

"Black power" mimicked notions of community control first conceived in the ateliers of white liberal policy wonks. (The War on Poverty was cobbled together without the participation of the civil rights movement.) A kind of masquerade, it left the ghetto as disempowered as ever. But it was at the same time a vehicle of empowerment for those enjoying the fruits of the civil rights breakthrough. Andrew Young, who as a young SCLC activist helped author that vision (and would go on to become UN ambassador) summed up its accomplishments, outlook, and limitations many years later: "I quantify revolution in dollar terms." "Now I see black people driving around Atlanta in cars that are worth one hundred thousand dollars. That's integration. I keep running into young people who are starting their own businesses. That's integration. I used to know everyone in black Atlanta who could afford to take an airplane. Now I see black folks I don't even know flying first class. These people are carrying on the struggle."[33]

Black power indeed! The dream was a worthy one. Yet its realization came at a steep price.

Conclusion
The Homeland

Even though we now have a Homeland Department of government, the word *homeland* strikes a dissonant note here in the United States. Scarcely ever used before September 11, 2001, it's a locution far more familiar abroad and has been for centuries. It connotes bloodlines and points to the familial, ethnic, and racial foundations of nation-states. It is interchangeable with references to the fatherland or the motherland. Such references have always seemed more than faintly foreign here. In the New World, the nation was seen more as a confected than a natural creation. Colloquially, it is common to think of America as the nation of nations. As in any other place on earth, there have been moments when that cosmopolitan openness has closed. Then the "foreigner" (either located abroad or here at home) has taken on the characteristics of some alien other, looming up as a primal threat not just to our way of life but to our native stock. So it is today that we grow increasingly comfortable with a word that once conjured up bellicose patriotism and much worse.

What usually has defined the American nation, however, has been precisely those core beliefs and desires we have come to see embodied in its colonial beginnings and constitutional genius, in its cowboy self-reliance and in the Statue of Liberty's global promise of liberty, in material abundance for all and a color-blind egalitarianism lauded by Nixon and King. The American, in her or his ideal state, was bloodless—or if not bloodless, then a representative human endowed by his or her creator not with organic ties to this or that community of skin or ancestry, but to the inalienable rights of the individual. So compelling were those elements of the national identity that they have managed to conceal from view a largely subterranean reality of social conflict. The pristine free individual of American myth was a cultural triumph that buried that discomfiting alternate reality. The chapters assembled here have thus been a work of disinterment.

Is There a Future for the Proletarian Metaphysic?

Our native notion of an immaculate nation, virginal, without classes, and for that matter without any telltale signs of earthier origins or makeup, has an odd affinity with what sometimes passes as the orthodox Marxist view of class. Precisely because the pure proletarian is stripped of all parochial attachments to kith and kin, to traditional customs and local loyalties, to specific work cultures and skills, to a "homeland," race or church denomination, he or she becomes the raw material of species consciousness: human, nothing less. The proletarian's loss would become humanity's great gain, or so the dialectic decreed.

Yet, like the mythic American, the mythic proletarian has turned out in real life to be pockmarked by all those historical bruises. Nothing could make that clearer than the 2016 presidential election. On the one hand, American workers were up in arms, hostile to the political class and to the financial/corporate elite it enabled. Some, however, seemed equally

exercised to defend their racial and gender "identities." Trump
fed on misogyny and racial fear as much as he did on the revul-
sion for the naked selfishness of the country's ruling classes.
His revanchist patriotism rooted its appeal in masculine nomenclature reveling in muscular "greatness." Opinion articulated through the outlets of mainstream news and culture depicted workers not so much as a class but as members of rival
tribes: white workers were alleged to be first of all white; blacks
were not even considered as workers, which, of course, is the
class they overwhelmingly belong to, but as members of a vic-
timized race. It was as if the zeitgeist was working overtime to
transmute proletarian angst into something more primeval.

Utopian notions notwithstanding, American society always has had to come to grips with social conflict. A favored
way of doing that has been to reconceive class divisions rather
as ones involving race or other forms of inherent or ascribed
or volitional identity. That has clearly been the case over the
last half century, with special emphasis on race; indeed, as its
biological underpinnings weakened and then vanished entirely, race as a social category grew ever more robust. This has
led, on the one hand, to great gains in recognizing the basic
humanity of nonwhite people, women, and others. It has also
functioned as an evasion. Class in this context can be made to
not matter. To speak of "wage slavery" and the "emancipation
of labor" today is to use a language far more foreign to American ears than it was a century ago. Meanwhile, the vocabulary
of racial and other difference grows ever more lush.[1]

Identity politics to one side, the disfigurement of the
proletarian as savior is further abetted by the vanishing of many
of the customary traits that once composed his profile. "He,"
for instance, is just as likely to be a "she." That runs up against
the distinct masculinity that for ages characterized the hero of

proletarian emancipation. Moreover, "she" as well as "he" is far less likely to work in heavy industry (due to deindustrialization), whose "heaviness" contributed to that muscular image of the hammer-wielding arm. Workers were collected together in mega-sized factories that were easy to conceive as the mobilization points for the great army of the proletariat aided by but not composed of or captained by women. The industries they "manned," if stopped, could unman the economy, the army's big weapon.

Now "wage slaves" are scattered about, employed in thousands of small retail operations or subcontracting firms, working at home as telecommuters, as "free-agent" truck drivers or freelance technicians, as home care nurses, at call centers or in the chronically shifting world of temporary employment. Not only does that dispersal reduce the leverage once exercised by industrial labor, more profoundly it eliminates that concentrated social geography that encouraged multitudes to get to know, trust, and depend on each other, to see themselves as a "class" at odds with another class.

Indeed, employment itself has become a sometime thing, a condition without any long-term assurance it will continue or, if it does, still carries with it a sense of permanent impermanence. A precariat has replaced or grown up alongside the proletariat. Can its footloose existence allow it to cohere as an organized presence in the public arena the way an older working class once did? Also, some suspect, the information economy has or will soon consign millions to marginalization, living outside the perimeters of gainful employment entirely. The fate long endured by the African American mudsills of American society threatens to descend on others. Estimates of the percentage of current jobs apt to be automated over the next two decades range from 47 percent to 80 percent. The very meaning of the word *proletariat* may revert to what it once was in ancient times: not a "working class" compelled to earn its keep in a capitalist production process it has no control over, but rather a surplus population without any means of support—superfluous, inessential, yet socially explosive. Under these circumstances, it is much harder to foresee a "red army" of the class conscious. Yet, as I hope these essays have suggested, class has always been an essential part of the warp and woof of American society. Sometimes squirreled away, at other times bursting onto the surface of public life, it has always mattered. Clearly it mattered in our recent electoral surprise, if it's not so clear just how it mattered and what it signifies for the future.[2]

The Utopian Dilemma

Because the American myth is a peculiarly utopian one, the understructure of class division has been a reality hard to reconcile. Capitalism is allegedly hardheaded. It is supposed to rest on animal appetites that the mechanisms of the market have domesticated. It disdains utopias as wooly-headed pipe dreams, socialism perhaps most of all. Yet in the New World, utopianism has always been there on the surface, sometimes even as a national boast.

Plymouth and Jamestown persist in memory as founding moments of democratic consent and self-reliance, pathfinders for the world. Yet they rested on forms of dependency and exploitation. The Constitution is thought to be the fruit of political genius, a near-perfect clockwork mechanism ensuring equilibrium in a society subject to chronic imbalance. Yet it was written in the full knowledge that some social groups would benefit and others lose if it were adopted. We have grown accustomed to believe that the Statue of Liberty commands New

York Harbor because its creators meant it as an offering to the rest of the world to come here and live the American Dream. Yet its conception and architecture were fueled by fears of class turmoil and a wariness about "huddled masses" from abroad. No figure has better captured the essence of *Homo Americanus* than the cowboy: free, on his own, brave, graceful, unpretentious, at one with nature, steely-eyed but with his heart in the right place. Still, he was after all a "boy," unlikely to mature into the self-sufficient manhood his popular reputation depicted, a rootless proletarian of the range more honored in his mythic afterlife than on the punishing cattle drives feeding global markets for meat. The Moscow kitchen and the kitchen I grew up with in suburbia were meant to prove that the New World housed the only society without classes: utopia realized. But within a few short years of the vice president's debate with the Soviet Union's premier, the United States was fissured by confrontations on all fronts. From the Lincoln Memorial, Martin Luther King Jr. called on the nation to redeem the promissory note issued at its founding, to let freedom ring. Yet even as he spoke, the freedom he dreamed of would fail to touch the sources of subjugation that left millions powerless and in slavish subordination.

Is this a case of utopia deferred, perhaps? Or is it utopia as obfuscation? Utopias often, if not always, may seem to be about emancipation. And they often are remembered for that inspiration. Less noticeable, however, is that they are also about control, about how to reconfigure the social cosmos so that harmony reigns. This can be said of Thomas More's famous book and even more emphatically about the most renowned literary utopia of the American imagination, Edward Bellamy's *Looking Backward*. Something is amiss in the old order, which is socially disruptive, morally delinquent, politically corrupt, and which corrodes human relations. A new world can be re-engineered into being. Utopia offers salvation not by licensing the unfettered will but by reconstructing the social order—that is, by instituting a new system of control more likely to result in the general welfare.

Control as much as freedom is what the American utopia fantasized. The propertied individual was the atomic nucleus where that control was born, resided, and exercised its energy. And that control carried with it distinctly male genetics. Utopias rarely (although there have been exceptions) envisioned women wielding the command mechanisms of their new societies. And that was true too here in the New World. John Smith's "every man a master" was a man. To be without property was to put manhood at risk.

Because the New World seemed to promise that propertied mastery could become a universal condition, the peculiar nature of the American utopian dream of individual freedom and self-reliance took on a deeply male coloration. Naturally, women can, did, and still do aspire to that same form of utopian control. There is nothing sexually essentialist about this New World utopia. Still, its traits, perhaps best exemplified by the cowboy, have historically been carried through time by the traditions of male culture. They have been reinforced by law and custom over generations. They imply or openly proclaim a domination over nature, over others, and above all over the self.

Dominion inhered in the colonial expedition. It breathed life into the Constitution. Liberty's statue presided over a national ideal purged of lower-order discord. Cowboys were nature's supermen. A benign American imperium, armed to the teeth, tutored the world in democracy and equality from its suburban kitchen. Equality under the law effaced persistent inequality and submission outside the law.

All of this was and remains plausible—indeed, more than plausible. As an ensemble, it comprises an article of faith. Women are invited now to swear allegiance to that faith and enjoy its empowerments. Many do, suggesting that after all there was never anything inherent but only something historical in that masculinized way of being. But at its heart is still that lone figure, the solitary self-sufficient, the new human unfazed by any impediment whether raised up by custom, social hierarchy, or political coercion. To keep that utopian vision aloft has required heavy labor. To honor its promise of individual emancipation, it has had to repress or deny the social emancipation of millions. The American utopia is a house divided against itself.

Notes

Introduction. The Enigma of Class in America

1. This line is borrowed and slightly modified from a song called "Forget It" by Sixto Rodriguez, originally released in 1971, which appeared in the documentary film *Searching for Sugar Man.*

2. Correspondents of the *New York Times, Class Matters* (New York: New York Times Books, 2005); David D. Kirkpatrick, "New Populism Puts Old Guard on Defensive," *New York Times,* December 11, 2015.

3. Nelson D. Schwartz, "Economists Take Aim at Wealth Inequality," *New York Times,* January 3, 2016.

4. Smith, quoted in Stephen Innes, "Fulfilling John Smith's Vision," in *Work and Labor in Early America,* ed. Stephen Innes (Chapel Hill: University of North Carolina Press, 1988).

5. Terence McCoy, "How Joseph Stalin Invented 'American Exceptionalism,'" *Atlantic,* March 15, 2012.

6. Max Lerner, *American Civilization: Life and Thought in the United States Today* (New York: Simon and Schuster, 1957).

7. Paul Fussell, *Class: A Guide through the American Status System* (New York: Simon and Schuster, 1983), 15. If I were writing about why class matters in general, not only here in the United States but elsewhere in the Western world and outside the West as well, this approach would not make as much sense. Other nations have labored less hard or not at all at this work of denial. They are not thought of as "exceptional," nor do they think of themselves that way, at least insofar as acknowledging the presence and importance of class in their social physiognomies, political makeup, economic divisions, and cultural tastes and prejudices.

8. Chris Lehmann, *Revolt of the Masscult* (Chicago: Prickly Paradigm, 2003), 67; Hannah Arendt, *The Human Condition* (Chicago: University of Chicago Press, 1998), 218; André Gorz, quoted in Paul Mason, *Postcapitalism: A Guide to Our Future* (New York: Farrar, Straus and Giroux, 2015), 179; Louis Menand, introduction to *Masscult and Midcult: Essays against the American Grain*, by Dwight MacDonald, ed. Louis Menand (New York: New York Review Books, 2011).

9. Joshua Clover, *Riot, Strike, Riot: The New Era of Uprisings* (London: Verso, 2016), 27.

10. Thomas Jefferson, quoted in Alex Gourevitch and Aziz Rana, "America's Failed Promise of Equality Opportunity," *Salon*, December 2, 2012.

Chapter 1. East of Eden

1. Godfrey Hodgson, *A Great and Godly Adventure: The Pilgrims and the Myth of the First Thanksgiving* (New York: Public Affairs, 2006), 38–40.

2. Nick Bunker, *Making Haste from Babylon: The Mayflower Pilgrims and Their World* (New York: Knopf, 2010), 51; Innes, "Fulfilling John Smith's Vision"; Edmund Morgan, *American Slavery, American Freedom: The Ordeal of Colonial Virginia* (New York: Norton, 1975), 24, 65–67.

3. Hodgson, *Great and Godly Adventure*, 61–63, David A. Price, *Love and Hate in Jamestown: John Smith, Pocahontas, and the Heart of a New Nation* (New York: Knopf, 2003), 7, 16–17; Innes, "Fulfilling John Smith's Vision."

4. Innes, "Fulfilling John Smith's Vision," 3; David Vickers, "Working the Fields in a Developing Economy," in Innes, *Work and Labor in Early America*; Bunker, *Making Haste from Babylon*, 55.

5. Vickers, "Working the Fields."

6. Ibid.; Bunker, *Making Haste from Babylon*, 240, 250; Price, *Love and Hate in Jamestown*, 36, 51, 55; Hodgson, *Great and Godly Adventure*, 144–46, 357–58.

7. Hodgson, *Great and Godly Adventure*, 45, 47, 54, 55; Bunker, *Making Haste from Babylon*, 240, 250; Price, *Love and Hate in Jamestown*, 16–17.

8. William Cronon, *Changes in the Land: Indians, Colonists, and the Ecology of New England* (New York: Hill and Wang, 1983), 73–75.

9. Innes, "Fulfilling John Smith's Vision"; Karen Ordahl Kupperman, ed., *Captain John Smith: A Selected Edition of His Writings* (Williamsburg, VA: Institute of Early American History and Culture, 1988), 194.

10. Bunker, *Making Haste from Babylon*, 248; Price, *Love and Hate in Jamestown*, 7–8, 77, 108, 230–31; Kupperman, *Captain John Smith*, 20–21, 187.

11. Hodgson, *Great and Godly Adventure*, 99; Price, *Love and Hate in Jamestown*, 70–71, 77–78, 129; Cronon, *Changes in the Land*, 100.

12. Hodgson, *Great and Godly Adventure,* 45, 47, 54–55; Bunker, *Making Haste from Babylon,* 13, 250.

13. Hodgson, *Great and Godly Adventure,* 144–46.

14. Ibid., 57; Bunker, *Making Haste from Babylon,* 284–86.

15. Bunker, *Making Haste from Babylon,* 284–86; Hodgson, *Great and Godly Adventure,* 43–45, 74–75.

16. Hodgson, *Great and Godly Adventure,* 57, 74.

17. Eric J. Sundquist, *King's Dream: The Legacy of Martin Luther King's 'I Have a Dream' Speech* (New Haven: Yale University Press, 2009), 110; Cronon, *Changes in the Land,* 109; Price, *Love and Hate in Jamestown,* 1–5, 112, 127, 129, 146–47; Innes, "Fulfilling John Smith's Vision."

18. Alan Axelrod, *A Savage Empire: Traders, Trappers, Tribes and the Wars That Made America* (New York: St. Martin's, 2011), 7–13.

19. Bunker, *Making Haste from Babylon,* 232–40, 246–48, 262; Axelrod, *A Savage Empire,* 7–13.

20. Bunker, *Making Haste from Babylon,* 246–48, 351–52.

21. Cronon, *Changes in the Land,* 83, 92, 94–95; Hodgson, *Great and Godly Adventure,* 45; Bunker, *Making Haste from Babylon,* 9, 350.

22. Cronon, *Changes in the Land,* 92–102.

23. Ibid., 83, 90, 91.

24. Ibid., 95–99, 101–4; Hodgson, *Great and Godly Adventure,* 113–14, 115.

25. Cronon, *Changes in the Land,* 64–65, 67–68, 102–4, 118, 170.

26. Ibid., 162, 165.

27. Kupperman, *Captain John Smith,* 141–44; Cronon, *Changes in the Land,* 53, 55, 56, 57, 90; Hodgson, *Great and Godly Adventure,* 115, 120.

28. Hodgson, *Great and Godly Adventure,* 47, 120.

29. Ibid., 63, 115, 120; Bunker, *Making Haste from Babylon,* 289.

30. Kupperman, *Captain John Smith,* 8, 23, 144, 145.

31. Price, *Love and Hate in Jamestown,* 7–8, 36, 40–41, 70–71, 77, 108, 128–29, 186, 87, 196–97; Kupperman, *Captain John Smith,* 8, 10, 154, and introduction.

32. Cronon, *Changes in the Land,* 73.

33. Ibid., 73–77, 83; Vickers, "Working the Fields"; Hodgson, *Great and Godly Adventure,* 136, 139, 140, 141–43; Price, *Love and Hate in Jamestown,* 230–32; Kupperman, *Captain John Smith,* 45.

Chapter 2. We the People in the City of Brotherly Love

1. Woody Holton, *The Unruly Americans and the Origins of the Constitution* (New York: Hill and Wang, 2007), 1–2.

2. Pauline Maier, *Ratification: The People Debate the Constitution, 1787–1788* (New York: Simon and Schuster, 2010), 72–73.

3. Ibid., 10.

4. Holton, *The Unruly Americans*, 12; Gary B. Nash, *The Unknown American Revolution: The Unruly Birth of Democracy and the Struggle to Create America* (New York: Penguin, 2005), 448; Alan Taylor, "Agrarian Independence: Northern Land Rioters After the Revolution," in *Beyond the American Revolution: Explorations in the History of American Radicalism*, ed. Alfred E. Young (De Kalb: Northern Illinois University Press, 1993); Maier, *Ratification*, 15.

5. Jackson Turner Main, *The Anti-Federalists: Critics of the Constitution, 1781–1788* (New York: Quadrangle Books, 1964), 103, 104–5.

6. A fictional but deeply researched and richly descriptive and evocative portrait of this hinterland can be found in John Ehle's novel *The Land Breakers* (New York: New York Review Books, 2014), originally published in 1964.

7. Holton, *The Unruly Americans*, 276–77; Main, *The Anti-Federalists*, 116.

8. Maier, *Ratification*, 12, 72–73.

9. Adam Smith, quoted in Holton, *The Unruly Americans*, 453.

10. Holton, *The Unruly Americans*, 4, 5, 7, 23, 25–26, 64, 87.

11. Main, *The Anti-Federalists*, 162 (quoting "Plato" in the *U.S. Chronicle*, April 10, 1787), 163.

12. Holton, *The Unruly Americans*, 9; Gary Gerstle, *Liberty and Coercion: The Paradox of American Government* (Princeton: Princeton University Press, 2016), 21; Maier, *Ratification*, 32, 52.

13. Holton, *The Unruly Americans*, 10.

14. Ibid., 11–12.

15. Maier, *Ratification*, 69, 134; Holton, *The Unruly Americans*, 13.

16. Main, *The Anti-Federalists*, 103–5, 106, 131, 132–33, 142, 165–66; *Virginia Independent Chronicle*, October 31, 1786; Maier, *Ratification*, 121.

17. Main, *The Anti-Federalists*, 270–72, 277; Maier, *Ratification*, 72–73.

Chapter 3. Wretched Refuse

1. Edward Berenson, *The Statue of Liberty: A Transatlantic Story* (New Haven: Yale University Press, 2012), 98, 120; Edward Burrows and Mike Wallace, *Gotham: A History of New York City to 1898* (New York: Oxford University Press, 1999), 1115; Candace Falk, ed., *Emma Goldman: A Documentary History of the American Years* (Urbana: University of Illinois Press, 2008); Emma Goldman, *Living My Life* (1931; repr., New York: Arno, 1970), 2, 716–17; Alexandra Kollantai, "The Statue of Liberty," in *Articles and Speeches* (New York: Progress, 1984).

2. Berenson, *The Statue of Liberty*, 8–9, 13, 25–26; Yasmin Sabina Khan, *Enlightening the World: The Creation of the Statue of Liberty* (Ithaca: Cornell University Press, 2010), 109; Marvin Trachtenberg, *The Statue of Liberty: A Centenary Edition of a Classic History and Guide* (New York: Penguin, 1986), 29.

3. Berenson, *The Statue of Liberty*, 13, 25–26.

4. James B. Bell and Richard I. Abrams, *In Search of Liberty: The Story of the Statue of Liberty and Ellis Island* (Garden City, NY: Doubleday, 1984), 18; Berenson, *The Statue of Liberty*, 13–14; Trachtenberg, *The Statue of Liberty*, 28–29.

5. Berenson, *The Statue of Liberty*, 11, 13, 16, 28; Bell and Abrams, *In Search of Liberty*, 25.

6. Bell and Abrams, *In Search of Liberty*, 85; Berenson, *The Statue of Liberty*, 11–14, 28; Khan, *Enlightening the World*, 2–4, 109; Trachtenberg, *The Statue of Liberty*, 29, 32.

7. Bell and Abrams, *In Search of Liberty*, 19–21; David Glassberg, "Rethinking the Statue of Liberty: Old Meaning, New Contexts," University of Massachusetts, Amherst, December 2003m archives.inpui.edu/b. + stream/handle/2450/0781/Rethinking the Statue—Glassberg; Berenson, *The Statue of Liberty*, 69.

8. Berenson, *The Statue of Liberty*, 35, 39, 69, 76.

9. Timothy J. Gilfoyle, "Reminiscences of Gotham," *Atlantic*, February 1999.

10. Burrows and Wallace, *Gotham*, 1033–34, 1037.

11. Berenson, *The Statue of Liberty*, 33, 35, 76; President Grant's letter of January 1884 is at the Gilder Lehrman Institute of American History, New York.

12. Steve Fraser, *The Age of Acquiescence: The Life and Death of American Resistance to Organized Wealth and Power* (New York: Little, Brown, 2015), 169, 171.

13. Bell and Abrams, *In Search of Liberty*, 75; Burrows and Wallace, *Gotham*, 181; Berenson, *The Statue of Liberty*, 70, 80, 88; Kathy Weiser, Legends of America: New York Legends: "Liberty Island and the Statue of Liberty," May 2012, legendsofamerica.com/aboutus.html; "Happy 100th Birthday," National Park Service Centennial: "Native Americans and Historic Uses of Liberty and Ellis Islands," National Park Service Centennial; Bell and Abrams, *In Search of Liberty*, 75.

14. Berenson, *The Statue of Liberty*, 3, 76, 80, 81, 83, 95, 98; Bell and Abrams, *In Search of Liberty*, 35, 36, 41, 73.

15. Burrows and Wallace, *Gotham*, 1117; Fraser, *Age of Acquiescence*, 54–55; Bell and Abrams, *In Search of Liberty*, 73; Berenson, *The Statue of Liberty*, 104, 108.

16. Berenson, *The Statue of Liberty*, 108, 110; Marianne Debruzzy, "A Nation Intended for a Race of Free Men," in *In the Shadow of the Statue of Liberty:*

Immigrants, Workers, and Citizens in the American Republic, 1880–1920, ed. Marianne Debruzzy (Urbana: University of Illinois Press, 1992), 232, 234.

17. Bell and Abrams, *In Search of Liberty,* 55, 58; Burrows and Wallace, *Gotham,* 123; Trachtenberg, *The Statue of Liberty.*

18. Burrows and Wallace, *Gotham,* 1115.

19. Khan, *Enlightening the World.*

Chapter 4. There Was a Young Cowboy

1. Contemplator.com/tunebook/Laredo.htm; Frank Maynard, *Cowboy's Lament: A Life on the Open Range* (Lubbock: Texas Tech University Press, 2010), 134–35.

2. Joe B. Frantz and Julian Ernest Choate, *The American Cowboy: The Myth and the Reality* (Norman: University of Oklahoma Press, 1955), 3–6; Richard White, *It's Your Misfortune and None of My Own: A History of the American West* (Norman: University of Oklahoma Press, 1991), 613; Patricia Nelson Limerick, *Something in the Soil: Legacies and Reckonings in the New West* (New York: Norton, 2000), 283–85.

3. Andy Adams, *The Log of a Cowboy: A Narrative of the Old Trail Days* (Lincoln: University of Nebraska Press, 1903), 1, 7, 14; Tom Engelhardt, *The End of Victory Culture: Cold War America and the Disillusioning of a Generation* (New York: Basic Books, 1995).

4. Harold McCracken, *The American Cowboy* (New York: Doubleday, 1973), 74–75; Frantz and Choate, *American Cowboy,* 34, 73; Charles A. Siringo, *A Texas Cowboy; or, Fifteen Years on the Hurricane Deck of a Spanish Pony* (1886; repr., New York: Penguin, 2000).

5. McCracken, *The American Cowboy,* 70, 73, 75; Frantz and Choate, *American Cowboy,* 16, 32; White, *It's Your Misfortune,* 236.

6. John Williams Malone, *The Album of the American Cowboy* (New York: Franklin Watts, 1971); McCracken, *The American Cowboy,* 137; Frantz and Choate, *American Cowboy,* 16, 33–34; White, *It's Your Misfortune,* 26, 150.

7. Malone, *Album of the American Cowboy;* Frantz and Choate, *American Cowboy,* 133–34; White, *It's Your Misfortune,* 57, 59, 127–28, 150; Jane Kramer, *The Last Cowboy* (New York: Harper and Row, 1977), 10.

8. Frantz and Choate, *American Cowboy,* 114–15, 117.

9. Malone, *Album of the American Cowboy;* McCracken, *The American Cowboy,* 99, 102, 106; White, *It's Your Misfortune,* 222–23.

10. Malone, *Album of the American Cowboy;* McCracken, *The American Cowboy,* 123, 132, 134–36; Frantz and Choate, *American Cowboy,* 52, 55; White, *It's Your Misfortune,* 261–62, 268, 270–71; Kramer, *The Last Cowboy,* 38–39.

11. White, *It's Your Misfortune*, 271–73; Kramer, *The Last Cowboy*, 38–39; J. Evetts Haley, *The XIT Ranch of Texas; and the Early Days of the Llano Estacado* (Norman: University of Oklahoma Press, 1929), 3, 5, 56–57, 69, 72, 77, 88, 96–97, 103, 125.

12. Frantz and Choate, *American Cowboy*, 114; White, *It's Your Misfortune*, 270, 344–46; McCracken, *The American Cowboy*.

13. Malone, *Album of the American Cowboy*; McCracken, *The American Cowboy*, 119–30; Frantz and Choate, *American Cowboy*, 34, 36–37.

14. Malone, *Album of the American Cowboy*; McCracken, *The American Cowboy*, 16, 87, 95; Adams, *Log of a Cowboy*, 105–6, 123–25, 210, 275, 364.

15. Frantz and Choate, *American Cowboy*, 5, 36, 39, 41, 46, 55, 56–59, 60–61; Malone, *Album of the American Cowboy*; McCracken, *The American Cowboy*, 87; Adams, *Log of a Cowboy*, 77–81, 105–6, 211; Haley, *The XIT Ranch*, 116.

16. Adams, *Log of a Cowboy*; Malone, *Album of the American Cowboy*; McCracken, *The American Cowboy*, 137; White, *It's Your Misfortune*, 345–46; Kramer, *The Last Cowboy*, 7, 10.

17. Frantz and Choate, *American Cowboy*, 74, 77, 80, 117; White, *It's Your Misfortune*, 344, 346; Henry Nash Smith, *Virgin Land: The American West as Symbol and Myth* (Cambridge, MA: Harvard University Press, 1975), 81, 109; Adams, *Log of a Cowboy*, 77–81.

18. Malone, *Album of the American Cowboy*; Adams, *Log of a Cowboy*, 14, 180–81, 182.

19. Owen Wister, *The Virginian: A Horseman of the Plains* (New York: Macmillan Reference, 1967).

20. Malone, *Album of the American Cowboy*; McCracken, *The American Cowboy*, 11, 12; Frantz and Choate, *American Cowboy*, 80, 81–83; White, *It's Your Misfortune*, 310–12, 330.

21. Malone, *Album of the American Cowboy*; Frantz and Choate, *American Cowboy*, 155; Smith, *Virgin Land*, 110–11; White, *It's Your Misfortune*, 620, 621–22, 626; Eric Hobsbawm, "The American Cowboy: An Intellectual Myth?" in *Fractured Times: Culture and Society in the 20th Century* (New York: New Press, 2013); Limerick, *Something in the Soil*, 277; E. N. Feltskog, introduction to *The Oregon Trail*, by Francis Parkman, ed. E. N. Feltskog (Lincoln: University of Nebraska Press, 1994).

22. Frantz and Choate, *American Cowboy*, 13, 65–66, 80, 85, 155, 200; Smith, *Virgin Land*, 81, 84, 107, 109, 111; McCracken, *The American Cowboy*.

23. Wister, *The Virginian*; Frederic Remington drawings in Malone, *Album of the American Cowboy*.

24. William MacLeod Raine, *A Texas Ranger* (New York: Grossett and Dunlap, 1911), 226–27.

25. Frantz and Choate, *American Cowboy,* 59–60, 60–61.

26. McCracken, *The American Cowboy,* 12–14, 106–7, 119–32, 137; Wister, *The Virginian;* a novel by Oakley Hall entitled *The Badlands* (Chicago: University of Chicago Press, 1978) provides a vivid depiction of these conflicts; Frantz and Choate, *American Cowboy,* 3, 52; White, *It's Your Misfortune,* 223–25, 345–46; Smith, *Virgin Land,* 109.

27. Hobsbawm, "The American Cowboy"; White, *It's Your Misfortune,* 560; Limerick, *Something in the Soil,* 81; Kramer, *The Last Cowboy,* 51, 69, 133.

28. Kramer, *The Last Cowboy,* 4, 51, 113.

29. Richard's descriptions of his odyssey out west come from two letters written to the author.

Chapter 5. John Smith Visits Suburbia

1. Elaine Tyler May, *Homeward Bound: American Families in the Cold War Era* (New York: Basic Books, 1988), 20–21.

2. Ibid., 20–21; "Better See Once," *Time,* August 3, 1959; William Safire, "The Cold War's Hot Kitchen," *New York Times,* July 23, 2009; "The Nixon-Khrushchev Debate," July 24, 1969, CNN Transcript Cold War, at Temple.edu; Andrew Glass, "Nixon and Khrushchev Hold 'Kitchen Debate,'" *Politico,* July 24, 2009; Monte Olmsted, "Nixon, Khrushchev, and Betty Crocker at the 1959 Kitchen Debate," Taste of General Mills, at General Mills.com; Ruth Oldenzied and Karen Zachmann, introduction to *Cold War Kitchen: Americanization, Technology, and Europe,* ed. Ruth Oldenzied and Karen Zachmann (Cambridge, MA: MIT Press, 2009); Kevin D. Bodin, "The American National Exhibit and Kitchen Debate: How the World's Superpowers Portrayed the Events of 1959 to Meet National Needs" (senior thesis, Gettysburg College, 2015).

3. Safire, "The Cold War's Hot Kitchen"; "Khrushchev-Nixon Debate"; Glass, "Nixon and Khrushchev Hold 'Kitchen Debate.'"

4. Safire, "The Cold War's Hot Kitchen"; "Better See Once"; Bodin, "The American National Exhibit."

5. Victor Lebow, "Price Competition in 1955," *Journal of Retailing,* Spring 1955; *House Beautiful,* quoted in Lizbeth Cohen, *The Consumer's Republic: The Politics of Mass Consumption in Postwar America* (New York: Knopf, 2003), 125; U.S. Labor Department, *How Buying Habits Change* (Washington, DC: Bureau of Labor Statistics, 1959); Eisenhower, quoted in Cohen, *Consumer's Republic,* 125; "Worker Loses His Class Identity," *Business Week,* July 11, 1959; May, *Homeward Bound,* 20–21.

6. What might be described as a nonfiction novel by Francis Spufford, entitled *Red Plenty* (Minneapolis: Graywolf, 2010), captures the striking

self-confidence about the future characteristic of the Soviet *nomenklatura* in this period.

7. Cohen, *Consumer's Republic.*

8. Ibid., 121–32, 195–96; "The New America," *Newsweek*, April 1, 1957.

9. Cohen, *Consumer's Republic*, 292; "USA: The Permanent Revolution," *Fortune*, February 1951.

10. Louis Hartz, *The Liberal Tradition in America: An Interpretation of American Political Thought since the Revolution* (San Diego: Harcourt Brace Jovanovich, 1991); David Potter, *People of Plenty* (Chicago: University of Chicago Press, 2009); John Kenneth Galbraith, *The Affluent Society* (Boston: Houghton Mifflin, 1958); Daniel Boorstin, *The Genius of American Politics* (Chicago: University of Chicago Press, 1953); Clinton Rossiter, *Seedtime in the American Republic: The Origins of the American Tradition of Political Liberty* (New York: Harcourt Brace, 1953); Vance Packard, *The Hidden Persuaders* (New York: D. McKay, 1957); David Riesman, *The Lonely Crowd: A Study in the Changing American Character* (New Haven: Yale University Press, 1950); Bell, *End of Ideology;* Herbert Marcuse, *One Dimensional Man* (Boston: Beacon, 1964); Chris Lehman, *Revolt of the Masscult* (Chicago: Prickly Paradigm, 2003), 38–39; R. Jeffrey Lustig, "The Tangled Knot of Race and Class in America," in *What's Class Got to Do with It?"* ed. Michael Zweig (Ithaca: Cornell University Press, 2004); Cohen, *Consumer's Republic,* 33.

11. Marx, quoted in Stathis Kouvelakis, *Philosophy and Revolution from Kant to Marx* (London: Verso, 2003), 294; George Lichtheim, *New Europe: Today and Tomorrow* (New York: Praeger, 1963); Howard Brick, *Transcending Capitalism: Visions of a New Society in Modern America* (Ithaca: Cornell University Press, 2006), 6, 8, 199–200, 207–8, 229, 248–49, 268.

12. George Lipsitz, *Rainbow at Midnight: Labor and Culture in the 1940s* (Urbana: University of Illinois Press, 1994), 282; Riesman, *Lonely Crowd;* Lehman, *Revolt of the Masscult,* 38–39, 67.

13. Robert O. Self, *All in the Family: The Realignment of American Democracy since the 1960s* (New York: Hill and Wang, 2012), 223–32.

14. Paul Fussell, *Class: A Guide through the American Status System* (New York: Simon and Schuster, 1983), 18, 19, 21, 39.

15. Cohen, *Consumer's Republic,* 159, 161, 195, 309–10.

16. David Brion Davis, *In the Image of God: Religion, Moral Values, and Our Heritage of Slavery* (New Haven: Yale University Press, 2001), 357; Packard, *Hidden Persuaders;* William H. Whyte, *The Organization Man* (New York: Simon and Schuster, 1956); David Riesman, "Work and Leisure in Post-industrial Society," in *Mass Leisure,* ed. Eric Larabe and Rolf Meyersohn (Glencoe, IL: Free Press, 1958).

17. MacDonald, *Masscult and Midcult*, 8, 11–13, 56; Lehman, *Revolt of the Masscult*, 29–30, 38–39, 67.

18. Arendt, *The Human Condition*, 218, 219; Lipsitz, *Rainbow*, 192; *The Public Papers of the Presidents of the United States: Dwight D. Eisenhower, 1955* (Washington, DC: Government Printing Office, 1956), 852–53; Cohen, *Consumer's Republic*, 152.

19. Fraser, *Age of Acquiescence*, 305–7; Lehman, *Revolt of the Masscult*; Marcuse, *One Dimensional Man*, ix, x, 8, 9, 31, 48–49, 56–57, 61, 79, 241, 256–57.

20. "Unknown Teacher Changes 'Shapes,'" *Barnard Bulletin*, February 11, 1965.

21. Marcuse, *One Dimensional Man*, 250–51.

Chapter 6. Free at Last?

1. Drew D. Hansen, *The Dream: Martin Luther King, Jr. and the Speech That Inspired a Nation* (New York: Ecco-HarperCollins, 2003), 159; Taylor Branch, *Pillar of Fire: America in the King Years, 1963–65* (New York: Simon and Schuster, 1998), 362, 374.

2. Eric J. Sundquist, *King's Dream* (New Haven: Yale University Press, 2009), 1–3, 8, 15; Michael Eric Dyson, *I May Not Get There with You: The True Martin Luther King, Jr.* (New York: Free Press, 2000), 26; CNN.com/2013/011/19/us/mlk-conservative.

3. Nicholas Lemann, *The Promised Land: The Great Migration and How It Changed America* (New York: Knopf, 1991), 17–18, 47; Greta de Jong, *You Can't Eat Freedom: Southerners and Social Justice After the Civil Rights Movement* (Chapel Hill: University of North Carolina Press, 2016), 1–2.

4. Steve Fraser, "The Politics of Debt in America: From Debtor's Prison to Debtor Nation," tomdispatch.com, January 29, 2013.

5. Hansen, *The Dream*, 1–4.

6. Aldon Morris, *The Origins of the Civil Rights Movement: Black Communities Organizing for Change* (New York: Free Press, 1984), 3–8.

7. Lemann, *Promised Land*, 5–6, 10, 17–18, 50.

8. Morris, *Origins*, 41; Robert Korstad and Nelson Lichtenstein, "Opportunities Found and Lost: Labor Radicalism and the Early Years of the Civil Rights Movement," *Journal of American History*, December 1988; Lemann, *Promised Land*, 17–18.

9. James R. Grossman, *Land of Hope: Chicago, Black Southerners and the Great Migration* (Chicago: University of Chicago Press, 1997), 213, 243, 244.

10. Lemann, *Promised Land*; Grossman, *Land of Hope*, 213, 243.

11. Lemann, *Promised Land*, 70; de Jong, *You Can't Eat Freedom*, 3–4, 12.

12. Risa L. Goluboff, *The Lost Promise of Civil Rights* (Cambridge, MA: Harvard University Press, 2007), 5, 7, 9, 11, 17.

13. Reuel Schiller, *Forging Rivals: Race, Class, and Law and the Collapse of Postwar Liberalism* (Princeton: Princeton University Press, 2016); Korstad and Lichtenstein, "Opportunities Found and Lost"; Goluboff, *The Lost Promise*, 11–12, 17, 37, 38, 51.

14. Goluboff, *The Lost Promise*, 5, 6, 9, 17, 18, 27, 29, 35, 52, 56, 113, 139, 143; "New Attack upon Liberties," *Social Action*, January 10, 1936.

15. Sundquist, *King's Dream*, 51; Taylor Branch, *Parting the Waters: America in the King Years, 1954–63* (New York: Simon and Schuster, 1988), 883; Goluboff, *The Lost Promise*, 217–20, 225.

16. For a treatment of how intellectual and academic discussion of the "race question" was similarly hobbled, see the excellent study by Leah N. Gordon, *From Power to Prejudice: The Rise of Racial Individualism in Midcentury America* (Chicago: University of Chicago Press, 2015); Goluboff, *The Lost Promise*, 12, 14, 16, 104, 105–7, 137, 212–20, 235, 237, 239, 264–65, 269.

17. Sundquist, *King's Dream*, 45, 102, 154, 156; Hansen, *The Dream*, 13, 16; Dyson, *I May Not Get There with You*, 19–24; Goluboff, *Lost Promise*. The stature of the proclamation endures despite the caveats that accompanied its passage: it was issued as a "military necessity," it was preceded by a one-hundred-day grace period during which emancipation would be forestalled if the South laid down its arms, and it did not apply in the border states fighting for the Union or in southern states already under Union control.

18. Hansen, *The Dream*, 44–48; Branch, *Parting the Waters*, 880.

19. Sundquist, *King's Dream*, 15; Clayborne Carson, "Rethinking African-American Political Thought," in *The Making of Martin Luther and the Civil Rights Movement*, ed. Brian Ward and Tony Badger (New York: New York University Press, 1996); Martin Luther King Jr., *Stride toward Freedom: The Montgomery Story* (Boston: Beacon, 2010); Dyson, *I May Not Get There with You*, 6, 19; Grossman, *Land of Hope*, 243.

20. Sundquist, *King's Dream*, 61, 63, 73, 110–11, 138; Dyson, *I May Not Get There with You*, 19; Hansen, *The Dream*, 16, 183; Lemann, *Promised Land*, 159–60; Branch, *Parting the Waters*, 539.

21. Richard Yeselson, "When Labor Fought for Civil Rights," *Dissent*, Winter 2017; Schiller, *Forging Rivals*; Branch, *Parting the Waters*, 269, 847; de Jong, *You Can't Eat Freedom*, 1–2, 12; Hansen, *The Dream*, 13, 14, 40.

22. Adolph Reed, *Stirrings in the Jug: Black Politics in the Post Segregation Era* (Minneapolis: University of Minnesota Press, 1999).

23. For King and others keeping guns, see Lemann, *Promised Land*, 160–62.

24. De Jong, *You Can't Eat Freedom*, 3.

25. Sundquist, *King's Dream*, 20, 59, 61.

26. Dyson, *I May Not Get There with You*, 21, 28–29, 77–79, 83–88; Sundquist, *King's Dream*, 150, 211–12; Hansen, *The Dream*, 185–86, 190–92, 201, 220–21.

27. Hansen, *The Dream*, 167; Dyson, *I May Not Get There with You*, 6, 80; Clover, *Riot, Strike, Riot*, 112–13.

28. Lemann, *Promised Land*, 112, 154.

29. Ibid., 131, 149, 151.

30. Reed, *Stirrings in the Jug*, 57; Lemann, *Promised Land*, 201.

31. Lemann, *Promised Land*, 90–94, 195.

32. Ibid., 192, 195; Reed, *Stirrings in the Jug*, xi, 5–6, 15, 47, 49, 57, 60–63, 67.

33. Dyson, *I May Not Get There with You*, 87–88, 92; Lemann, *Promised Land*, 159, 164; Goluboff, *Lost Promise*, 264–69; Reed, *Stirrings in the Jug*, 62–63, 67, 70.

Conclusion. The Homeland

1. Walter Benn Michaels, *The Trouble with Diversity: How We Learned to Love Identity and Ignore Inequality* (New York: Metropolitan Books, 2006), 2–3.

2. "The New Non-workers—Uber, et al.," *New York Times*, February 13, 2016; Nick Srnicek and Alex Williams, *Inventing the Future: Postcapitalism and the World of Work* (London: Verso, 2015), 88.

Index